Advanced Imagineering

Advanced Imagineering

DESIGNING INNOVATION AS COLLECTIVE CREATION

Edited by

Diane Nijs

Breda University of Applied Sciences, the Netherlands

EE Edward **Elgar**
PUBLISHING

Cheltenham, UK • Northampton, MA, USA

Published by
Edward Elgar Publishing Limited
The Lypiatts
15 Lansdown Road
Cheltenham
Glos GL50 2JA
UK

Edward Elgar Publishing, Inc.
William Pratt House
9 Dewey Court
Northampton
Massachusetts 01060
USA

A catalogue record for this book
is available from the British Library

Library of Congress Control Number: 2018960803

This book is available electronically in the **Elgar**online
Business subject collection
DOI 10.4337/9781788976244

ISBN 978 1 78897 623 7 (cased)
ISBN 978 1 78990 285 3 (pbk)
ISBN 978 1 78897 624 4 (eBook)

Typeset by Servis Filmsetting Ltd, Stockport, Cheshire
Printed and bound in Great Britain by TJ International Ltd, Padstow, Cornwall

Contents

List of figures   vii
List of tables   viii
List of boxes   ix
List of contributors   x
Foreword by Benyamin Lichtenstein   xii
Preface by Diane Nijs   xiv
Acknowledgments   xxi

1 Introduction: towards a new design discipline   1
   Diane Nijs

PART I FOUNDATIONS OF IMAGINEERING

2 LANDSCAPE: a big shift in society – growing complexity and
   the innovation opportunity   22
   Diane Nijs

3 LENS: a big shift in science – seeing change and innovation as a
   matter of emergence   41
   Diane Nijs

4 LOGIC: a big shift in design – Imagineering, beyond
   conventional Design Thinking   60
   Diane Nijs

PART II THE SYSTEMIC DESIGN APPROACH OF IMAGINEERING

Introduction to Part II   85

5 A-ppreciating: how to discover the generative core   90
   Celiane Camargo-Borges

6 B-reathing: how to understand the bigger picture   105
   Lilian Outtes Wanderley and Fabio Campos

7 C-reating: how to define vision and concept/Creative
   Tension Engine   119
   Frank Ouwens

8 D-eveloping: how to deal with the challenge of making it real
   and involving others   138
   Geoff Marée

9   E-nabling: how to enable co-creation   151
     Angelica van Dam

10   F-lourishing: how to nurture the system into becoming a learning
     community   167
     Liliya Terzieva

Afterword by Diane Nijs   183

Index   185

Figures

1.1 The evolution of innovation models (Rothwell, 1992) and the dominant logic of value creation in relation to growing complexity and openness   6

1.2 Creative Tension Engine (CTE) as a core element in innovating from the experience perspective   13

3.1 The rabbit–duck illusion is an ambiguous image illustrating that a same reality can be diagnosed as being a rabbit or a duck   42

6.1 System frame for better services at Neighborhood 4811 TC   115

6.2 System frame populated with some actors   115

7.1 The Concept Continuum   129

7.2 Atoms of Molecule Principle applied to Red Bull   135

8.1 The Innovation Engine   139

8.2 Four realms of experience   142

8.3 The Interactive Experience Model   143

9.1 The DART model   157

9.2 The ecosystem of the engagement platform   159

10.1 The four conditions of the Imagineering F-lourishing step   170

Tables

1.1	Rothwell's five generations of innovation models	5
2.1	Two complementary models of value creation	31
4.1	Relating conventional Design Thinking and the Systemic Design Approach of Imagineering	67
4.2	The Systemic Design Approach of Imagineering	75
9.1	The ACTIVE model	156
10.1	The nine leadership behaviors in an Imagineering translation	176

Boxes

1.1   Imagineering snapshot: innovating the ever more deserted
      city center   3
1.2   Imagineering snapshot: Fashion District Arnhem   3
1.3   Imagineering snapshot: the emergence of the first national park
      in Belgium   11
2.1   Characteristics of complicated (technical complex) and complex
      (social complex) issues   24
2.2   Metcalfe's law on the value of networks   28
4.1   Imagineering snapshot: helping troubled families   78
5.1   Two examples of determining values   95
7.1   Some examples of purpose formulations   123
7.2   Examples of principles   124
7.3   Examples of promises   124
7.4   Imagineering snapshot: Burning Man   128
7.5   Imagineering snapshot: the Creative Tension Engine of
      'Peace Parks' in South Africa   132
8.1   Imagineering snapshot: El Bulli   140
8.2   Imagineering snapshot: the Constellation   145
8.3   Imagineering snapshot: Ritz-Carlton   146
8.4   Imagineering snapshot: Alessi   148
9.1   Imagineering snapshot: Nike Plus   152
9.2   Imagineering snapshot: SEATS2MEET   155
9.3   Imagineering snapshot: Center Parcs   163
10.1 Feed the Future: Barack Obama's agricultural promise   174

Contributors

Celiane Camargo-Borges is a lecturer, researcher, Brazilian Country Expert and practitioner working at the interface of psychology, health/wellbeing, community building, education, process design and organizational development. Her work focuses on relational forms of practices creating a more effective means of collaboration and decision making. She is interested in exploring how individuals can come together through dialogic relations – improving interaction and collaboration. She is also very focused on participatory ways of developing research such as community practices, arts-based research, narrative research and storytelling.

Fabio Campos is a lecturer, researcher and practitioner on applied design methods, education, innovation, entrepreneurship and social projects. He has contributed to the design, implementation and management of many small and large innovative and prize-winning projects in those areas, around Brazil, working with CESAR, a Brazilian innovation institute. Among other positions, Fabio has coordinated the CNPq Consulting Committee in Industrial Design, the first Brazilian bachelor in Web Design and the first Design PhD program from a Brazilian Federal University. Fabio holds a PhD in Computer Science, a MSc in Electronic Engineering and is currently a professor of Design at the Federal University of Pernambuco – Brazil.

Angelica van Dam has a background in film production and the pop venue industry. After 16 years at Breda University of Applied Sciences (BUas) (Netherlands), she is a lecturer in Imagineering and chairs the Imagineering competency group for the bachelor program. In recent years, she has investigated how to apply Imagineering to its fullest in education as well as in the way of working of organizations. She has done this by researching the concept of 'platforming' in general and involving the whole organization, so they can create their own enabling environment where people are inspired to learn from each other and work on a more collaborative basis. Angelica holds a master's degree in Imagineering.

Geoff Marée teaches creativity, innovation, design and imagineering in the fields of hospitality and facility management at BUas. A former president of his office for industrial design, Geoff is also a trainer and public speaker. He is a visiting professor at Haaga–Helia University of Applied Sciences in Helsinki since 2007. He has written several book chapters on innovation and design in hospitality and co-authored a book on organizational concepts: *Work in Wonderland* (2009). He publishes regularly in professional magazines. Geoff is a certified LEGO® Serious Play® facilitator. His research focuses on design-thinking, and creativity skills and processes.

Diane Nijs is the BUas professor of Imagineering. Since joining BUas in 1986, Diane has worked as Academy Director, lecturer, researcher and since 2003 as professor. Working at the interface of complexity science, creative industries, innovation (as whole system healing) and design, her research focuses on the use of liberating practices to unleash collective creativity in strategic desired directions. In 2006 she founded the (Executive) Master Imagineering, a Business Innovation program that was awarded Top Educational Master Program in the Netherlands in 2015. Diane received her PhD in Organization, Complexity and Innovation from the University of Groningen (2014). She regularly speaks at industry and academic conferences and has (co)authored several academic and professional books and articles.

Frank Ouwens finished his bachelor degree in Leisure Management at BUas in 1995, after which he successively graduated for his Master in European Leisure Resource Management at the University of Wales in Swansea. From 1996 to 2008 he has been globally and full-time involved as a practitioner for several live communication agencies in the conceptualization, creative direction and production of large-scale events for brands such as Mercedes-Benz, Deloitte, Allianz, Philips, Pfizer, BMW, Volkswagen AG, Bertelsmann and Volvo. Since 2009 he has operated as a freelance concept developer, creative director and Imagineer for agencies and brands alike such as NIKE EMEA. He combines over 20 years of concepting and experience design in the industry with teaching Imagineering, Experience Design, Concepting and Event Management at the Academy for Leisure of BUas and the Conservatory ArtEZ in Eschede (NL).

Liliya Terzieva is a lecturer, researcher and practitioner in the field of organizational behavior, leadership, andragogy, entrepreneurship and strategic design in the context of tourism, leisure and hospitality. Liliya is a Bulgarian Country Expert with substantial experience in international environment collaboration, and is a member of diverse European Union (EU) networks for project development and implementation as well as of the global network of e-coaches and e-auditors certified by the British Chamber of Commerce and Industry. She holds a PhD in the field of Economic and Organizational sciences of Leisure, Hospitality and Tourism. Apart from the leisure and tourism background, Liliya holds a second master's degree in 'Management of Adult Education'.

Lilian Outtes Wanderley is a lecturer in Corporate Social Responsibility (CSR). Lilian holds a PhD in Management Studies from the University of Cambridge – Cambridge/UK (2005), a MSc in Management from the Universidade Federal do Rio Grande do Sul – Porto Alegre/Brazil (1996) and a BSc in Business Administration from the Universidade Federal de Pernambuco – Recife/Brazil (1994). Her research interests include CSR, Climate Change, Sustainable Transport/Tourism and Development Studies.

Foreword

Benyamin Lichtenstein, University of Massachusetts, Boston, USA

Our world is changing in important ways, with increasing complexity, international social media networks, and more critical attention on the changing climate. How can we incorporate these into our thinking and action? Up to now our thinking – the way we understand our world – has been guided by a Newtonian logic, whereby problems are met with solutions in a relatively linear way. However, straight 'solution thinking' can limit the system when it emphasizes technical challenges but leaves out subtle social drivers of these complex systems.

In response, a new style of design thinking has emerged, represented by **Imagineering**, which offers new ways to generate knowledge. At the core of Imagineering, and other new models, is a 'dynamic agency' – the agents, together, generate new order in the system. Whereas Newtonian thinking tends to emphasize reductionism through analysis, these dynamic models offer a different path, a path of up-building and connecting that helps organizations and social systems. For students who have been taught reductionism as the key method for coping with problems, Imagineering and Generative Emergence open opportunities to think and act in a more nuanced way. These complement a Newtonian approach, offering ways to integrate complex social systems into natural systems, combined with a personal awareness of this process.

The drivers of these models are fully consistent. In Imagineering *Collective Creativity* generates new synergies, as a group of people collectively envision and enact a new idea. In *Generative Emergence* (Lichtenstein, 2014), a parallel approach is offered – a 'cycle of order creation' – and tangible examples show how each step in the cycle can be produced. Another dynamic model is *Effectuation* (Sarasvathy, 2001), which shows how an entrepreneur's resources and enactments can generate emergences. Another, *Self-organization*, explains how far-from-equilibrium dynamics can transform social systems. All of these models turn on how our agency can generate truly unique emergences. All of these models incorporate non-linearity, non-predictability, and distributed agency for explaining and enacting new order.

These dynamic models are emerging at a critical moment in our society. Globalization demands new methods of organizing; moreover, the range of stakeholders and the growth in value chains now extend around the entire world. In the short term we are seeing the emergence of more autocratic and nationalist governments, requiring new ways to invigorate more democratic thinking. In a broader sense, 20th-century economics and trade has made it possible for so many people to purchase so many products; so much so that the earth itself is becoming damaged by the success of this growth-oriented Newtonian worldview. A goal of these new models is to provide an alternative that can complement these mainstream approaches, and thus create a wider range of useful ideas.

How can we characterize these new models? Overall, their main driver is order creation. One could say the goal of these models is to increase the *capacity* of the system, to extend its capabilities beyond what individuals might expect on their own. In Collective Creativity, for example, the new capacity for group-level creativity opens up whole new layers of insight, inspired solutions and innovations. Order creation is also expressed by the resulting positive change and organizational innovation.

Another characteristic is visioning: these models help us dream of new possibilities. They support John F. Kennedy's claim for people 'who can dream of things that never were and ask, "Why Not"?.' *Generative Emergence* starts by envisioning the system in a new way, and to imagine innovation across organizations and systems. *Imagineering* develops a collective – the distributed creativity of the many – to see something new in the old, sparking them to improve their reality.

Overall, our work is for empowering those brave souls who dare to dream, those who dare to leave the beaten path for a more effective one. May this book provide insight and guidance on that path, and may it provide a powerful step in your own journey.

Reference

Lichtenstein, B. B. (2014). *Generative emergence: a new discipline of organizational, entrepreneurial, and social innovation.* Oxford University Press (UK).

Sarasvathy, S. D. (2001). Causation and effectuation: Toward a theoretical shift from economic inevitability to entrepreneurial contingency. *Academy of Management Review,* 26(2), 243–263.

Preface

Diane Nijs, Breda University of Applied Sciences, the Netherlands

This book is for the next generation of managers

This book has been written for the next generation of managers. We strongly believe that when it comes to innovation they need to be educated with something more than the traditional Newtonian scientific framework. The managers of today need to understand the power and hope that comes from looking at the world though the framework of living systems. The book has been written with students in mind and specifically for those in programs in which experience and service design are central, such as leisure, tourism, events, hospitality, games and media, and entertainment management. These types of programs have an untapped 'systemic potential' as we will demonstrate in this book, a potential to educate students and executives to reframe and transform whole systems by inspiration and creative liberation instead of obligation and ever more rules and regulations.

This book on *Advanced Imagineering* aims to show these and other students, managers and entrepreneurs that designing and managing experiences is not just an end in itself in the experience industries, as has been articulated in the Imagineering books so far. This book articulates that, increasingly, designing and managing experiences is a means to an innovation-end in all kinds of other industries and systems. With this book we show the reader that the competence of Imagineering has more uses and is more broadly and widely applicable in a networked world than just the experience industries with which Imagineering is often spontaneously associated.

This book is written for open-minded managers who sense that they are on a threshold of something new and are looking for fresh know-how in order to become more effective in today's dynamic and complex, networked world. For these managers, this book links the Big Shift in society today with the Big Shift that is going on in science and describes the connection in terms of managerial operating logic. The design logic of thinking and acting towards evolution rather than towards a solution will make them more effective in today's world with disruption emerging all around them and in all industries. This book ultimately shows how strategically well-designed and well-managed poetic language can turn a conventional bureaucracy into what Charles Landry (2018) calls a 'Creative bureaucracy'. This is a bureaucracy in which the collective creativity is liberated in strategic ways so as to be able to flourish in a networked world. The book shows that poetic language has not only the capacity to move people, to make them see the world anew, but that it has also the potential to mobilize collectives to act differently.

The first part of this book will appeal to those who are interested in the science and philosophy underlying Imagineering and how it relates to conventional

Design Thinking and innovation. It is probably ambitious for most bachelor students but necessary in the longer term for them to become truly effective social architects. The second part of the book will appeal to those who want to use the design approach of Imagineering in practice. This second part is very much a 'how to' guide including frameworks and checklists. The aim is to bring the Imagineering concepts alive by illustrating them with real-life examples.

This book is about innovation and design in a networked world

The world is transitioning from an industrial era characterized by its mechanical focus on innovation as 'expert innovation' to a networked era characterized by its ecological focus on 'experience innovation'. Expert innovation was largely confined to research and development (R&D) departments; we are all involved in experience innovation as co-creators. Accordingly, innovation and design are entering the social sciences and the management and business schools. All too often, however, this new, emerging field of study is approached through the existing mechanical view on Design Thinking, service design and even experience design. This is understandable perhaps since this view stems from the roots of 'industrial design' as developed in previous decades at the more technically oriented universities.

This book is meant to complement the 'material' view on innovation and design with a 'human systems' view. Innovating a human system is simply not the same as innovating material systems. Design in Systems Thinking is simply not the same as design in conventional Design Thinking. I believe that in contrast to material innovators, human system innovators usually aim to design and do something today that improves the system tomorrow.

The existing 'mechanical' view of the world locks today's managers and politicians into a 'hyper-simplification that makes us blind to the complexity of reality'. This often leads to what French philosopher Morin calls 'mutilating actions'. The 'mechanical' view of the world leads to a limited, linear and material view on innovation and design. There are examples of this all around us that appear daily in the media – for instance the suggestion to build a wall or a fence as a solution for migration or to build shelters as a solution for homelessness. These are 'touchpoint solutions' that fail to take into account the deeper reasons for why these problems exist in the first place; these 'solutions' can actually harm the system further instead of healing it. If we have a 'mechanical' view of the world, we are obsessed with 'solving' problems. The obsession prevails even when the problems at stake cannot be solved but must be coped with in terms of empowerment and evolution. Fortunately, the emerging 'ecological' view of the world can throw a whole new, complementary light on innovation and design in a hyperconnected world.

The journey that led to this book

This book began with my experiences at the turn of the 21st century applying 'High Concept Thinking' in everyday organizations outside the creative industries, trying to help them flourish again. Thinking in terms of a High Concept is a typical and crucial part of the creative industries. You need to boil down your ideas to their absolute essence and then try to verbally capture an imagined world in such a way that it inspires people both internally as co-creators and externally as participants, visitors or spectators. High Concept Thinking is always about inspiring people on both 'sides' to create a new world of value. A High Concept is just like poetry in that its aim is to stimulate the reader to think in new ways, and to make them feel something new so as to make them act differently. A well-designed High Concept can set the stage for generating a new, desired reality and trigger 'innovation as collective creation'.

The experiments with High Concept Thinking in everyday organizations, such as retail chains and cities, have fascinated me for nearly two decades now. I have discovered that this kind of Design Thinking that is typical for the creative industries also has the power to innovate whole systems. I discovered that the experience perspective is a very powerful frame of reference for innovation in times of hyperconnectivity. In such times, innovation is no longer solely about producing better smartphones; it is about innovating with many people together as is the case, for example, in organizational innovation or whole system innovation. Imagineers as social architects can design a High Concept that sets the stage for 'innovation as collective creation' in all kind of industries. This book is the result of our research, experiments and reflections on the innovation potential of the experience perspective.

Our first book on Imagineering, entitled 'Creating Worlds of Experiences', was written in Dutch in 2002 together with my Breda University of Applied Sciences colleague Frank Peters. Right after it was published I received an invitation from the Strategic Director of one of the biggest advertising agencies in Belgium. He had read our book and was struck in particular by one of the examples we highlighted: KetnetCool*** in the Sportpaleis in Antwerp, which is a large event for kids from the Flemish public TV-channel. Ever since its first edition in 1998, this event has attracted some 50,000 participants each year. There are more than 300 co-creators involved and there are kids themselves reporting on screen and in print. It always brings fascinating family warmth to the Christmas holidays. This all felt like 'magic' to the Strategic Director, who worked daily with organizations that were struggling with the impact of growing connectivity. He felt that it was a kind of 'collective art' that he wanted to understand more about.

So I was invited, together with his Creative Director, to consider what High Concept Thinking could do for some of their most challenging accounts. The first account we looked at was the Belgian retail chain Veritas, which at that time was nearly bankrupt. Veritas was then over 100 years old and had some 60 shops selling sewing materials for women who made their own clothes. The CEO of Veritas told me candidly that he tried all the conventional strategies and that he was willing to do whatever it took if I could come up with just one good idea to help the retail chain flourish again. This was the start of a revolutionary experiment. Even today, shifting the mental models and the business models from profit to purpose still feels revolutionary.

The revolution for Veritas started in 2003. We reframed the identity of the company and described the envisioned experience world in the poetic words: 'Veritas, Express Yourself'. People internally and externally started to wonder what this might mean for their daily actions. External people started to see the retail chain differently. Internal staff started to act creatively together in Friday afternoon design team sessions. What emerged was a whole new world of experiences. There were maker workshops in the shops; an atelier; a magazine that was produced and distributed by Sanoma, and a TV spin-off called *The Designers* on Flemish commercial TV. The whole system of Veritas started to self-organize its way to recovery. Veritas became the retail chain of the year in 2011 and even today the chain is still flourishing.

Shortly after the Veritas experience, I read the afterword that organizational scientist Peter Senge (2005) wrote in a new book that appeared at that time: *The World Café: Shaping our futures through conversations that matter*, by Juanita Brown and David Isaacs (2005):

> All my life I have been drawn to the puzzle of collective creating. How is it that sometimes, as if by magic, people create something together, which has beauty, power and life? A sports team that suddenly moves to another plateau where the game is no longer the game but a vehicle for an aesthetic statement (and yet the game is still there). A symphony orchestra that disappears into the music. A dance troupe that ceases being individual dancers. An individual racer who joyously hugs her 'opponents' at the end of the race, knowing that it was only from their collective striving that her performance was possible.
>
> This question has drawn me and guided me, but it has worried me as well. Do the recurring examples of collective creating only happen in sporting events or in the performing arts? Is this why singing, dancing, drumming, running, and jumping have bound human cultures together for all our history? But these activities are less central in modern cultures, and as adults, we are more likely to encounter them as spectators than as participants. Instead, our lives revolve around teaching, parenting, doctoring, and coping with countless daily stresses. As one of many who have argued that collective creating can be cultivated in our daily working lives, I worry that the case has been overstated. While the possibility is undeniable, the practices for reliably realizing that possibility have remained elusive.

Recognizing what Peter Senge was worrying about, we started to organize our research at Breda University around the following question: how can the design approach of Imagineering help a bureaucracy transform into what Charles Landry calls a 'creative bureaucracy'? Or to put it another way, how can High Concept Thinking and poetic language effectuate experience innovation leading to 'innovation as collective creation'? This question has kept us busy ever since (including a doctoral thesis) and will most probably do so for the rest of our professional lives. However, a recent conversation convinced me that we should pause our research for a bit and concentrate on writing this book.

The conversation was with one of the members of the Board of Surplus. Surplus is a healthcare organization in the south of the Netherlands with 3,000 employees and 3,000 volunteers that we have had the privilege to work with over the past two years. He said:

> I know that together we have discovered a major key in how to transform bureaucracies into 'creative bureaucracies'. Reframing the identity of a health care system in poetic language as we did with 'See Me' [see Chapter 4 for more about this case and a reference to a 20-minute movie] is a very powerful way to unlock and sustain collective creativity in a more desired direction. Well-designed and well-managed poetic language can set the stage for the collective creation of 'beauty' and heal the system at the same time. It is indeed beauty that I see appear everywhere in the organization. Besides of the emergence of beauty, we can report a structural improvement in the rate of absence of employees in the departments that are already operating with 'See Me'. And no, we are not there yet. And we have to stay humble since all innovation is human endeavor and therefore vulnerable. But I know this system is healing itself now and it is moving 'From Rules to Relation' as all actors in the healthcare system in the Netherlands are aiming for this.

I realized that the field of innovation urgently needs to become a matter of collective creation.

The core argument of this book

We have a design problem today, rather than a management problem. So says Paul Hawken in *The Ecology of Commerce* (Hawken, 1993:55). He believes that we must learn to design systems 'where doing good is like falling off a log, where the natural, everyday acts of work and life accumulate into a better world as a matter of course, not a matter of conscious altruism'. The concept of Design Thinking is indeed rising up the agenda of management. Nevertheless, Design Thinking remains overlooked and oversimplified in much of today's management practice and education as it is often defined as the process of empathizing and rapid prototyping in relation to products and services. As such, the impact on managerial decision thinking has been limited.

We argue that, in order to be effective in management, conventional 'Newtonian' Design Thinking should be extended with complex systems Design Thinking. It should also be executed by the CEOs, strategists and policy makers themselves. In this book we present the argument that 'High Concept Thinking' is a way forward to do just that. Managers in today's networked world must learn to set the stage to make something that feels like magic: a small intervention that generates an important, big effect. They have to learn to set the stage for 'innovation as collective creation'. They are the ones that can help 'people create something together which has beauty, power and life' (Senge, 2005). It follows that management education must develop its own Design Thinking 'toolbox'.

What Imagineering can bring you

'We are still in the Barbarian times of our thinking' according to the French philosopher Morin (2008:6). I think he is telling us in a deliberately shocking way that we might be less sophisticated in our thinking than we think we are right now. Most people are still locked into mechanistic logic in all that they do. They do not even realize that their worldview is somewhat outdated. My colleagues and I at Breda University believe that it is time to become more nuanced in our thinking. We think that studying the basics of complexity science in relation to innovation and design can open our eyes in the right direction. Our opinion is that we have celebrated the genius of the few for way too long without seeing the potential of the many. This has to change because innovation is in the DNA of all of us. New and different ideas emerge when we collaborate in coping with complex issues and a new future becomes possible for us all. We strongly believe that knowledge matters.

We have observed over the last decade that the young people we teach often become very inspired with Imagineering. The discovery that the analytic, reductionist scientific perspective has a complement in the living systems is something that clearly resonates with their experiences in the networked society. They see that this new perspective works in a holistic, systemic way to generate new order instead of fragmentation. However, it is the principle that small interventions can result in big effects that inspires them the most. They discover that they can play a role in society and they feel that even young people can make change happen. From this moment on, they seem to loosen up and their study becomes a real engagement for life. We are very confident that students who study Imagineering and its impact will as a result act differently as leaders and managers.

When working with executives, we have observed that many organizations do a fairly good job of using certain elements of innovation. However, the piecemeal approach is rarely effective in today's connected society. Today, more than ever, systems are the frameworks of our lives. The solar system, the organizations, the human body – these are all living systems in which all the component parts work together to keep the body flourishing. Innovation in this context is so much more than realizing better products, processes or services; innovation becomes first and foremost about optimizing (some scholars even speak about 'healing') the system as a whole. Imagineering is an experience-based systems approach to innovation and creativity management. It is uniquely suited to the values, beliefs and organizational challenges that face managers, politicians, entrepreneurs and leaders today. Imagineering is a design process for whole system innovation that can enable you to:

- not only do the work better, but do better work;
- cope effectively with the new players in your industry;
- learn faster and innovate faster than your competitors;
- become a continuous innovator in a strategic, desired direction;
- unlock collective creativity in that same desired direction;
- engage your workforce in a more meaningful way; and

- engage internal as well as external stakeholders in co-creating value with you.

We are perfectly aware that a book cannot change your actions directly but we hope that it can change your mind. This book is intended to trigger you to think differently and to see things in a different way. From then on it is up to you to decide whether what you read is so fascinating that you try to act upon your new insights or not. We, of course, hope you will.

References

Brown, J., and Isaacs, D. (2005). *The world café: Shaping our futures through conversations that matter.* Berrett-Koehler, Inc.

Hawken, P. (1993). A declaration of sustainability. *Utne Reader*, September/October: 54–61.

Landry, C. (2018). Creative bureaucracy. Available: http://charleslandry.com/themes/creative-bureaucracy/ (accessed October 8, 2018).

Morin, E. (2008). *On complexity.* Hampton Press.

Nijs, D., and Peters, F. (2002). *Imagineering. Het creëren van belevingswerelden.* Amsterdam: Boom.

Senge, P. (2005). Afterword: Discovering the magic of collective creativity. In: Brown, J., and Isaacs, D. *The world café: Shaping our futures through conversations that matter.* Berrett Koehler, Inc, pp. 217–220.

Acknowledgments

I want to thank the remarkable people who I have had the privilege to work with over the last two decades. There are many people that could be mentioned here but some stand out in particular for their contribution to this book and the thinking behind it. I would like to thank Johan Leyssen and Tom Andries who were both directors at the advertising agency LDV-Bates in Antwerp when I started to experiment. I have many others from industry to thank but most especially Marc Peeters, former CEO of Veritas; Anton van Mansum and Anthonie Maranus, President and member of the board of Surplus; Marieke Beekers, Chief Connecting Officer and Nadine Gooijers, Strategic Advisor, both at the city of Breda; Dirk Diels, Director Entrepreneurship and Innovation at the city of Antwerp; and Annemie Lemahieu, Director Innovation at Unizo Belgium.

I would like to thank the Board of Breda University and in particular Dr. Elisabeth Minnemann and Nico van Os for their ongoing commitment to Imagineering. Then there is, of course, my great international team of co-writers and researchers that I would like to thank here: Celiane, Lilian and Fabio all from Brazil; Frank, Geoff and Angelica from the Netherlands; and Liliya from Bulgaria. In addition, I explicitly want to thank my colleagues Frank Crucq, Gert-Jan Remmers, Suzan Lindhout, Pim Dopheide and Koert de Jager (former Director of Breda University) for their ever eye-opening work so relevant to the topics in this book. And last, but definitely not least, I would like to thank Jonathan Clark for taking care of the editing of this book at a time that was very challenging for him personally: Jonathan, that our work may also be a tribute to the ones we love.

I have had extremely valuable academic feedback along the road to this new field of complexity, innovation and design. With this in mind I have a large number of great scholars to thank. In the Netherlands, Jo van Engelen, Professor of Integrated Sustainable Solutions, and Ena Voute, Dean of the Faculty of Industrial Design, both at the University of Delft; Sjoerd Romme, Professor of Entrepreneurship and Innovation at the Technical University of Eindhoven; Danielle Zandee, Professor of Sustainable Organizational Development at Nyenrode University and Ton Jorg, former Senior Complexity Researcher at the University of Utrecht. In Belgium, I want to thank Koen Vandenbempt, Dean of the Faculty of Business & Management of the University of Antwerp.

In the UK, I would like to thank Eve Mitleton-Kelly, Professor and Director of the EMK Complexity Group at the London School of Economics, and Robert Young, Professor of Design Practice in the Department of Design, Faculty of Arts, Design and Social Sciences, Northumbria University. In South Africa, I would like to thank Ronel Rensburg, Professor and Director of the Centre for Communication and Reputation Management. In China, I would like to thank my former colleague, Dr. Wendong Deng and Ken Friedman, Editor-in-Chief of *She Ji: The Journal of Design, Economics, and Innovation*, and Professor of Design at Tongi University. Finally, in the US, I would like to thank my former colleague at the Master Imagineering and awards winning author at Fast Company, Soren Kaplan; Alfonso Montuori, Professor in the Transformative Inquiry Department at California Institute of Integral Studies and co-supervisor of my PhD-study; and finally, but definitely not the least important, Benyamin Lichtenstein, Associate Professor of Entrepreneurship and Management at the University of Massachusetts, Boston, and author of the most inspiring Oxford book on Generative Emergence. Benyamin never ceased giving me very valuable feedback for this book.

Special thanks go of course to my family and friends; to my children, Kaat and Michel, my partner Johan, and my close friends Axelle, Veerle, Tanja and Jo for all the beauty we have together.

1

Introduction: towards a new design discipline

Diane Nijs

Innovation is at the top of the management agenda in nearly every company today. However, despite significant investments in innovation, results remain largely disappointing. Today's product and service innovations, like the growth they generate, are often incremental, fleeting and marginal. According to recent research (Jaruzelski et al., 2015), worldwide research and development (R&D) spending on innovation rose 5.1 percent in 2015 and yet revenue for the same companies increased by less than 1 percent. Times are changing fundamentally and what we need now is a more holistic approach to innovation first. To say it metaphorically: we need to stop rearranging the deck chairs, while in many industries we are on the Titanic. To become more effective in product and service innovation, we need to focus on innovation from the experience perspective first.

Innovating from the experience perspective is fundamentally different from innovation from the expert perspective. Expert, mechanistic innovation happens mainly in R&D departments and is often about fixing problems. Innovation from the experience perspective is emergent and joined-up in nature. Instead of being an isolated project or event, experience innovation is an unfolding journey of people thinking and acting differently. The emergence of novelty results from an articulated ideology that inspires many fine-grained, creative human inter-actions, each building upon one another in complex innovation eco-systems. Innovations such as the slow-food movement, Ben & Jerry's (Lead with your values and make money too), Harley-Davidson (independence, freedom, express yourself) and Starbucks (creating a third place, a place away from home and work), start from a better ideology rather than a better technology.

The concept of experience innovation needs some deeper clarification first while it is central to this book and is used with different meanings in different streams of literature. In the literature on the hedonic sectors, such as entertain-ment and hospitality, the concept refers to innovating experiences (Jernsand, Kraff and Mossberg, 2015) while in the literature outside these sectors, experi-ence innovation refers to innovating strategically through experience staging (Candi, Beltagui and Riedel, 2013). This book focuses on the latter meaning: innovating strategically from the experience perspective. Writing this book is the more relevant while there is a growing recognition of the opportunities for experience innovation but the literature so far is failing to address how firms and organizations outside the hedonic sectors can join, what Pine and Gilmore (1999) coined as the experience economy. Pine and Gilmore argued that strategists that ignore the experience perspective in value creation risk falling into the trap of competing purely on price, resulting in ever dwindling profit margins and disconnection with the market in the long term.

The experience perspective on innovation has always existed but it often goes unrecognized and has remained somewhat unexplored in the non-hedonic sectors. With growing connectivity in society, however, times are changing fast. Today we all know some iconic experience innovators: Uber, Airbnb, and many more startups. Car service Uber did not innovate the taxicab product by changing the vehicle or retraining the drivers. It fundamentally redesigned the experience: the way you order, meet and pay for rides, and also how you assess your driver after a ride, which might generate even more business for him or her. Airbnb did not innovate the hotel or the travel portal. Without owning any lodgings itself, it completely redesigned how people find somewhere to stay. Moreover, it also created a way to make new friends all over the world by renting the house of a local.

Of course, these iconic experience innovators, as with all structural innovations, challenge the status quo of society too. But this does not prevent the list of startup experience innovators becoming longer by the day: Spotify and iTunes changed music consumption, Snapchat changed news consumption, SocietyOne changed banking, Netflix redesigned the movie industry, and while producers such as Gillette are still looking for one more variation in the assortment, experience innovators such as the Dollar Shave Club shake up the market with simple, low-cost mail subscription business models (Marshall et al., 2016).

This is not a new phenomenon. As early as 2003 management scholars Prahalad and Ramaswamy (2003:12) announced experience innovation as the next development in, and the future of, innovation. They noted that growing connectivity in society was transforming the meaning and process of innovation in such a way that it becomes ever more difficult to realize profitable business and growth through traditional means only. According to them: 'The next practices of innovation must shift the focus away from products and services and onto experience environments – supported by a network of companies and consumer communities – to co-create unique value for individual customers.' Designing innovation as an opportunity for collective creation by a community of creation (Sawhney and Prandelli (2000:24) able to 'benefit from the creativity, diversity, and agility' of partners and customers, however, is as yet in its infancy. Communities of creation, different from traditional communities of practice, are communities that span as well functional organizational boundaries. They integrate the broad diversity of actors in a system to create common knowledge and value.

Let's first illustrate the need for complementing expert innovation with experience innovation in a practical situation that we can all relate to (Boxes 1.1 and 1.2).

The problem of inner city centers is just one of the many examples that illustrate the ineffectiveness of our conventional, expert innovation today. In the

---

BOX 1.1

IMAGINEERING SNAPSHOT: INNOVATING THE EVER MORE DESERTED CITY CENTER

There was a time when city centers were vibrant places. But the centers of most Western cities today are ever more deserted: 10 percent and sometimes up to 30 percent of the business units stand empty. Why? Two major forces affecting high streets are the growth of online shopping and the emergence of out-of-town shopping centers. City councils in hollowed-out towns are unhappy with this evolution since the high street has always been an indicator of how well a city is doing and boarded up shop fronts simply don't look attractive. There are plans in almost every city to try to reverse the rot. Millions are invested in a High Street Innovation Fund most often to realize infrastructural improvements: for example, building a large covered market in the city center. But these 'infrastructural' plans are made on the 'supply-side' only; they are unlikely to save city centers since they don't bring people back. The conventional, 'mechanistic' way that expert innovators cope with this kind of complex eco-system problem is no longer effective. We need complementary thought and action if we want to become more effective in coping with this kind of systemic issue. We need to complement expert innovation with experience innovation.

BOX 1.2

IMAGINEERING SNAPSHOT: FASHION DISTRICT ARNHEM (IN DUTCH: MODE KWARTIER ARNHEM)

Arnhem as a city has a history and reputation in fashion and design. At the turn of the 21st century, the local government decided that the livability of one of the neighborhoods, the 'Vogelaarswijk' (Vogelaars Neighborhood), should be improved. A public housing corporation bought some ten units and started to rent them out to fashion and design entrepreneurs at a reduced tariff. In 2006 the first four fashion shops opened their doors. In 2007 a disused postal distribution center from another location was broken down into 125 pieces and re-erected in the district as 'Station Klarendal', a fashion center with several shops and a café–restaurant. In 2012 the central square was named 'Elly Lamaker', referring to the founder of the Fashion Academy of the regional Art University (ArtEZ). Increasingly, decisions in this neighborhood drew their inspiration from the field of fashion to further develop the authentic (at least to the city of Arnhem) and inspiring identity of the district. Today there are some 50 shops and some 70 fashion and design business units mixed with regular houses to avoid the conventional high street idea. Fashion District Arnhem is now a vibrant place. It has already won several prizes for inspiring urban renewal projects.

---

network economy, coping with many of our 'unsolvable' problems is no longer a question of fixing the past but requires re-inventing and re-creating the future together. It requires a mindset of experience innovation first. The fact that so many city centers continue to struggle with revitalization raises the question why these cities do not make this seemingly simple choice.

There are several reasons perhaps. Firstly, there is the scenario of simply not knowing; ideological, cultural and experience opportunities have often gone unrecognized because of the dominance of the conventional, engineering paradigm that is oriented towards economies of scale and safeness. Secondly, even if those responsible do recognize the potential of mind-shifting experience strategies, they often have no idea how to shift from a mind-sharing to a mind-shifting paradigm since it is systemic in nature; an individual shop-owner cannot turn the tide of urban decline. And, thirdly, it seldom happens that 'emergent' experience innovation, also called value-driven innovation (Lindhult et al., 2015), emerges 'spontaneously', as was the case in Arnhem. Emergent innovation, innovation from the experience perspective, must be designed for consciously or unconsciously. Fashion District Arnhem emerged from unconscious design. In this specific case, many creative actions consistently took further the unconscious, intuitive choice for fashion that was taken by the public housing corporation leading to an ever stronger, emergent whole system innovation.

This chapter will unfold as follows: first, we will focus on the evolution of innovation in society in order to understand that to become more effective innovators we should learn to talk in a more nuanced way about the phenomenon of innovation. With a more nuanced view on the phenomenon of innovation, we will discuss the need to extend our thinking with what Lichtenstein (2014) calls 'generative emergence', a new discipline of organizational, entrepreneurial and social innovation. Aligned with this thinking, we will argue in Section 1.3 that we too need a new discipline of design in order to unlock generative emergence which Nijs (2014) calls 'Imagineering': unlocking and orchestrating whole system experience innovation by designing and using properly a generative image that shifts the collective focus from problem to aspirational future. We will finish this chapter with an overview of the structure of the rest of the book (Section 1.4).

1.1   The evolution of innovation

The example of the revitalization of the inner cities illustrates that the challenges we face in society and the nature of the micro-innovation processes we can use to cope with them, co-evolve with the socioeconomic context that characterizes the economy, in this case the network economy (Teece, 1987; Bessant, 1991; Dodgson et al., 2005). Innovation scholars have recognized this evolution. Rothwell (1992, 1994), a British sociologist and pioneer in understanding innovation management, documented this evolution in five generations of micro-innovation models (see Table 1.1). His five generations model provides a historic overview of innovation management in the Western world between the 1950s and 1990.

Rothwell observed that more effective innovation processes lead to a decrease in time to market and a reduction of costs. These five generations of models, going from 'supply push, technology-driven innovation models' (1G) in the 1950s and 1960s to 'strategic, integrated and open, ideology-driven models' (5G) of innovation in the 1990s, appear with a different timing in different countries, industries, segments and policies.

One of the main changes evident across these five generations of

Table 1.1 Rothwell's five generations of innovation models

Generation	Key features
1st: supply push	Technology-driven push: simple linear sequential process
2nd: market pull	Need pull: simple linear sequential process
3rd: coupling model	Recognizing interaction between different elements and feedback loops between them, the interaction between different departments, all within a firm
4th: collaborative model	Interaction upstream with suppliers and downstream with demanding and active customers, emphasis on linkages and alliances
5th: collective model	Whole eco-system integration, extensive networking model with continuous innovation ever more ideology-driven A strategic, integrated and open model

Source: Based on Rothwell (1992).

micro-innovation processes is the shift from closed, technology-push, expert models to progressively more open, whole system experience innovation models of collective creation, in which the boundaries of the innovating organization become ever more porous. Each new generation retains the key features of the one before, but adds ever-greater interaction and feedback. This increase in openness and complexity (everything relates to everything else) creates strategic innovation challenges, mostly around orchestration of the initiatives. Further, each generation of innovation model is harder to adopt than the previous one, as ever more actors are involved.

The shift from closed, first-generation, expert models to open, later-generation, experience models is also visible in the evolution of the definitions of innovation. From the original distinction made by Schumpeter between invention ('the occurrence of a new idea for a new product or process') and innovation ('the first attempt to carry it out in practice') (Fagerberg, 2004), more recent definitions of 5G experience innovation embrace the demand side. Innovation now is defined as 'the adoption of a new practice by a community' and it focuses on the mobilization of new, collective and creative behavior (Denning and Dunham, 2010) and the use of generative innovation practices (Tanev and Frederiksen, 2014; Tanev et al., 2011) to augment the effectiveness of the innovation micro-processes. Such recent, behavioral-oriented definitions and the aligned generative practices to foster innovation in a sustainable way emphasize the critical role of all the actors involved (hence a collective model): the innovators, the entrepreneurs, the customers and the policy makers.

While 1G expert innovation processes take place in a single department in a single organization, 5G experience innovation processes mean that innovation and value creation become ever more connected in ever more complex ways to other actors in the innovation and creation eco-system (Dougherty, 2016; Vargo et al., 2015). Thus, coordination and orchestration across the actors become a core part of the 5G innovation process. 5G experience innovation processes are at the frontier of today's best practices in business innovation. They are

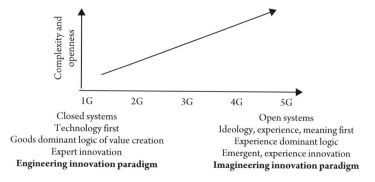

Figure 1.1 The evolution of innovation models (Rothwell, 1992) and the dominant logic of value creation in relation to growing complexity and openness

strategically fully integrated network-based, open creation and innovation processes, integrating both knowledge and creativity from inside as well as outside actors in processes that are central to what the organization does (Figure 1.1).

The new technologies that dramatically lower the cost of communication, research, and distributed learning and production are central to the emergence of 5G experience innovation processes. This generation of innovation processes enables collective creation and collaboration as never before. 5G experience-innovation processes (think, for example, of social, public, organizational or whole system innovation) require special skills and practices. Indeed, this is so much so that scholars argue that we face a paradigm shift from closed to open innovation systems for which we need a new innovation discipline, a discipline which Lichtenstein (2014) proposes to call 'generative emergence' (Section 1.2). Within that framework we need a new design discipline that Nijs (2014) proposes to call Imagineering (Section 1.3).

1.2   A new discipline of innovation: generative emergence

The paradigm shift from closed to open innovation that is manifesting itself in the network economy has far-reaching implications for both practice and science. Digitalization is not only a major driver of this growing connectivity, openness and complexity, but it is also leading to the deeper scientific understanding of our world. The huge computational power we have today means that scientists can start to decode the non-linear phenomena that are central to all living systems, such as the weather, the economy and other living phenomena, to complement the conventional, linear Newtonian worldview (see Chapter 3). Goldstein et al. (2010:5) write: 'finally it is important to note that organizations have always been complex. What has changed is our ability to understand them as complex systems and thereby influence them'. The emerging complementary worldview of the living systems (introduced in Chapter 3) leads scientists to a more in-depth understanding and to new thinking, not in the least concerning 5G experience-innovation practices and the implications for management and innovation policy.

Scientists have started to make a distinction between two types of science: an equilibrium science of forces through the mechanistic science perspective that began with Newton, and a new, emerging science of rules based on living systems

(Potts, 2017) – also called complexity science (introduced in Chapter 3). To put it simply these two complementary worldviews lead to two complementary frameworks for innovation policy and management: a framework for reallocating resources (such as realizing infrastructural innovations or realizing taxes and other regulations on the empty shops in the inner city case) and a framework for redesigning rules to generate new order in living systems (Colander and Kupers, 2014; Potts, 2017). This is similar to the choice of fashion as an experience rule of thumb for rethinking critical actions in the Arnhem case. While conventional design, which makes use of the imagination and creativity of involved experts, operates in the first framework, the design approach of Imagineering makes use of the imagination and creativity of all the involved actors, and thus operates in the second.

The real challenge, of course, is to master this second perspective on innovation by redesigning rule(s) consciously; this is the intention of the design approach of Imagineering. While the case in this chapter has been chosen for clarity, most of the other examples in this book were consciously designed for; indeed some have been designed for by the authors of this book themselves.

1.2.1 From emergent, experience innovation to generative emergence

According to complexity scientist Lichtenstein (2014), emergent 5G experience innovation processes should be approached as a matter of 'emergence' and not as the mechanistic concept we call 'innovation'. Lichtenstein argues that to become more effective in organizational, entrepreneurial and social innovation, and in all these new innovation challenges that typically emerge with the network economy, we need to build a new discipline of innovation. This will be a new field of study based on insights from the science of the living systems – a discipline of 'generative emergence'. Let's first understand the concept of emergence and its relevance for organizations and then we will turn to the characteristics of 'generative emergence' (Chapter 3 is totally devoted to this new scientific worldview).

'Emergence' is a property of all complex adaptive systems (adaptive systems are systems that can learn – human systems for instance). Emergence is the coming-into-being of a sustainable dynamic state arising out of the interactions among components (agents) that make up the system itself (Lichtenstein, 2014). Emergence is a natural pattern of change that can easily be recognized in times of 'emergency', which is a closely related word and phenomenon. In case of emergency, a disturbance interrupts ordinary life and all people spontaneously take on different tasks. This natural way of changing provides an alternative for the mechanistic thinking about change and innovation. Simply put, emergence is order arising out of chaos. Emergence is a phenomenon that has always existed. It is the reason a tree can grow from a small seed or a chicken can grow from an egg: two biological events that clearly cannot be explained based on the laws of gravitation. Emergence is not only the reason why there are hurricanes but also why there are social phenomena such as traffic congestions, rock concerts, and democracies.

'Generative emergence' then 'explores the dynamics of creation and re-creation of and in organizations, ventures, projects, initiatives, and social endeavors of all kinds' (Lichtenstein, 2014:3). 'Generative emergence' refers to social entities that 'arise and remain stable through intentional creative agency and organizing'. While emergency is triggered by a dramatic event, generative emergence, the emergence of an entity (e.g. an organization) is triggered by aspiration – 'to provide some kind of value, that is [. . .] valued by other agents' too (Lichtenstein, 2014:17).

1.2.2 Differentiating generative emergence from change and transformation

According to Lichtenstein (2014:5), the concept of emergence throws organizational change and transformation into a whole new light. Emergence presents itself as a third distinct process. Lichtenstein mentions four crucial differences between emergence as a process of generative, complex innovation and the two other processes, namely change and transformation:

First, while change and transformation always involve the modification of existing elements after a crisis dislodged the inertia of the system, emergence is **always creation**, and never simply change or transformation. 'Emergence is the invention of something new, the origination of a distinct system and/or the structures within it.' Consider again the case of the inner city, where the emergent entity is not the result of a change. Although the behavior of the individual actors in the system changes, there is also a new situation that arises based on the design of the mind-shifting concept of 'Fashion District Arnhem'.

The second difference with change and transformation lies in the trigger for the emergence of a new system, which is **aspiration** (Simon, 1955). Lichtenstein (2014:5) interprets:

> The vision and enactment of a new opportunity to be capitalized on. [. . .]
> Whereas crisis leads to a reactive attempt to save the organization, aspiration is an entrepreneurial desire to create new value, to make a new, meaningful contribution to a community or market. For this reason, emergence and re-emergence are often initiated when nothing is wrong per se in the organization; they are not triggered by a problem or urgent issue. And if they are, they turn the reactivity into procreative action. [. . .] One of the benefits of aspiration is that it can generate a projected future that may have fewer constraints and more creativity for the organization.

Articulating the concept of 'Fashion District Arnhem' in that specific context was the aspirational, creative spark that shifted the collective focus and triggered the emergence of an important development that would not have happened otherwise. However, emergence is not a matter of planning, meaning that the articulation of this concept won't have the same effect in every situation; what emerges is dependent on the unique situation and can never be predicted.

'Thirdly, this spark of creativity produces a whole different set of behaviors than is likely in crisis-driven change' (Lichtenstein 2014:5). Instead of evoking 'reactive creativity', which is characterized by negativity and desperation, it evokes **'proactive creativity'**, which is characterized by 'intrinsic motivation, positive affect, and focused self-discipline' (Heinzen, 1994:140). In 'Fashion District Arnhem' both employees and visitors will act differently in that region than they did before the reframing of the identity of the system. Moreover, talking about a 'Fashion District' in different settings will lead to different policies than would have been the case when seeing this region as a fragmented and deteriorated neighborhood. The aspirational shift in the collective focus will lead to previously unthought-of creative actions and interactions.

Fourth, contrary to the common modes of change and transformation, 'emergent structures **expand the capacity of the system** by an unprecedented amount, vastly increasing the capacity of the system to accomplish its work' (Prigogine and Stengers, 1984; Swenson, 1988, 1989 in Lichtenstein, 2014:6). A process of emergence improves the efficiency, adaptability and performance of the system in ways that would be impossible through common modes of change. In Arnhem, the reframed identity of the deteriorated eco-system made it possible for this region to become an example of economic, social and environmental development and to flourish. This new identity expanded the capacity of the system in many ways.

1.2.3   Beyond self-organization

From the foregoing it becomes obvious that emergent, experience innovation, or rather 'generative emergence', is at the same time a matter for the forest and for the trees. It is only by reframing the identity of the system (the forest) that individual actors (trees) are enabled to rethink decisions and actions in view of the collective aspiration (it is possible to plant new trees that together make the 'new' forest come alive).

The big question that arises is then: how do we design consciously for generative emergence? The aspect of reframing or redefining the forest (the whole entity) is often hard to grasp as conventional problem solving approaches have taught people to solve problems by analyzing them to see where improvements are needed. Generative emergence, however, is not a matter of fixing the past, nor is it a matter of pure self-organization or dismantling hierarchically directed command and control structures. Instead, it is about shifting the collective focus as to create the the context in which all actors are inspired to act differently. It is a matter of setting the stage to enable innovation as self-organizing collective creation – exactly the opposite of laissez-faire (Goldstein, 2011; Goldstein et al. 2010; Goldstein, 2005; MacIntosh and MacLean, 1999).

Complexity researchers agree unanimously that it is a serious misunderstanding that emergence in organizational settings could be the result of self-organization only – 'a term that suggests spontaneity and the inner-driven onset of new order' (Goldstein, 2005:3). They argue that the emergence of new order is always appropriately constructed (Goldstein, 2005) or conditioned (MacIntosh and MacLean, 1999). According to Lichtenstein (2014:204), 'generative emergence is always driven by agency, in the form of a vision for how to improve the social ecology by creating new value, and an aspiration – a motivation and intention – to pursue that vision'. In other words: Generative emergence needs design, a design for evolution. This then brings us to the core of this book: the design approach of Imagineering.

1.3   A new discipline of design: Imagineering

Imagineering is a blend word of imagination and engineering: generating optimized realities by making use of the imagination of all involved actors (see Chapter 4). According to Simon (1969) to design is to devise courses of action aimed at changing existing situations into preferred ones. In 1G expert innovation situations, design is a matter of experts using their imagination and creativity to come up with better solutions. In 5G emergent, experience innovation processes, design is a matter of shifting the collective focus in an aspirational way as to create the context in which all the involved actors are inspired to use their own imagination and creativity to generate a more desired reality together. Designing to evoke generative emergence is a matter of designing for evolution. Design here is about setting the stage to enable innovation as collective creation. Nijs (2014) proposes calling this design discipline Imagineering: designing and using a 'Creative Tension Engine' (CTE) to catalyze innovation as collective creation.

Designing to evoke generative emergence is still a rather new field waiting to be discovered. In Chapter 4 we will articulate the history of the word, the coming-into-being of the design approach of Imagineering and in Part II we articulate the design approach in practice. For now we will focus on the central mechanism of all Imagineering, namely the CTE. CTEs are presented in this book as a central mechanism through which innovators contextualize all innovation with aspirational meaning (Garud et al., 2014; Garud and Giuliani, 2013; Garud et al., 2010 and 2011). Let's start with an example and zoom in on the micro-processes of innovation that unfold from the design and use of a CTE to then describe exactly what it is (Box 1.3).

Examples such as the slow-food movement, AirBnB, Arnhem Fashion Quarter, the first national park perhaps give the impression that Imagineering is fun and easy. It is most definitely fun but it is not at all easy. Challenge yourself for a moment to discover the complexity of the design work. Think for example about the center of the city you live in that might also suffer with too many empty shops and try to design an appropriate CTE to turn the tide. And no, you may not copy-paste the 'Arnhem Fashion Center' idea since this is highly unlikely to work for your own city. Or think of a CTE that might turn the tide for a local library that most probably suffers from a diminishing number of people still making use of it. Or think of a conventional school and realize how hard it is to come up with a great CTE to set the stage for innovation as collective creation. Designing a CTE such as 'First National Park' is definitely simple in hindsight (and indeed the best CTEs are very simple by nature), but it is much harder when facing the original problem at the start. Most probably this is what Oliver Wendell Holmes (1897), a physician and one of the best regarded American poets of the 19th century, had in mind when he said: 'For the simplicity on this side of complexity, I wouldn't give you a fig. But for the simplicity on the other side of complexity, for that I would give you anything I have.' Let's discover the concept in more depth.

BOX 1.3

IMAGINEERING SNAPSHOT: THE EMERGENCE OF THE FIRST NATIONAL PARK IN BELGIUM

In the 1990s, at the very moment that all the coalmines closed down in the province of Limburg (Belgium) leaving 40,000 people unemployed, Ignace Schops and a group of friends were dreaming of 'making nature conservation sexy'. First, they developed the (marketing) concept: Hoge Kempen, Groene Kans (Hoge Kempen, Green Chance). But nothing happened until the friends, who regularly visited national parks during their holidays, started to dream of having the first national park in Belgium in their own region of Limburg. It was a rather strange idea but they imagined that, if all the fragmented land in the coalmine region could be brought together, this could result in the first national park. Reconnecting land instead of fragmenting it further for development is something rarely done. Bringing back nature to make the system healthy and flourishing again was something the friends really believed in as being a viable business model.

Their belief, together with their previous professional experience of developing high-quality biking routes and selling biking cards, convinced them of the fact that developing a national park was a viable route to building local economy by conserving nature. The '(Re)connection model' they believe is applicable for all value creation in society is based on four principles: reconnecting people with nature, reconnecting nature with nature, reconnecting business with biodiversity and reconnecting policy with practice.

The national park was opened in 2006 and looking back, Ignace highlights three principles as being core to their success: first, there is a real, big ambition that is easy to articulate (the first national park) and inspires many people, businesses and governments to join forces; second, all actors that decide to join forces should win through participating; third, there is M3: 'Mensen, middelen en mandaat' (people, resources and legitimacy). Let's explain and illustrate these three principles with some examples.

1. Real big ambition, aspiration, easy to articulate

'Our own national park' was a sufficient set of words to set people wondering how this could be a viable option in their region. Nearly everyone had positive associations with these words and were in favor of its realization as long as it brought them something and did not cost too much. As a result, all meetings were about the 'how' not about the 'what'. They made an initial master plan that had a long-term viewpoint (for example, a small industrial location in the park was planned to disappear in 25 years and the maintenance of the park stays with the Flemish Agency for Nature and Forests (ANB)). This plan convinced local governments as well as the provincial and national authorities to give them a budget on the condition that they had to match the amount with their own, commercial-generated funding. Which they did.

2. All actors that join the movement should win

All actors in the network learn by doing that they all can win by serving a better cause than by focusing shortsightedly on direct income.

➡

Nearly all participation is free. Even the entrance to the park is free. Visitors pay only for extra activities, which are mostly organized by third parties who can earn money. An example is the city of Zutendaal, which created 'the bare foot path'. This little village has only 7,000 inhabitants but the activity attracts more than 150,000 visitors each year who each pay 3 euro, which adds up to a significant income for the village. In addition, these special activities act as sweet spots that keep the majority of visitors near to the villages instead of having them spread over the whole of the park, which might be damaging for nature in the long term. Moreover, the value of land neighboring the national park is reported to have increased.

Hotels in the neighborhood of the park may use the park-registered logos free as long as they act according to agreed guidelines. Failure to follow the guidelines can result in losing the right to use the logos. Even though these participating hotels have their own communication budgets, they all report rising figures from the very start of the park. They are even now in favor of other good causes as long as they see a positive return in the end. All actors in the network learn through their participation that they should take a short-sighted view on direct income but that serving a better cause can lead to a much larger indirect income. Some hotel owners have now redesigned their properties to make a better fit with the national park and its visitors.

From the very beginning Ignace worked with the regional universities on rolling sets of experiments with a focus on monitoring and measuring success. New experiments are continuously being designed, for example there is one now on social value. Ignace deliberately placed extra-large benches in the park because this encourages people to share them with strangers. The hypothesis is that this will stimulate them to talk with one another and share experiences leading to them becoming happy ambassadors of the venue. Ignace has another interesting hypothesis around healthcare: how does the emergence of the national park influence healthcare in the province?

3. People, resources and legitimacy

To be successful you must be able to work with passionate people. You also need to have resources to start with and the ability to grow the resources in the long term. Finally, you should not even consider starting the whole process without the support of the most senior people in charge of the endeavor. Research shows that the inspiring work of Ignace and his team realizes yearly a (direct and indirect) return of 191 million euro and that it generates 5,000 connected jobs (Otte, 2011).

Their 'dream' became the dream of many participants, who in turn made their own dreams come true in their sub-systems. The first national park in Belgium acted as a 'CTE' making it possible to use nature conservation as a catalyst to create a more flourishing eco-system. It enabled the attraction of 1.2 million visitors to the region. It created hundreds of jobs directly and even more indirectly. It made the actors (governments as well as commercial) in the neighborhood more entrepreneurial. It increased the value of the neighboring land. Finally, it enabled the regeneration of the social beauty of this multicultural setting and the natural beauty of the region. In 2008 Ignace won the Goldman Environmental Prize in San Francisco.

(Personal interview with Ignace Schops on February 13, 2018)

1.3.1 Creative Tension Engine

Senge (1990, 2014; Senge et al., 2015) defines creative tension as the gap between the current reality and the aspirational future. According to him, this gap creates energy and it exists in 1G expert innovation as well as in 5G experience innovation. As with all tension in life, people want to solve the tension that they experience. Tension is what keeps people thinking. In the context of expert innovation, it will be the engineers and/or the economists that feel challenged to resolve the tension. In experience innovation, we argue that the design and use of a CTE can create the context in which all actors in a system feel challenged to help resolve the tension. A famous illustration of the latter is the CTE created and used by Martin Luther King: 'I have a dream'.

In 'Letter from Birmingham Jail', Martin Luther King (2000:67–68) wrote:

> I must confess that I am not afraid of the word 'tension'. I have earnestly opposed violent tension, but there is a type of constructive, nonviolent tension, which is necessary for growth. Just as Socrates felt that it was necessary to create a tension in the mind so that individuals could rise from the bondage of myths and half-truths to the unfettered realm of creative analysis and objective appraisal, we must see the need for nonviolent gadflies to create the kind of tension in society that will help men [sic] rise from the dark depths of prejudice and racism to the majestic heights of understanding and brotherhood.

His critics, afraid as they were of the tension his movement created, urged him to slow down, to be patient. They told him that the wounds of segregation would eventually go away and that all people would be equal in the end. Despite all of this, Dr King deliberately decided to identify and name the tension in order to use it as a tool for creative transformation. The tension created by his words offered the opportunity to open up a dialogue where there was none before. Creative tension is not an end in itself but, when well designed and managed, it can engage and mobilize a whole system in the desired direction.

A CTE is an 'engine' that catalyzes 'emergent, experience innovation'. It is a verbalized, generative image that frames or reframes an existing mental model. It provides a new conceptual and metaphoric landscape and thereby enables new thinking, talking and doing. When managed 'generatively', it can create the flexible context in which novelty can take shape, as shown in the example of the first national park in Belgium. A CTE can enable whole system innovation (Figure 1.2).

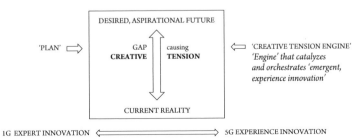

Figure 1.2 Creative Tension Engine (CTE) as a core element in innovating from the experience perspective

1.3.2 Creative Tension Engine and whole system innovation

Much has been written in the organizational learning literature on how to use the creative tension between vision and reality. The Appreciative Inquiry (AI) Summit is an approach that embodies creative tension. It has emerged in the last decades as a very powerful design methodology for helping large, multi-stakeholder initiatives. The AI Summit consists of a 4D-process developed by Whitney and Cooperrider (2011): Discover, Dream, Design and Destiny. It is an organizational approach that holds that improvement in social settings is more engaging when the focus is on the generative strengths rather than on the weaknesses. Contrary to conventional problem-oriented approaches, AI prevents the emergence of resistance and opens the organization up to new thinking. AI involves the systematic discovery of what gives 'life' to a system when it is at its very best, and to take that further into a flourishing future for the system.

Imagineering has much in common with the organizational design approach of AI but Imagineering is not specifically an organizational approach both examples in this chapter show. Imagineering is a whole system approach. In coping with 5G innovation processes, Imagineering brings the tension out of the organization into the broader societal context. As we will see in Chapter 4, Imagineering makes use of poetic or daily language so as to include all people, laymen as well as professionals, in the innovation movement. Imagineering enables whole system innovation as collective creation.

We agree with Senge (Senge et al., 2015) when he argues that system leaders have three core capabilities: the ability to see the larger system; the ability to foster generative conversations; and the ability to shift the collective focus from reactive problem solving to co-creating the future. We extend those ideas to claim that even though people like Schops and King are an enormous blessing, a well-designed and well-managed CTE can have an equally strong effect in producing collective leadership for whole system innovation. Thus, rather than a book about conventional leadership, we are proposing a model for designing and innovating systems. This is a much-needed 'new' management competency with great potential in today's networked society.

While experience is a mental phenomenon (Sundbo and Sørensen, 2013) caused by external mind-shifting stimuli, Imagineering makes use of appealing and mind-shifting narratives to tap into the imagination of the many 'to catalyze in real life the potentials we are imagining' (Atlee, 2007, 2014). We argue that the design of a CTE such as the 'first national park' or 'I have a dream' makes many involved actors wonder how they can contribute creatively to help resolve the tension and make that aspirational future come true. This then is the first step in the design approach we like to call Imagineering: designing and using a CTE that shifts the collective focus from a problematic situation to an aspirational future and sets the stage for innovation as collective creation. to set the stage for innovation as collective creation. Contrary to the conventional engineering paradigm in which design operates with a solution orientation, the Imagineering paradigm design operates with an evolution orientation. Imagineering is about appealing to the imagination of the many to generate collectively, and over time, a more desired reality.

As a CTE, a generative image such as 'national park' or 'Arnhem Fashion Quarter' is meant to do five specific things well:

- **Mind-shifting**: it creates a strategic mind-shift in an aspirational direction (from problem to opportunity) in all the people involved, each with their own experience archive that feeds the interpretation in context. This enables an enormous richness in daily dialogues and interactions as people see and interpret their interactions in a new strategic light.
- **Integrating**: it allows people to see the bigger picture, to approach system optimization in an integrated way. It brings departments together and as such functions as an antidote to silo thinking and acting. Moreover, new initiatives can build upon one another as the reframing is sustained over the long term.
- **Mobilizing**: the collective aspiration inspires engaged collective action, since all participants know that interpreting and acting is relevant for the whole system. It shows their creativity and their care for the whole system and it is strategically supported (so it is also safe to act).
- **Sustaining**: articulating this image and integrating it in the core of the system sustains innovative long-term action, making it possible for the innovation thoughts and initiatives to build upon one another.
- **Imaginative**: it allows all actors to see a new opportunity horizon which they can relate to, and creatively re-interpret daily activities and interactions.

It is obvious that a strategic generative image does not work just by being there. It has to be applied and managed in an appropriate 'generative' way in order to encourage movement in the envisioned direction. In Chapter 4 and in Part II of this book, we will dig deeper into the logic and the dynamics that are seen as central in taking care for the eventual emerging processes.

1.3.3 Creative industries as Creative Tension Engine

Recently the relationship between the art world and the market economy gave rise to new academic thinking. In *The Rise of the Joyful Economy*, cultural economist and economic sociologist Hutter (2015) runs the argument that these two worlds have been seen so far as statically distinct but that they are dynamically coupled. It are the dynamics of tension and resolution, created by interactions between different 'logics of worth' that drive the evolution of humanity. In this same sense, Jason Potts, an evolutionary economist and complexity scientist, recently made a remarkable statement (2007:9). According to him, 'the "play" industries [being the creative industries and by extension also the broader leisure industries] are not just into economic significance as a set of industries, but more deeply into the main driver of the market-economy engine, the ultimate engine for generating new order in society'. The importance of the arts for innovation has been highly underestimated so far. The 'play' industries, unlike all others, have 'dynamic' value for society at large. They act as a CTE on a macro level in society. They are the industries that keep people wondering. They are essential for all evolution.

The creative industries are not responsible for creativity in society. All industries (agrarian industry, biomedical industry, etc.) are as creative as they are. Yet the creative industries play a crucial role like no other as a permanent infrastructure that facilitates the processes of origination, experimentation, adoption and retention (Potts, 2007, 2009, 2012). They give rise to three different sorts of creativity:

- **Generative creativity**: the 'original' form of creativity associated with the development of a novel idea.
- **Adoptive or adaptive creativity**: the creative discovery of new ways of adopting those novel ideas and the development of new processes to facilitate that process (for example the adoption of a rule).
- **Retentive creativity**: the creativity with respect to the embedding of novel ideas into consumer lifestyles and into the routine operations of firms (for example, the installation of a social coordinating mechanism that effectuates the normalization or institutionalization, something which is often overlooked but core to sustainable evolution).

These three types of creativity are considered crucial to the sustainable emergence of novelty in society on a macro level. It is our hypothesis that these three types of creativity are also crucial for the sustainable emergence of novelty on a micro-organizational level and that on this level a CTE can play a similar 'infrastructural role'. A CTE can set the stage for sustainable whole system innovation.

1.4   Conclusion and structure of this book

Concluding this first introductory chapter, we have seen how the evolution from 1G closed to 5G open and complex innovation processes demands a new discipline of innovation, which Lichtenstein (2014) calls generative emergence. We have seen how viewing organizations as living systems and approaching innovation in terms of generative emergence demands a new discipline of design, which Nijs (2014) calls Imagineering. Imagineering is a design approach that generates new order through the use of a CTE that reframes an existing complex issue in a way that it appeals to the imagination of all involved actors in the system and that enables and sustains long-term collective creativity and collective leadership.

Senge et al. (2015:28) note that 'we are at the beginning of the beginning in learning how to catalyze and guide' emergent, systemic change. Accordingly, the purpose of this book is to share what we have learned in the previous decades about fostering innovation as collective creation from the experience perspective. Whole system innovation from the experience perspective, also called 'cultural innovation', 'emergent innovation' or even better 'generative emergence' is a new approach. It is innovation that must be designed for either unconsciously or, more effectively, consciously. Being able to design for generative emergence will complement our design toolbox and allow us to become more effective innovators able to cope with the growing complexity in society.

This book is split into two parts. Part I covers the 'Foundations of Imagineering' and has three chapters. Chapter 2 presents a broad view on the big shift in society and in the landscape of value creation. In doing so, the chapter explains why it makes more sense now than ever to study the design approach of Imagineering. Chapter 3 covers the big shift in science that is taking place at this very moment. It gives an overview of the key concepts and principles of complexity science as the lens of the living systems. This chapter shows how it leads to a whole new perspective on how living systems can be influenced to become more healthy flourishing systems. Chapter 4 considers the big shift in design logic that is taking place and it describes the complexity-inspired design logic of Imagineering. It articulates how Imagineers try to generate new order when facing social (or organizational) complexity.

Part II, 'The Systemic Design Approach of Imagineering', consists of six chapters. It explains the design approach of Imagineering, which combines the three phases of a regular design approach (inspiration, ideation and implementation) with the scientific framework of complexity science, resulting in an A–B–C–D–E–F design approach:

Phase 1: Inspiration

- Chapter 5: **A**ppreciating – answers the question: 'How do you try to understand a problematic situation in an appreciative way?'
- Chapter 6: **B**reathing – answers the questions: 'Before jumping to solutions, I try to get a deep understanding of the bigger picture: "What is going on in this living system?" "Which small intervention might 'heal' or 'appeal to' the system in a very evident way?"'

Phase 2: Ideation

- Chapter 7: **C**reating a vision and a concept – answers the question: 'Which principle might work for the experience and what narrative might ignite the system in the envisioned direction by mobilizing the individual actors creatively?'
- Chapter 8: **D**eveloping the experience – answers the question: 'How can the working principle be translated into very concrete, consistent experiences?'

Phase 3: Implementation

- Chapter 9: **E**nabling – answers the question: 'How can the experience platform (physical as well as digital) connect and enable the involved stakeholders?'
- Chapter 10: **F**lourishing – answers the questions: 'How can the system be nourished on the longer term for sustainable flourishing?' 'How can the emerging processes be managed dynamically?'

By describing the design approach of Imagineering in these six activities, we hope to extend your design toolbox and to make you a more effective innovator, better able to cope with the growing number of complex issues in society.

References

Atlee, T. (2014). *The Tao of democracy: Using co-intelligence to create a world that works for all.* North Atlantic Books.

Atlee, T. (2007). *Imagineering, The First Annual Story Field Conference.* At: https://www.co-intelligence.org/Imagineering.html (accessed October 8, 2018).

Bessant, J. R. (1991). *Managing advanced manufacturing technology: The challenge of the fifth wave.* Wiley-Blackwell.

Candi, M., Beltagui, A., and Riedel, J. C. (2013). Innovation through experience staging: Motives and outcomes. *Journal of Product Innovation Management, 30*(2), 279–297.

Colander, D., and Kupers, R. (2014). *Complexity and the art of public policy: Solving society's problems from the bottom up.* Princeton University Press.

Denning, P. J., and Dunham, R. (2010). *The innovator's way: Essential practices for successful innovation.* MIT Press.

Dodgson, M., Gann, D., and Salter, A. J. (2005). *Think, play, do technology, innovation, and organization.* Oxford University Press on Demand.

Dougherty, D. (2016). *Taking advantage of emergence: Productively innovating in complex innovation systems.* Oxford University Press.

Fagerberg, J. (2004). *Innovation: A guide to the literature.* Georgia Institute of Technology.

Garud, R., Gehman, J., and Giuliani, A. P. (2014). Contextualizing entrepreneurial innovation: A narrative perspective. *Research Policy, 43*(7), 1177–1188.

Garud, R., and Giuliani, A. P. (2013). A narrative perspective on entrepreneurial opportunities. *Academy of Management Review, 38*(1), 157–160.

Garud, R., Gehman, J., and Kumaraswamy, A. (2011). Complexity arrangements for sustained innovation: Lessons from 3M Corporation. *Organization Studies, 32*(6), 737–767.

Garud, R., Kumaraswamy, A., and Karnøe, P. (2010). Path dependence or path creation? *Journal of Management Studies, 47*(4), 760–774.

Goldstein, J. (2011). Emergence in complex systems. In: Allen, P., Maguire, S., and McKelvey, B. (eds.) *The Sage handbook of complexity and management.* Sage Publications, pp. 65–78.

Goldstein, J., Hazy, J., and Lichtenstein, B. (2010). *Complexity and the nexus of leadership: Leveraging nonlinear science to create ecologies of innovation.* Springer.

Goldstein, J. (2005). Emergence, creativity, and the logic of following and negating. *The Innovation Journal: The Public Sector Innovation Journal, 10*(3), 1–10.

Heinzen, T. E. (1994). Situational affect: Proactive and reactive creativity. In: Shaw, M. P., and Runco, M. A. (eds.) *Creativity and affect.* Ablex Publishing Corp., pp. 127–146.

Holmes, O. W. (1897). *The Path of the Law*, 10HARV. *L. REV*, 457–469.

Hutter, M. (2015). *The rise of the joyful economy: Artistic invention and economic growth from Brunelleschi to Murakami*. Routledge.

Jaruzelski, B., Schwartz, K., and Staack, V. (2015). Innovation's new world order. *Strategy+Business*, (81). At: http://www.iberglobal.com/files/2015/ Innovations_New_World_Order.pdf (accessed October 8, 2018).

Jernsand, E.M., Kraff, H., and Mossberg, L. (2015). Tourism experience innovation through design. *Scandinavian Journal of Hospitality and Tourism*, 15(sup1), 98–119.

King, M. (2000). Letter from Birmingham jail. In: Luther King, M. Jr. (ed.) *Why we can't wait*. Signet Classics, Penguin Group, pp. 64–84.

Lichtenstein, B. B. (2014). *Generative emergence: A new discipline of organizational, entrepreneurial, and social innovation*. Oxford University Press (UK).

Lindhult, E., Hazy, J. K., Midgley, G., and Chirumalla, K. (2015, January). Value-driven innovation in industrial companies: A complexity approach. In: *ISPIM Conference Proceedings*. The International Society for Professional Innovation Management (ISPIM), p. 1.

MacIntosh, R., and MacLean, D. (1999). Conditioned emergence: A dissipative structures approach to transformation. *Strategic Management Journal*, 20(4), 297–316.

Marshall, J., Stone, R., Wise, R., and Wright, J. (2016). *Experience innovation, the next frontier to differentiate and drive growth*. Lippincott – Global Creative Consultancy.

Nijs, D. E. L. W. (2014). *Imagineering the butterfly effect: Complexity and collective creativity in business and policy: designing for organizational emergence* (Doctoral dissertation, University of Groningen Library).

Otte, A. (2011, October 29). Hoge Kempen, Hoge Baten. *De Tijd*.

Pine, B. J., Pine, J., and Gilmore, J. H. (1999). *The experience economy: Work is theatre & every business a stage*. Harvard Business Press.

Potts, J. (2017). Complexity, economics, and innovation policy: How two kinds of science lead to two kind of economics and two kinds of policy. *Complexity, Governance and Networks*, (1), 22–34.

Potts, J. (2012). 13 creative industries and innovation in a knowledge economy. In: Rooney, D., Hearn, G., and Kastelle, T. (eds.) *Handbook on the Knowledge Economy*, Vol. 2. Edward Elgar Publishing, pp. 193–203.

Potts, J. (2011). *Creative industries and economic evolution*. Edward Elgar Publishing.

Potts, J. (2009). Why creative industries matter to economic evolution. *Economics of innovation and new technology*, 18(7), 663–673.

Potts, J. (2007). Art and innovation: An evolutionary view of the creative industries. *UNESCO Observatory*, 1(1), 1–18.

Prahalad, C. K., and Ramaswamy, V. (2003). The new frontier of experience innovation. *MIT Sloan Management Review*, 44(4), 12–18.

Prigogine, I., and Stengers, I. (1984). *Order out of chaos*. Bantam.

Rothwell, R. (1994). Towards the fifth-generation innovation process. *International marketing review*, 11(1), 7–31.

Rothwell, R. (1992). Successful industrial innovation: Critical factors for the 1990s. *RandD Management, 22*(3), 221–240.

Sawhney, M. and Prandelli, E. (2000). Communities of creation: Managing distributed knowledge in turbulent markets. *California Management Review, 42*(4), 24–54.

Senge, P., Hamilton, H., and Kania, J. (2015). The dawn of system leadership. *Stanford Social Innovation Review, 13*(1), 27–33.

Senge, P. M. (2014). *The fifth discipline fieldbook: Strategies and tools for building a learning organization.* Crown Business.

Senge, P. (1990). *The fifth discipline. The art and practice of learning organization.* Doubleday Currence.

Simon, H. A. (1969). *The sciences of the artificial.* MIT Press.

Simon, H. A. (1955). A behavioral model of rational choice. *The quarterly journal of economics, 69*(1), 99–118.

Sundbo, J., and Sørensen, F. (2013). Introduction to the experience economy. In: Sundbo, J., and Sørensen, F. (eds.) *Handbook on the experience economy.* Edward Elgar Publishing, pp. 1–18.

Swenson, R. (1989). Emergent attractors and the law of maximum entropy production: Foundations to a theory of general evolution. *Systems research, 6*(3), 187–197.

Swenson, R. (1988). Emergence and the principle of maximum entropy production: Multilevel system theory, evolution, and nonequilibrium thermodynamics. In *Proceedings of the 32nd Annual Meeting of the ISGSR, 32,* 32.

Tanev, S., and Frederiksen, M. H. (2014). Generative innovation practices, customer creativity, and the adoption of new technology products. *Technology Innovation Management Review, 4*(2), 14–20.

Tanev, S., Knudsen, M. P., Bisgaard, T., and Thomsen, M. S. (2011). Innovation policy development and the emergence of new innovation paradigms. *Technology Innovation Management Review, 1*(2), 14–19.

Teece, D. J. (ed.). (1987). *The competitive challenge.* Ballinger.

Vargo, S. L., Wieland, H., and Akaka, M. A. (2015). Innovation through institutionalization: A service ecosystems perspective. *Industrial Marketing Management, 44,* 63–72.

Whitney, D., and Cooperrider, D. (2011). *Appreciative inquiry: A positive revolution in change.* ReadHowYouWant.com.

Part I

Foundations of Imagineering

2

LANDSCAPE: a big shift in society – growing complexity and the innovation opportunity

Diane Nijs

Virtually everyone agrees that systems we depend on such as the healthcare system, the educational system and the retail system, as well as other service-sector systems are in trouble. But there is little agreement on the nature of the trouble. Managers and politicians often point to the financial crisis and the economic downturn when talking about the challenging times we are going through. At the same time, most of us realize that we are in the midst of a much deeper, longer-term and more pervasive change that is driven for the most part by socio-technological innovations. This is what Hagel calls the 'big shift' (Hagel et al., 2009). It is a big shift in the value-creating landscape: a big shift in how we create value, do business and govern our institutions. In this chapter we intend to offer you a comprehensive and coherent picture of this shifting landscape in order to answer the 'why-question': why do we need new approaches such as Imagineering to become more effective innovators?

The answer to this question is in fact simple and clear: because we face growing complexity in society. However, this simple answer raises more questions than it answers: what is complexity, why is it growing and what are the implications of growing complexity for value creation and for the logic with which we operate in organizations? Growing complexity presents us with challenges but it also provides opportunities. Those who understand both are better placed to take advantage of the opportunities.

We start this chapter by introducing a preliminary distinction between complicated issues and complex ones. We will demonstrate how the former calls for expert-driven design approaches and the latter demands experience-driven design approaches. Then we show how hyperconnectivity is accelerating the growth of complex issues in society and how this growing complexity has implications for the logic with which we create value and manage organizations. We finish the chapter by reflecting on the implications and opportunities for innovating under complexity, and why it makes ever more sense to develop the competency of Imagineering.

2.1   Complicated and complex issues

The difference between complicated and complex issues is illustrated very well by the work of Rittel and Webber (1973), two Berkeley professors in urban planning. They made a distinction between tame and wicked problems. A tame problem according to them may be complicated but, while the degree of uncertainty is limited, it is resolvable through unilinear acts and it is likely to have occurred before. Examples of tame problems are timetabling the railways, planning heart surgery, negotiating your salary or building a nuclear plant.

Wicked problems on the contrary are complex issues that are difficult or impossible to solve because of incomplete, contradictory, and changing information and complex interdependencies (Grint, 2008). There are no clear cause-and-effect relationships. Moreover, the effort made to solve one aspect of a wicked problem may reveal or create other problems. Such problems cannot be removed from their environment, solved and returned without affecting the environment. These issues simply cannot be solved or fixed. Examples of wicked problems are global warming, obesity or violence, as well as institutional innovation (i.e. corporate, public, social or system innovation). Coping effectively with these issues calls for a different operating logic. It calls for thinking and acting in terms of evolution instead of solutions. Imagineering provides just such an approach.

The organization scholars Vasconcelos and Ramirez (2011:1–2) turned to LEGO to help explain the difference between tame and wicked problems. They write as follows:

> Suppose you have a LEGO-style construction set, and that should complete two tasks:
>
> • Build the tallest stable tower with the available blocks.
> • Build the best toy for children with the available blocks.
>
> Upon getting started, you will notice that these two exercises imply two completely different challenges. In order to build the tallest stable tower with the given blocks, one analyzes several tower designs and compares them with a fixed set of restrictions. The definition of this exercise is objective: Algorithms that exist are capable of discovering the best way to carry out the task. All relevant parameters are set and are not subject to discussion.
>
> However, the second task involves a completely different challenge. To build a toy with the pieces of a construction set one may consider, among others, the following questions. (1) What is a toy? (2) What are the criteria for a good toy? (3) Which kind of toy to build? (4) How can I assemble a toy with the pieces I have? (5) Will the children like it? And are they the only stakeholders to consider – what about the parents? (6) Will the children recognize the toy as such? (7) Will they learn how to play with the toy?
>
> Building a toy from a construction set is not only a matter of optimizing resources (blocks) for a given end. This activity is a matter of building the objectives based on incomplete or contradictory information and constructing a solution – not necessarily optimal – to attain these objectives. The key processes involved, in other words, are not just finding the best algorithms and of optimizing

resources. Instead, establishing communication, interpreting desires, clarifying intent and building on ambiguity are the key elements involved. In this case the priorities among ends are neither well defined nor given in advance. When facing such problems managers create solutions because they must take into account elements that are not direct logical consequences of the problem. These elements emerge from the interaction between the problem and the actors who work on it, often changing the meaning of the terms used to describe it.

Vasconcelos and Ramirez further argue that the two tasks are examples of two different kinds of complexity, respectively called algorithmic and natural complexity. In this book we use the term 'complicated' to describe algorithmic, technical complex issues; and we will refer to natural, social complex issues simply as 'complex'. In the LEGO construction set example, building the tallest stable tower is an example of a problem that addresses 'complication' (i.e.: technical complexity). Building a good toy is an example of a problem that addresses 'complexity' (i.e.: social complexity) (Box 2.1). Note that we prefer to speak about 'issues' or 'challenges' instead of 'problems' since complexity is not *a priori* a problem.

Another example (Glouberman and Zimmerman, 2002) that is often used to illustrate the difference between the complicated and the complex compares

---

BOX 2.1

CHARACTERISTICS OF COMPLICATED (TECHNICAL COMPLEX) AND COMPLEX (SOCIAL COMPLEX) ISSUES

2 completely different challenges:

Building the tallest stable tower

vs

Building the best toy for children

COMPLICATED ISSUES **Technical complexity**	COMPLEX ISSUES **Social complexity**
A well-defined problem	A wicked problem (impossible to 'solve')
One best answer	Many questions to answer on the forehand – criteria
Existing knowledge	Incomplete and contradictory information
All parameters are set	Many good answers possible
Not subject to discussion	Many stakeholders involved

Source: Based on Vasconcelos and Ramirez (2011). Images designed by Joris Putteneers.

the challenge of sending a rocket to the moon (a complicated issue) to raising a child (a complex issue). The rocket challenge can be solved perfectly well by experts; indeed, incorporating non-experts would make things unnecessarily more difficult. However, issues like raising a child are undertaken successfully by non-experts (i.e. first-time parents!). Moreover, such challenges are best done by engaging others constructively in the endeavor. Of course, this does not preclude that parents become better at raising children over time; developing expert-knowledge certainly makes sense even for complex issues. However, the process and context of raising a child will continually change; after all, a second child rarely behaves in a similar way to their older sibling in a similar situation. Continually changing contexts demand that we evolve our thinking. In this case, distributed intelligence and co-creation makes much more sense than searching for a best 'solution' or a best 'recipe for success'.

A metaphor that is often used to illustrate why complicated and complex issues call for different approaches is the road intersection. Observation shows that traffic flow at intersections is a highly complex situation. More often than not stop–go traffic lights are placed at intersections in order to regulate the traffic – an example of an expert-driven design approach. However, time and again experiments have shown that a well-constructed roundabout can lead to fewer traffic jams and accidents, and less environmental pollution. This is a very good illustration of the fact that, in coping with complex issues, creating the context such that the individual actors are enabled to interpret the situation for themselves can lead to greater effectiveness. The traffic light takes away decision making from the driver, the roundabout gives it back. Thus we should consider experience-driven design approaches instead of expert-driven design approaches to cope more effectively with complex issues.

2.2 The century of complexity

The preeminent English astrophysicist and well-known Cambridge professor Stephen Hawking announced in the year 2000 that the 21st century will be the 'century of complexity'. Thus far, the world population has exceeded 7 billion people, the proportion of elderly people is growing fast in Western countries, we are facing growing ethnic and cultural diversity worldwide, and climate change continues to generate global challenges. This is indeed complexity on a level that the world has never seen before. Information and Communications Technology (ICT) plays an increasingly important role in this picture, not only as the enabling technology for the generation of big data, but also for sustainable research, development and innovation.

2.2.1 Hyperconnectivity

An important part of today's accelerating complexity is due to what Fredette et al. (2012) call 'hyperconnectivity' or the 'hyperconnected world' – in other words the 'increasing digital interconnection of people and things, anytime, anywhere'. We see new channels for sharing and socializing, new ways of advertising and shopping, new ways of consuming, and new business models for selling, all emerging at an enormous pace. For example, music can now be purchased by monthly subscription or single-song download; television has come out of the living room and onto multiple screens usable on demand; breaking news can be followed on Twitter. We now have ample possibilities to make use of latent resources – from renting out our spare bedrooms, our parked cars, our free time, to crowd sourced funding and design (Akamai, 2012).

'Hyperconnectivity' is said to be 'the single most important trend in today's world' (Fredette et al., 2012). It is shifting the power away from organizations and institutions towards individuals in networks, which brings with it a serious challenge of governability. The hyperconnected world makes all of us potential innovators but no one is in control of what happens. Instead of problems of scarcity that we had in the past, we now have problems of coordination (Dum, 2015). All this calls for developing new knowledge, new thinking and new practices in order to be able to handle hyperconnectivity effectively.

We must learn to think in terms of catalyzing instead in terms of controlling. For business, hyperconnectivity means a shift from considered and long-term decision making to real-time management. It means fast decision taking, reacting to events as they happen, and it implies that the people within an organization have as much power as their leadership. It follows that the only way to 'control' a business is through a culture of openness, inspiration and transparency.

For governments (Fredette et al., 2012), hyperconnectivity makes it possible to improve communication with their citizens by sharing information more quickly and transparently. In addition, it allows the relationship between governments and those they govern to be turned upside down! Citizens can be given the ability to take the initiative and be supported by their government in doing so, rather than the other way around, as has traditionally been the case. At the very least it can make services more readily available and enable what is called 'smart governance': an administration that applies and integrates information, communication and operational technologies to address the challenge of planning and managing operations across multiple domains. At the other end of the spectrum hyperconnectivity unleashes unknown possibilities for value creation that make use of collective and distributed intelligence, possibilities that will be discovered in the coming decades. Governments will also be confronted by complexities such as real-time protests and social media democracy. WikiLeaks has shown that when privacy is removed the quality of information deteriorates; high-quality information can be communicated in private, whereas, in public, clarity and meaning suffer through over-simplification. Handling hyperconnectivity for both commercial organizations and governments comes down to trust, transparency and openness.

Without question hyperconnectivity also brings hyper-accelerated innovation to all of us. As we use a growing collection of devices to stay connected – from laptop to tablet to phone to TV, we are changing the way we work, play, communicate and consume. Organizations must co-evolve with ever more demanding consumers and co-creators. From young startups to long-standing multinationals, organizations of all sizes across all industries are innovating, transforming or being transformed at an unprecedented rate. If they do not innovate they run the risk of going out of business.

This vast demand for organizational or institutional innovation and whole system innovation also creates opportunities to make the world a better place if only we can develop approaches to make them come true. Expert-design approaches do not seem to be able to cope effectively with complex issues, so the time is ripe for exploring experience-driven design approaches, approaches that enable the individual actors as co-creators of value. Let us explore the potential and challenges of hyperconnectivity and then turn to the implications for the logic with which we operate to create value and to manage our institutions and endeavors.

2.2.2   The challenges and potential of hyperconnectivity

Accelerating interconnectedness is creating a new environment that strategic business leaders already in the 1990s started to call a 'VUCA' environment. VUCA is a military-derived acronym that stands for volatility, uncertainty, complexity and ambiguity. These terms describe an increasingly unstable and rapidly changing world and by extension the business environment we find ourselves in. The characteristics of this new environment have fundamental implications for leadership, for strategy, for organizations and for innovation. Fundamental new thinking is emerging around the focus and methods used in all these disciplines. We see new concepts developing with names such as 'new leadership', 'new strategy', 'the new organization' and 'new innovation'. The implications of growing complexity with its necessary culture of openness and transparency are central to all of this thinking. The VUCA-world has become the 'new normal' (Lawrence, 2013).

Volatility refers to the rate of change or the turbulence. Turbulence is a phenomenon that occurs now more frequently than in the past. Drivers of turbulence in business today are digitization, connectivity, trade liberation and global competition (Reeves et al., 2012).

Uncertainty points to the fact that the present is unclear. There is a lack of predictability. Past issues and events can no longer be used as predictors of the future, making strategic forecasting extremely difficult if not impossible.

Complexity indicates that there are no clear cause-and-effect relationships. It is often impossible to determine what is cause and what is effect. The relationships between multiple key decision factors are unclear.

Ambiguity describes the lack of clarity on the meaning of an event. Events are open to interpretation. Forecasting and planning become difficult and the relationship between variables is very hard to decipher.

With these four factors at play, business leaders and politicians are confronted with progressively more complex organizations and a growing ineffectiveness of conventional thinking and acting to deal with it all. The idea that the world works like a machine, that with good analysis we can predict the future, decide how to intervene, make and execute plans, and control and measure outcomes is no longer valid. The VUCA-world cannot be understood by breaking problems down into constituent parts to be dealt with in piecemeal fashion.

The mechanistic, linear worldview still maintains its attraction given that it provides a sense of order, purpose and control, but we must admit that times are changing fundamentally and that a complex world needs new thinking and new ways of acting. Instead of breaking things down we have to approach them in an interconnected way. A complex world needs systemic thinking and acting. A VUCA-world needs bigger picture thinking and acting. A VUCA-world calls not only for a zooming-in to analyze issues, but also a zooming-out to see the overall view. In addition, a VUCA-world requires whole Systems Thinking (see Chapter 6) to understand the patterns, processes and relationships. It is essential to have a good understanding of the big picture in order to be able to intervene in small ways that improve the whole system without harming it in the long term.

It is not all about challenges; there are also plenty of opportunities that come with growing connectivity. Hyperconnectivity in essence augments the potential for value creation. Metcalfe's Law explains why this is possible (Box 2.2): a network's value increases exponentially with its size, meaning that the more people who use a specific network, the more their participation enhances the network and the more the network can become more valuable to the community. It follows therefore that accelerating interconnectedness brings with it the potential to optimize value creation.

That growing connectivity is augmenting the potential for value creation and thus for economic growth was recently illustrated by research done by Mandel (2014) for LinkedIn. His research suggested that connected cities are economically more healthy cities based on the fact that four-year job growth was significantly higher (8.2 percent) in the most connected US metro areas (measured on LinkedIn profiles) than in the least-connected areas where job growth was only 3.5 percent. If future research confirms the relation between connections and job growth, Mandel speculates that we might have a new tool for creating jobs: areas that help residents extend their personal networks could see an employment payoff.

BOX 2.2

METCALFE'S LAW ON THE VALUE OF NETWORKS

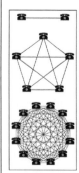

Metcalfe's law states that the value of a telecommunications network is proportional to the square of the number of connected users of the system (n2). [. . .]

The law has often been illustrated using the example of fax machines: a single fax machine is useless, but the value of every fax machine increases with the total number of fax machines in the network, because the total number of people with whom each user may send and receive documents increases. Likewise, in social networks, the greater number of users with the service, the more valuable the service becomes to the community. [. . .]

Source: https://en.wikipedia.org/wiki/Metcalfe%27s_law (accessed October 8, 2018).

In addition to the first-level network effects that augment value creation, Hagel et al. (2009) signal a second level of augmented value creation, namely the learning effects. Participating in rich networks gives us all the ability to learn faster than ever before. Richard Florida's (2014) theory of innovation in urban areas builds on both these levels. Large, diverse and tolerant cities can act as engines of innovation and at the same time they allow for countless unexpected, novel combinations of people, ideas, cultures, practices and resources. Networks can act as creative spaces that enable and harness collective intelligence and collective creativity as well as its learning effects. Collective intelligence and collective creativity then is the intelligence and creativity that emerges from the interaction between the different actors. It was simply not there at the beginning.

In summary, accelerating complexity has its good and bad sides. It can be a source of innovation that offers us a greater capacity to change, adapt and evolve, but it can also lead to greater opacity. So much happens between the system's densely connected components that it becomes impossible to see what is going on inside the system. The result is deep uncertainty. It is harder to predict what the effect of an intervention will be but at the same time it is easier than ever before to influence the system in a desired direction. It is easier than ever before to unlock the unlimited potential of our organizations and ourselves. Organizations making no use of these dual network effects are missing out. They will face fierce competition and dominance from the ones who can. Coping with complexity calls for a different and complementary operating logic that is different from the one we have inherited from earlier, more static industrial times. Let us explore the implications of hyperconnectivity for this operating logic.

2.3   The implications for the operating logic

The operating logic is the logic with which managers and leaders act and engage with the world. The 'dominant logic' of an organization, according to Prahalad and Bettis (1986), is in essence the DNA of the organization.

> 'It reflects how managers are socialized. It manifests itself often in an implicit theory of competition and value creation. It is embedded in standard operating procedures, shaping not only how the members of the organization act but also how they think. Because it is the source of the company's past success, it becomes the lens through which managers see all emerging opportunities. This engrained lens makes it hard for incumbent companies to embrace a new and broader logic for competition and value creation' (Prahalad, 2004:172).

A dominant logic helps sustain organizations and strategy in stable environments because it is internally consistent, but it can also blind an organization when times are changing and new entrants to the industry challenge the dominant logic. Prahalad (2004) finds that changing the dominant logic is extremely difficult for a company. In order to do so managers and leaders must accept that their inherited logic is suddenly devalued and that they have to change or complement it to stay smart.

To see just how difficult it can be to accept a new dominant logic, consider today's long-standing taxicab companies and tourism organizations and how they struggle to embrace the value-creating logic of new entrants in their industries such as Uber and Airbnb. They realize that this is not simply a matter of adding a new website or app, but they often have no idea about the logic they should adopt in order to flourish in the hyperconnected business landscape. Let us take a closer look at some essential parts of the operating logic, namely the value-creating logic and the managerial logic, so as to understand the challenges and opportunities for innovation as collective creation.

2.3.1 A big shift in value creation

According to Ramirez (1999), human beings have always created things that are valued by others in two ways: simultaneous in value-creating networks (Value Creation Paradigm) and sequential in value-creating chains (Exchange Paradigm). In previous decades the sequential mode has been dominant and our industrial focus enabled sequential value creation in unprecedented dimensions. However, earlier in our history, simultaneous value creation was dominant. It happened mostly in local settings but sometimes in astonishing ways. It is said for instance that in medieval times the Chartres Cathedral was built without any architectural plan. Many people working together, simultaneously, have created huge, monumental creations long before the emergence of our hyperconnected world. In a network context, whether in the real world or the digital world, simultaneous value creation is dominant over sequential value creation.

In the industrial context, however, our managerial mind became molded on the assumptions and the models of the industrial economy (Ciborra, 1996). The industrial-based conceptual frameworks and icons (such as the assembly line) persuaded us to think that we should study production and consumption separately and statically instead of studying them as dynamic relational processes (Sheth and Uslay, 2007; Ramirez, 1999; Normann and Ramirez, 1993; Normann, 2001). In this traditional view, consumers consume value and companies occupy positions in the value chain and they 'add' value to their inputs before passing them downstream to the next actor in the value chain until finally it is the consumer who consumes the value. In the modern world the simultaneous mode of value creation has the potential to be unlocked again by growing connectivity, but this time on a global scale. We can finally liberate ourselves from the limited, industrial interpretation of value creation and enjoy again the dominance of simultaneous value creation.

Today's value-creating environment can be typified by four characteristics, as described below.

Simultaneous value creation is enabled as never before

Value creation in networks is not only faster than value creation in chains but it invites us to rethink the roles and relationships. Intermediate roles are no longer needed and all actors can become co-creators of value. Travel agencies, for example, have a tough time when people can search and book their travel on their own without expert help. Moreover, people become more knowledgeable and start to create other kinds of value as they surf and book online – they gather data as they go. Consumers are no longer simply consuming value but they are creating new value. This can be financial value or social value and it is sometimes also environmental value in the event they make more informed and planet-friendly choices.

The future is less predictable but easier to influence and more 'shapeable' than ever before

There are many connections in value creation in networks that influence one another and make it almost impossible to see clear cause-and-effect relation-ships. As a consequence, it is not possible to predict the effect of new actions. But this does not mean that we cannot influence the future. Influencing is in fact easier than ever before, since all the actors in a system have more individual power than ever before. Moreover, interventions can 'ripple through' networks, sometimes generating exponential effects. The big challenge in networks then is to influence emerging processes in a desirable direction (Table 2.1).

A stakeholder orientation (that includes shareholders) is a better fit than a shareholder orientation

The growing possibilities of interaction and the fact that the costs for commu-nication reduce to nearly zero, enable decentralized approaches. Thus, collec-tive intelligence and collective creativity become a newly available resource. However, co-creation will only appeal to the imagination of stakeholders if they have a vested interest. Stakeholder co-creation will not be activated by a purely shareholder orientation. We can already see the economic impact of collective intelligence and collective creativity in the increasing popularity of such concepts as wikinomics, open source, communities of practice, user-driven innovation, peer production, social entrepreneurship, collaborative design, and so forth.

Table 2.1 Two complementary models of value creation

Exchange paradigm	Value creation paradigm
Sequential mode of value creation	Simultaneous mode of value creation
Exchange: the act of giving and taking in return for something	Initiators and participants create value together
Firms create value, consumers consume/destroy value	The purpose of consumption is not 'having' but 'being' and 'becoming'
Self-interest	Mutual interest
Shareholder perspective: profitability dominates responsibility	Stakeholder perspective: responsibility emphasized over profitability
Value creation in chains	Value creation in networks
Limited roles and responsibilities	Broader roles and responsibilities

Source: Nijs (2014).

In a hyperconnected world, according to Wilson (2004:22), 'if a corporation cannot come up with a better definition of its social purpose than profit, it risks alienating itself from key stakeholder groups, including employees, customers and community members'. This pivot from a shareholder value orientation to a stakeholder value orientation (in which shareholders are an important group of stakeholders) is a matter of rethinking relevance for society at large. It is a matter of re-orientating from profit first to purpose first.

That this shift in managerial thinking from profit to purpose is no longer 'theoretical' thinking but simply big business thinking is proved by the recent annual letter of BlackRock's (a $6.3 trillion asset managing company) CEO and Board Chair Larry Fink (2018) to the corporate CEOs in the company's vast portfolio entitled 'A Sense of Purpose'. According to BlackRock's Fink:

> Companies must ask themselves: What role do we play in the community? How are we managing our impact on the environment? Are we working to create a diverse workforce? [. . .] As we enter 2018, BlackRock is eager to participate in discussions about long-term value creation and work to build a better framework for serving all your stakeholders. Today, our clients – who are your company's owners – are asking you to demonstrate the leadership and clarity that will drive not only their own investment returns, but also the prosperity and security of their fellow citizens. We look forward to engaging with you on these issues.

Being open and co-evolving continuously is a necessity in turbulent and dynamic circumstances

It is this move from profit to purpose that enables 'meaningful value creation', which is essential for mobilizing collective intelligence and collective creativity. Successful companies increasingly do not simply add value but they reinvent value creation. They inspire and orchestrate whole networks of value-creating stakeholders in which the consumer becomes an active participant in value creation.

2.3.2   A big shift in marketing academia

This shift in the dominant value-creating logic has been articulated in marketing academia by Vargo and Lusch (2004) as a shift from a Goods Dominant Logic (GDL) to a Service Dominant Logic (SDL). In today's hyperconnected context, it is service and not goods that is the starting point for all value creation and this holds true for marketing too. Service is an interactive process of 'doing something for someone' that is valued by all actors involved. In SDL service becomes the unifying purpose of any business relationship and goods are just part of the bigger integrative context of service.

In 2004 Vargo and Lusch decided to call this new marketing paradigm 'Service Dominant Logic' and not 'Experience Dominant Logic' (EDL). In their 2008 paper (2008:9) they state that they made this choice 'partly because of the fact that we have found when many people encounter the term "experience," it often evokes connotations of something like a "Disneyworld event." Of course, the word experience has several other meanings as well, including previous interaction. However, [. . .] we are comfortable with the terms being used interchangeably, as we have done on a number of occasions.'

Together with scholars such as Schembri (2006), Peñaloza and Venkatesh (2006), Wilden et al. (2017) and Hietanen et al. (2017), we think that words do make a difference and that the choice for 'service' potentially keeps managers locked into the dualistic transaction paradigm. Consequently, they continue to think in terms of discrete consumers and producers instead of seeing what Küpers (2000) calls prosumers – seeing both as co-constructors of the service experience. As Schembri (2006:389) argues: 'Services are experiential and this is the case for both consumers and organizations.' Whether calling it SDL or EDL, it is evident that this new lens challenges marketing orthodoxy and invites future innovation in both theoretical and practical terms. Here is a practical illustration to help us understand the big shift in value creation.

At the time of the financial crisis in 2008 when many banks reported devastating results and some even went out of business, a few banks did remarkably well. Banks such as Triodos Bank in Europe, which positions itself as the most sustainable bank in the world, or the state-owned Bank of North Dakota, a bank that stimulates local economies without handing over millions in profit to Wall Street, or Grameen Bank, a Nobel Peace Prize-winning microfinance organization and community development bank for the poor in India all did very good business during the financial crisis. These banks operate with a clearly articulated purpose for society and appear to their customers to be trusted, transparent and open. Their logic of serving society seems to have given them a better 'fit' to flourish in hyperconnected times.

Another illustration of purpose-oriented shift in business was the September 2015 edition of *Fortune* that was totally devoted to nothing less than 'Change the World' (Porter and Kramer, 2015). This multinational business magazine released its first ever 'Change the World List', a ranking of businesses that are doing well by doing good. They called this new emerging evolution 'the next and best movement in the business world': 'A quiet corporate revolution is underway: Companies are beginning to compete to change the world for the better. The drive for profit, often criticized for coming at society's expense, is driving and enabling solutions to many of the world's most challenging problems.' The drive for profit cannot be the ultimate purpose of any organization.

Harvard Business Review recently published a study researching the impact of CEOs on both financial and non-financial criteria of their companies. Their reasoning was that CEOs and their companies are increasingly being 'called to account for their impacts on employees, communities, governments, and society at large' (Fombrun, 2015). A corporation is not a social welfare institution, but it is a social institution – that is, an institution designed to serve a social purpose. An organization will not 'fit' today's networked reality if this fact is not clearly articulated in the core of its value creation system. This is not simply a matter of coping more effectively with openness and transparency. It is first and foremost a matter of being able to cope with the ability to innovate continuously by tapping into distributed, collective creativity and to learn continuously.

Value co-creation and the fact that value is embedded in personalized experiences according to Prahalad (2004:172) 'requires greater sensitivity to what is happening at the periphery'. It asks for another managerial logic too.

2.3.3 A shift in managerial logic

What then are the implications of the 'big shift' in value creation for the managerial operating logic? How are the organizations that flourish with the value co-creating template managed differently? According to Ramirez (1999), the shift in value creation as a consequence of hyperconnectivity has implications in at least four fields of practice:

- the way we define or conceptualize the business (and the business model);
- the way we organize work;
- the way we manage; and
- the way we transform or innovate.

Let us explain and illustrate each of these aspects.

The way we (re-)define or (re-)conceptualize the business

Hyperconnectivity calls for (re-)defining or (re-)conceptualizing the business in order to 'fit' the Value (Co-)Creation template. It calls for a pivot from a shareholder perspective to a stakeholder perspective so as to inspire and enable value co-creation. This goes far beyond changing the structure of corporate governance, tightening audits and accounting procedures or adding technology to the existing way of doing business. For existing organizations it involves nothing less than rethinking the basic purpose and responsibilities of the organization and the role and relationships of all kind of actors in the system. In short, it asks for a rethinking and reframing of relevance, roles and relationships.

Imagine a producer of hearing aids no longer defining itself as a producer of hearing aids but as a 'caretaker for hearing issues'. In doing so, this organization at once gains a whole new perspective on innovation and the costs of operation. Reframing its identity in this way completely changes its logic of value creation. It moves to an SDL or an EDL as explained above. 'Customers' are no longer seen as passive 'patients and consumers' but are asked to keep diaries of their hearing problem, for example, and in doing so they create the best possible research notes for the organization. Moreover, 'taking care of hearing issues' can cause the organization to no longer think in terms of 'patients' but in terms of 'prevention' (ear plugs for concerts and events perhaps) and in terms of 'fun' (earphones).

This example also illustrates that reframing the value-creating logic from profit to purpose first has consequences for the business model (the rationale of how an organization creates, delivers, and captures value in economic, social, cultural or other contexts). Reframing the identity towards 'Care taker for hearing issues' instead of producer of hearing aids will lead to new services, new experiences and to more inspiring business in general. A key benefit of an 'inspiring business' is that the content is the marketing. Or as Gilmore and Pine (2002) state, 'the experience becomes the marketing'. Being the caretaker for hearing issues is a positive, meaningful positioning that will make people talk about the organization in a constructive way, for example on social media. After all who wants to share the fact that they are someone with a hearing problem? Compare that to helping a company to solve hearing issues for everyone.

The way we organize work

Hierarchy as the dominant form of organizations is becoming irrelevant when faced with the challenges of the current tsunami of increasing complexity (Conklin, 1996). Firms are inventing new, more horizontal and flexible ways of organizing. They integrate by managing as much diversity as possible, which enables them to change and learn from each other. They organize and manage 'beyond' the traditional organizational boundaries. They are competent at dialogue avoiding the opportunity costs that bad, or no, dialogue causes. The networked value (co-)production framework does not discard the industrial manufacturing value creation framework, but considers it to be useful only in specific circumstances. It is simply a part of a wider and more diverse set of possible forms of value creation.

The way we manage

Growing complexity, with its co-creative template of value creation and more complex way of organizing, demands new managerial skills – skills such as interlinking, coordinating or orchestrating and (systemic) designing. Variables, their dimensions and purpose in the system are known in 'complicated systems', but this is not the case in 'complex systems'. Managing complex systems thus calls for managing ignorance. One way to manage ignorance is by engaging multiple views in order to decrease the risk of not knowing. Another way is to create the environments in which people become empowered to think and act strategically for themselves in context. This is what we understand as the core objective of the Imagineering, experience-driven design approach. We will dive deep into this subject in Chapter 4 on 'Logic' and discuss the fact that we should complement conventional managerial decision logic with the new logic of Design Thinking and doing.

The way we transform or innovate

It is time to admit that our conventional approaches to organization innovation and whole system innovation have not been very effective so far. New approaches that would help transform organizations and management are needed urgently. Good business is a business that is here today and here tomorrow. The big shift in value creation in society brings with it the possibility to make the world a better place if only we can become better at innovating whole systems. Organizations are the actors that can change the world. Nowhere do we spend more energy than in our organizations, so helping organizations reinvent the way they create value and liberating them from the limiting, selfish industrial logic is an important step in making the dream of a better world come true.

Despite the growing awareness of a 'misfit', existing companies and institutions are struggling with the process of strategic (system) innovation. Ramaswamy and Gouillart (2010) note:

> The new paradigm of co-creation presents an enormous opportunity for enterprises that can figure out how to harness it. Individuals are far ahead of most organizations in their eagerness to engage in co-creating value, and organizations must now respond. (Ramaswamy and Gouillart, 2010:109)

> [. . .] it is the enterprise that is quite not there yet – whether the enterprise is a 'profit. com', 'social.org', or 'public.gov'. The co-creation movement must be seen as a journey in organizational transformation to the next paradigm of value creation – one that can lead to new growth and new sources of competitive advantage. [. . .] Welcome to the opportunity to co-create the future of value creation! (Ramaswamy, 2009:17)

Being locked in an industrial operating logic (a logic ideally suited to cope with complicated issues) manifests itself as a 'chronic pain' in modern organizations according to Conklin (1996) and it is often hidden behind a quiet resignation. It is like the fish that does not realize the existence of the water; what always has been there is hard to see. The frustration of trying to do a complex job without the proper tools is very rarely discussed and is rarely the focus of management troubleshooting since it is ubiquitous. 'It extends from the janitor's closet to the executive suite. Being everywhere, it goes unnoticed.' Instead, there are complaints about being under intense pressure, about being absorbed by too many meetings that are too long and ineffective, about being asked to collaborate when there is no trust, about the feeling of chaos and senseless complexity. But often these people are a bit embarrassed and apologetic. They think that they just have to try a little harder and then everything will soon return to normal!

The way out is to begin to recognize and acknowledge the nature of our current, emerging business landscape and then to begin to accept that we urgently need a new operating logic to become more effective innovators. We must complement the mechanistic, linear operating logic with the networked, 'generative logic' (Denning and Dunham, 2010; Tanev and Frederiksen, 2014; Lichtenstein, 2014) or 'boosting logic' as this logic is sometimes referred to (Harquail, 2012). This is the subject of Chapter 3, but by way of introduction to 'boost logic' we will summarize briefly three core tactics that Scooter Braun employed in building the music business of his group of artists, which included Justin Bieber (Harquail, 2012 based on a the *New Yorker* article by Lizzie Widdecombe):

- **Interdependency – both economic and social**: Bieber and each of Scooter Braun's artists have a stake not only in their own business but they also have a financial stake in each other's success. This encourages the older, more experienced artists to help the younger ones. The same goes for the social dimension. The established artists lend their celebrity to the newcomers 'helping to legitimate the new artists as the next big thing'. Meanwhile they gain maturity themselves by being the mentor of the younger ones.
- **Transparency**: Braun takes care that his deals and revenue streams are straightforward and clear to all so that they can trust that they are getting and giving value throughout the network.
- **Creating and releasing shared value (a win–win–win orientation)**: The Braun artist network also contributes to the community outside their own business, mainly through charity. For example, a portion of the proceeds from sales of Bieber's perfume Someday was designated for a group of charities in which fans can get involved themselves. The result is a situation that is good for Braun/Bieber, good for the audience and good for the charity.

2.4   Conclusion: innovating under complexity

The networked landscape of value creation comes with its challenges and its opportunities. In this chapter we focused on the opportunities since these are the most important for designers that want to make the world a better place. We are, however, only too aware of the downsides. The networked world 'has also made it possible for shocks on one side of the planet to affect communities on another with frightening speed. In other words, these technologies can be at the same time either beneficial or harmful, empowering or dangerous' (Fredette et al., 2012:118). The only thing that government leaders and enterprise managers cannot do with these technologies is to make them go away. While these technologies offer the possibility to generate global wealth, the only mandate then is to become better at using them.

We have argued in this chapter that the big shift in the landscape of value creation comes with a big innovation opportunity. There is an opportunity to transform the logic of our organizations from profit to purpose, an opportunity to make better business by making the world a better place to live in too. We have described the two clear archetypes of value creation (Romme, 2003), the linear mechanistic, sequential one and the generative, simultaneous co-creative one. There is an important opportunity for imagineers to design a generative image that enables the transition from one to the other operating logic. Seen in this light, we can now understand the statement 'Digital isn't software, it is a mind-set' (Dignan, 2014). Transforming the enterprise logic to flourish in the networked society is not a matter of adding the digital infrastructure to the existing way of operating. It is about rethinking the very foundations of value creation in order to create the context in which all actors together can start to operate differently.

In this new landscape of value creation, organizations are confronted with ever-rising expectations of consumers as well as employees. They know that things can be done differently and they expect organizations to perform accordingly. For organizations this means they have to do a better job in a shorter timeframe within a context of declining budgets and declining numbers of employees. Customers as well as employees are calling for greater participation in the organization. This just adds to the growing complexity of managing organizations in a shifting landscape of value creation. These demands require organizations to develop a capacity for whole system transformation and call for a revolution in management thinking. Organizations must 'break through bureaucracy' (Barzelay, 1992) to realize what Landry (2018) calls a 'creative bureaucracy'. This is 'a bureaucracy that understands people are at the heart of the system'. Our conventional methods fall short of bringing about whole system innovation; we need fundamentally new thinking and doing. In this new landscape we need a new lens, a new pair of glasses one could say. We need nothing less than a new scientific framework to be able to think differently about organization and whole system innovation. This will be the subject of the next chapter.

References

Akamai (2012). *The hyper-connected world: A new era of opportunity*. White paper. At: http://media.economist.com/sites/default/files/debates/hyperconnec ted_world.pdf (accessed October 8, 2018).

Barzelay, M. (1992). *Breaking through bureaucracy: A new vision for managing in government*. University of California Press.

Ciborra, C. U. (1996). The platform organization: Recombining strategies, structures, and surprises. *Organization science*, 7(2), 103–118.

Conklin, J. (1996). *The Age of Design*. White paper. CogNexus Institute.

Denning, P. J., and Dunham, R. (2010). *The innovator's way: Essential practices for successful innovation*. MIT Press.

Dignan, A. (2014). Digital isn't software, it's a mindset. At: https://vimeo.com/88296842 (accessed October 8, 2018).

Dum, R. (2015). Presentation in the European Commission, Global Systems Science Programme, Data & Models & Systems, From scientific evidence to policy narratives. At: https://glocomnet.com/library/video-oecd-workshop-ralph-dum-senior-expert-digital-science-unit-dg-connect-european-commis sion (accessed October 8, 2018).

Fink, L. (2018, January 16). A sense of purpose. At: https://www.nytimes.com/interactive/2018/01/16/business/dealbook/document-BlackRock-s-Laurence-Fink-Urges-C-E-O-s-to-Focus.html (accessed October 8, 2018).

Florida, R. (2014). *The rise of the creative class – revisited: Revised and expanded*. Basic Books (AZ).

Fombrun, C. (2015, February 6). How do you rank the world's best CEOs? *Harvard Business Review*. At: https://hbr.org/2015/02/how-do-you-rank-the-worlds-best-ceos (accessed October 12, 2018).

Fredette, J., Marom, R., Steiner, K., and Witters, L. (2012). The promise and peril of hyperconnectivity for organizations and societies. In: *The Global Information Technology Report: Living in a hyperconnected world*. World Economic Forum, pp. 113–119. At: http://www3.weforum.org/docs/GITR/2012/GITR_ Chapter1.10_2012.pdf (accessed October 8, 2018).

Gilmore, J. H., and Pine, B. J. (2002). *The experience is the marketing*. BrownHerron Publishing.

Glouberman, S., and Zimmerman, B. (2002). Complicated and complex systems: What would successful reform of Medicare look like? *Romanow Papers*, 2, 21–53.

Grint, K. (2008). Wicked problems and clumsy solutions: The role of leadership. *Clinical leader*, 1(2), 54–68.

Hagel III, J., Brown, J. S., and Davison, L. (2009). *The big shift: Why it matters*. Deloitte Center for the Edge.

Harquail, C. V. (2012, September 5). Justin Bieber and The Boost Economy. Really. Authentic Organizations. At: http://authenticorganizations.com/harquail/2012/09/05/justin-bieber-and-the-boost-economy-really/#sthash. NvsgOYqb.dpbs (accessed October 8, 2018).

Hawking, S. (2000, January 23). I think the next century will be the century of complexity. *San José Mercury News, Morning Final Edition*.

Hietanen, J., Andéhn, M., and Bradshaw, A. (2017). Against the implicit politics of service-dominant logic. *Marketing Theory*, 18(1), 101–119.

Küpers, W. (2000). Embodied symbolic consumption. Phenomenological perspectives for an interpretative consumer research. In: Beckmann, S., and Elliott, R. (eds.) *Interpretive consumer research*. Copenhagen Business School Press, pp. 293–317.

Landry, C. (2018). Creative bureaucracy. At: http://charleslandry.com/themes/creative-bureaucracy/ (accessed October 8, 2018).

Lawrence, K. (2013). Developing leaders in a VUCA environment. *UNC Exec Dev*. At: http://www.growbold. com/2013/developing-leaders-in-a-vuca-environment_UNC.2013.pdf (accessed October 10, 2018).

Lichtenstein, B. B. (2014). *Generative emergence: A new discipline of organizational, entrepreneurial, and social innovation*. Oxford University Press (UK).

Mandel, M. (2014, November). Connections as a tool for growth: Evidence from the LinkedIn Economic Graph. At: http://www. slideshare. net/ linkedin/mandel-linked-in-connections-reportnov-2014 (accessed October 8, 2018).

Nijs, D. E. L. W. (2014). *Imagineering the butterfly effect*. Eleven International Publishing.

Normann, R. (2001). *Reframing business: When the map changes the landscape*. John Wiley & Sons.

Normann, R., and Ramirez, R. (1993). From value chain to value constellation: Designing interactive strategy. *Harvard Business Review*, 71(4), 65–77.

Peñaloza, L., and Venkatesh, A. (2006). Further evolving the new dominant logic of marketing: From services to the social construction of markets. *Marketing theory*, 6(3), 299–316.

Porter, M. E., and Kramer, M. R. (2015, September 1). Profiting the planet. *Fortune*, 64–65.

Prahalad, C. K. (2004). The blinders of dominant logic. *Long Range Planning,* 37(2), 171–179.

Prahalad, C. K., and Bettis, R. A. (1986). The dominant logic: A new linkage between diversity and performance. *Strategic Management Journal,* 7(6), 485–501.

Ramaswamy, V., and Gouillart, F. (2010). Building the co-creative enterprise. *Harvard Business Review,* 88(10), 100–109.

Ramaswamy, V. (2009). Co-creation of value – towards an expanded paradigm of value creation. *Marketing Review St. Gallen,* 26(6), 11–17.

Ramirez, R. (1999, January). Value co-production: Intellectual origins and implications for practice and research. *Strategic Management Journal,* 20, 49–65.

Reeves, M., Love, C., and Mathur, N. (2012). *The Most Adaptive Companies 2012: Winning in an age of turbulence.* Boston Consulting Group.

Rittel, H. W., and Webber, M. M. (1973). Dilemmas in a general theory of planning. *Policy sciences,* 4(2), 155–169.

Romme, A. G. L. (2003). Making a difference: Organization as design. *Organization science,* 14(5), 558–573.

Schembri, S. (2006). Rationalizing service logic, or understanding services as experience?. *Marketing Theory,* 6(3), 381–392.

Sheth, J. N., and Uslay, C. (2007). Implications of the revised definition of marketing: From exchange to value creation. *Journal of Public Policy & Marketing,* 26(2), 302–307.

Tanev, S., and Frederiksen, M. H. (2014). Generative innovation practices, customer creativity, and the adoption of new technology products. *Technology Innovation Management Review,* 4(2), 5–10.

Vargo, S. L., and Lusch, R. F. (2008). Service-dominant logic: Continuing the evolution. *Journal of the Academy of marketing Science,* 36(1), 1–10.

Vargo, S. L., and Lusch, R. F. (2004). Evolving to a new dominant logic for marketing. *Journal of marketing,* 68(1), 1–17.

Vasconcelos, F. C., and Ramirez, R. (2011). Complexity in business environments. *Journal of Business Research,* 64(3), 236–241.

Wilden, R., Akaka, M. A., Karpen, I. O., and Hohberger, J. (2017). The evolution and prospects of service-dominant logic: An investigation of past, present, and future research. *Journal of Service Research,* 20(4), 345–361.

Wilson, I. (2004). The agenda for redefining corporate purpose: Five key executive actions. *Strategy & Leadership,* 32(1), 21–26.

3

LENS: a big shift in science – seeing change and innovation as a matter of emergence

Diane Nijs

3.1 Introduction

Einstein already stated it 100 years ago: 'We cannot solve our problems with the same thinking we used when we created them'. With the landscape of value creation becoming ever more complex, we need new thinking to cope with some of the most challenging 5G innovation problems, issues we approach in this book as 'designing innovation as collective creation'. To cope effectively with challenges such as whole system innovation and public innovation, challenges which entail essentially 'breaking through bureaucracy' (Barzelay, 1992), we urgently need new thinking and doing.

In this chapter we present the science of the living systems, also called complexity science, as the science that offers a truly new lens or new glasses, to tackle more effectively these seemingly impossible issues, sometimes in a remarkably easy way as we will illustrate at the end of this chapter. This is a truly new lens as Stevenson and Harmeling (1990) articulate: perhaps the single most important shift in thinking that complexity theory provides is a movement away from explaining why change happens and toward explaining why and how order emerges in the first place. Complexity science is a scientific framework that informs 'innovation as collective creation'. This chapter answers the question: How can complex thinking make us more effective complex innovators?

The chapter is designed to offer those new to complexity science an understanding of the basic principles and processes. The definitions and descriptions are given in a popular way and are by no means exhaustive, as the purpose of this chapter is not a scientific one. Nevertheless, it is an important chapter to read for 5G-innovators, as without this basic all-round and proper understanding of the scientific background, it is not possible to design consciously for emergence and to effectively manage emerging processes without harming the social system one is trying to improve.

The chapter unfolds as follows: after explaining what a worldview or lens is and how they evolve in a very natural way (Section 3.2), we articulate what the complex systems lens is all about (Section 3.3) by describing basic metaphors, principles and dynamics of complexity science. Then we turn to the implications of the lens for management and leadership (Section 3.4) and we finish the chapter with reflecting on the implications of the lens for 5G, complex innovation challenges (Section 3.5). Finally, we illustrate our argument with two examples out of the field of healthcare.

3.2   Worldviews and their evolution

> The reform in thinking is a key anthropological and historical problem. This implies a mental revolution of considerable greater proportions than the Copernican revolution. Never before in the history of humanity have the responsibilities of thinking weighted so crushingly on us. (Morin, 2008:vii)

A worldview or paradigm is a way, a lens or else glasses, to look at the world. It is 'a connected set of beliefs or basic assumptions, or a dispositional stance about the nature and organization of the world, together with beliefs about how to best to investigate it' (Kuhn, 2007:156). Depending on the worldview or 'lens' one is using, the same reality can look totally different. In Figure 3.1, the same reality can be diagnosed as being a rabbit or a duck. Depending on the fact that you see it either as a duck or as a rabbit, you will think and act differently.

The same counts for business reality or whatever context you are working with, the lens you use will be decisive for what you will think and do. Worldviews, for example, differ between generations. Contrary to former generations for example, young people today grew up with the idea that many jobs are not forever and that there are plenty of opportunities to create new startups. The view we have of the world frames the way we do research, understand the world and the way we attempt to affect the world as designers. Worldviews differ between people and generations but they differ even more in society over centuries. There was a time, for example, that people thought that the earth was flat or that people thought that the sun was turning around the earth. Worldviews evolve and in today's networked world we are at the fringe of another shift in the way we view the world.

Figure 3.1 The rabbit–duck illusion is an ambiguous image illustrating that a same reality can be diagnosed as being a rabbit or a duck

3.2.1   The Newtonian, mechanistic worldview

Today we are using predominantly a mechanistic worldview, a view based on Newton's vision of an orderly and predictable reality. His vision on the processes of change in nature was based on his studies on planets and these objects in motion, which led him to see the world as an orderly machine that functioned in a deterministic and predictable manner. 'This worldview and value system, articulated between 1500 and 1700, caused a dramatic shift in the way people in Europe pictured the world and in their whole way of thinking. The new mentality and new perception of the cosmos gave the Western civilization the features and characteristic of the modern era' (Capra and Luisi, 2014:13). Scientists at that time saw the world as a big machine and they thought that if they took the machine apart and understood the parts, they would understand the whole. The Newtonian worldview inherited from previous generations, works in terms of equilibrium and deterministic cause-and-effect relationships. It made us evidently interpret everything around us in a linear and mechanical way, mostly without being aware of the inherited template (Mathews et al., 1999). In today's networked world, however, we increasingly discover the limits of this mechanistic lens.

3.2.2 The emerging, ecological worldview of complex, living systems

Since the second half of the 20th century, the calculating power of the computer has been available to scientists, enabling them to decode the non-linear processes and principles at work in complex living systems such as the weather and the economy. In a variety of sciences such as physics, chemistry and biology, scientists have discovered that the seemingly turbulent, chaotic and disorderly universe hides a deeper order of more complex patterns and processes. The study of complex, living systems brings forth a new imagery of processes, metaphors, descriptions and relations that allow one to see the world in a more systemic and dynamic way. It is these insights that can make us truly more effective innovators in coping with 5G innovation challenges. Instead of 'seeing the universe as a machine composed of elementary building blocks, we now discover that the material world, ultimately, is a network of inseparable patterns of relationships; that the planet as a whole is a living, self-regulating system' (Capra and Luisi, 2014:xi).

Understanding the concept of systems is core to the ecological worldview (Tsoukas and Dooley, 2011). A system has been defined as 'a grouping of component parts that individually establish relationships with each other and that interact with their environment both as individuals and as a collective' (Cavaleri and Obłój, 1993:13). A complex system has many interacting parts where cause-and-effect relationships are not clear and can be shifting all the time. A complex adaptive system, or else a complex evolving system (Mitleton-Kelly, 2003), is a system that can learn in interaction with its context. All non-linear systems share the characteristic that they can transform themselves into more complex forms, an insight that lays one of the foundation for a new worldview in facing growing complexity.

According to complexity scientist Ilya Prigogine, the Nobel Chemistry Prize winner in 1977, growing connectivity with its accelerating interdependency in society, makes that the world itself start to act as a living, complex system. Capra and Luigi Luisi (2014:xi) write:

As the twenty-first century unfolds, it is becoming more and more evident that the major problems of our time – energy, the environment, climate change, food security, financial security – cannot be understood in isolation. They are systemic problems, which means that they are all interconnected and interdependent. Ultimately, these problems must be seen as just different facets of one single crisis, which is largely a crisis of perception, a crisis of worldview. [. . .] There are solutions to the major problems of our time; some of them even simple. But they require a radical shift in our perceptions, our thinking, our values. Unfortunately, this fundamental change of worldview in science and society, has not yet dawned on most of our political leaders, [. . .] who fail to see how their so-called solutions affect future generations.

How is it possible that some of the major problems of our time can have simple solutions? For a first grasp of this contradiction, there is an interesting three-minute YouTube movie of consultant Nick Obolensky (2008). Under the title of 'Who needs leaders', this short movie illustrates in a fun way how the same challenge can be impossible and easy at the same time, depending on how you approach the issue. The challenge in this short movie is to put all the actors in a group the same distance from two other actors chosen at random from that group. The movie shows how it is impossible for one person to solve this complex challenge centrally but how the challenge is solved in less than a minute when making use of one simple rule that mobilizes the distributed intelligence of all actors in the system. It is an interesting illustration of how the concepts of complexity and simplicity relate to one another. Let's further explore the lens of complex systems, central to the new worldview.

3.3   The complex systems lens

Studying complexity has become one of the most ambitious and all-encompassing intellectual challenges of recent times. By studying complexity, scientists and researchers, in all kind of disciplines such as biology, chemistry and physics, are trying to understand how a group of independent agents can generate singular systems that evolve, and adapt to their environments. These insights come right in time to help understand and cope with the growing complexity of our time (Kuhn, 2007). Complex Systems Thinking or short 'Systems Thinking' is embraced as a tool for making sense in and of a changing world.

The lens of complex systems science or 'complex systems lens' refers to a wide set of concepts that can be used to explore the dynamics of living systems instead of the static building blocks of machines. Complementary to the Newtonian, mechanistic lens that makes us see the world as comprised of individual building blocks, the complex systems lens makes it possible to see the world as 'a reality of interactions, emergences and becoming' (Díaz, 2007:48).

The 'big shift' and also 'big shock' of 20th-century science has been that complex, living systems cannot be understood by the analyzing paradigm of the Newtonian lens. By taking out, for example, one part of a living body or one department of an organization, one no longer has a flourishing, living system.

On top of that, the properties of the parts can only be understood within the context of the larger whole. The complex systems lens is 'contextual' instead of analytical and it asks for mapping to understand instead of measuring to know. 'Analysis means taking something apart in order to understand it; (complex) systems thinking means putting it into the context of the larger whole' (Capra and Luisi, 2014:66) to understand it. Let's explore some of the basic metaphors and principles central in the complex systems lens.

3.3.1   Basic metaphors

One important way complexity science is influencing our thinking and behavior is by introducing metaphors in our language and our thinking. In this section three central metaphors are presented that are often alluded to in management literature and that are relevant for the articulation of the design approach of Imagineering: 'complex adaptive systems', 'emergence' and 'butterfly effects'.

Complex adaptive systems

A complex system is anything with multiple actors or agents, organized for a purpose – a school, a city . . . are all complex systems. An actor or agent is anything which acts within a system: individual, group, idea etc. Complex systems are essentially different from simple systems and we should think and act differently with both. Chapman (2002:40) explains the difference with a metaphor that stems from Richard Dawkins:

> A rock is a simple system. When you throw it, it will end up pretty much depending on your strength, aim and coordination. You can easily predict the trajectory. It could even be accurately modelled using maths and science. A bird, on the contrary, is a complex, living system. Throwing it (which one shouldn't do in practice), is something totally different. Even though the bird is subject to the same laws of physics as the rock, there is no way to predict the trajectory. However, you can try to influence the trajectory but this will ask for totally different thinking and acting: you might place food at the desired destination, but even then there are no guarantees.

A complex adaptive system (CAS) is more like a bird. It is dynamic and self-organizing, meaning it can be highly organized without any conscious leadership, direction, or management. The difference between a merely complex system and a CAS is the fact that a CAS can learn; a complex system cannot. A CAS can survive by changing its behavior and internal processes. 'A CAS exists within other interdependent systems and is driven by interactions between systems components and governed by feedback. Its complexity comes from these patterns of interactions. It is constantly adapting. Changes in one part of the system can cause changes in other parts of the system, often in nonlinear and unpredictable ways' (McKenzie, 2014:2).

Most of the things around us are CASs – the weather, environment, our immune systems, our bodies, brains, the economy, neighborhoods, governments, sporting events and, most important, the organizations in which we work. It is important to realize that a CAS is not a management process such as, for example, Total Quality Management, but that it is a concept which provides us with a fresh model for thinking about the world around us and not with a model for predicting what will happen. Viewing organizations as CASs opens new perspectives to act differently from according to the mechanistic paradigm. It enables us to act more in line with the logic of living systems.

The bird and rock analogy is, of course, an oversimplification, as every metaphor is. But this metaphor illustrates the key point that a CAS is able to adapt and thus survive by changing its behavior and internal processes in interaction with the environment (which makes some scholars speak about CES instead of CAS: Complex Evolving Systems). A rock simply can't do this. Why does the difference between birds and rocks matter for management? McKenzie (2014:3) argues:

> It matters because the way one would study, think about and work with a rock is different from the way one would (hopefully) interact with a bird. When implementing organizational change and policy reform, all too often we apply the wrong approach to the right idea. Why do we need TO THINK ABOUT systems? Our minds are full of concepts and constructs that humans have developed and passed down over millennia to make sense of the world around us. The problem is that our world today is full of challenges that have reached unsurpassed levels of complexity and uncertainty, and full of complex systems that are increasingly connected and interdependent.

Emergence

McKenzie (2014:2) goes on, in a CAS:

> the whole is more than the sum of its parts – something that is referred to as emergence. Emergence means that the characteristics or phenomena of the whole appear due to the collective behavior of the system. Like a flock of birds or an ant colony, the pattern that emerges cannot be seen through the analysis of any one of the individual parts. Only when the system is viewed as a whole does the behavior exist or emerge. [. . .] An action in one part of the system can have unanticipated effects on another seemingly unconnected part of the system. Results can be counterintuitive. You can make changes you want, but you might not end up in the place you would expect.[. . .] No single individual or organization has total oversight of how food for example arrives on our tables. And yet we all (those who can afford it) can eat every day, 24/7 if we want to. In the face of this complexity, traditional linear frameworks (where a+b=c) and reductionist mental models are insufficient. As the second decade of the 21st century progresses, it is clear that alternative approaches such as 'systems thinking' will play an increasingly important role in how we make sense of the world. [See Chapter 6 on Systems Thinking.]

In Chapter 1 we introduced the phenomenon of emergence as a property of all CASs. We defined it with Lichtenstein (2014) as *the coming-into-being of a sustainable dynamic state arising out of the interactions among components (agents) that make up the system itself.* Emergence, we stated, is order arising out of chaos and we also focused on the four crucial differences that Lichtenstein (2014:5) articulates between emergence and the more mechanistic concepts of change, transformation and innovation: emergence is always creation, triggered by aspiration, evoking 'proactive creativity' characterized by 'intrinsic motivation, positive affect, and focused self-discipline' (Heinzen, 1994:143), and expanding the capacity of the system to accomplish its work, its function. We also mentioned that processes of emergence don't start all by themselves but that they need to be triggered and contextualized. In short: they need to be designed for. In Chapter 1 we presented the concept of the 'Creative Tension Engine' (CTE) in this regard (see Chapter 4 for further explanation).

Butterfly effects

Butterfly effects have to do with 'extreme sensitivity to initial conditions'. Minimal changes in complex living systems' initial state can lead over time to large-scale consequences. It is called 'butterfly effect' because of the half-joking assertion that a butterfly stirring the air today in Beijing can cause a storm in Texas next month. From virtually the same starting point, two trajectories can evolve in a totally different way, making any long-range prediction impossible. This discovery (in weather forecasting) was shocking for the scientific community, as it seemed inconceivable that strictly deterministic equations of motion can lead to unpredictable results. The phenomenon is a striking example of how a simple set of non-linear equations can generate enormous complex behavior in open living systems. Small actions can be amplified and result in big effects (Capra and Luisi, 2014:114).

3.3.2 Basic principles

We discuss three basic principles that are core in the complex systems lens and that are revealing for the design approach of Imagineering, designing for generating (new) order, or else: designing innovation as collective creation. We discuss: open systems, order through fluctuation and non-linearity.

Open systems

Living systems (such as organizations in today's society) are open systems. Compared to a closed system like a rock or a table, an open system like a burning candle is a system that disposes itself of an external source of matter/energy. While a closed system is in equilibrium, the constancy of an open system's internal environment is not at all linked to such equilibrium. On the contrary, in an open system there is disequilibrium in the energetic flux that feeds it, and, without this flux, there is an organizational deregulation that quickly leads to decline. In an open system there is a 'nourishing disequilibrium' that allows the system to maintain an apparent equilibrium. This apparent equilibrium degrades if there is a closure of the system. Without an energy influx, a CAS cannot sustain its complexity. It will fall apart.

Co-creation and co-evolution are essential mechanisms to living systems in dynamic, turbulent environments. Open systems and co-evolution mean that every system as for example an organization exists within an environment which includes many other systems such as other organizations, the industry or the local economy. These other systems are constantly changing and for every organization to maintain best fit with the environment it must keep changing too. And by changing it also changes the environment because it is part of the environment. To survive an organization must do two things: change to meet the changes of the environment and change the environment to suit its own needs. Co-evolving is not just a matter of adapting but also a matter of influencing. It is an interactive process. The danger of making fixed plans then is that the attention goes to realizing the plan rather than changing to meet the changes in the environment.

Order through fluctuation

The original research that now underlies what is being called 'complexity' is the research of physical chemist Ilya Prigogine on 'dissipative structures'. It explains how regimes of order come into being and retain their form amidst a constant dissipation of energy and resources (Prigogine, 1955). His work was considered to be of such groundbreaking importance that it was awarded the Nobel Prize in 1978. It demonstrated that we live in a world of non-linear dynamic systems which are essentially always in motion and are able to transform themselves into emerging new states of being. Rather than living in a world where systems run down, subject to ongoing deterioration, we live in a world of constant generation and regeneration. Dissipative structures are the basic structures of all living systems, including human beings (McMillan, 2008). As the four dynamics of dissipative structures are central in all 'emergency praxis', we shortly present them here. In Section 3.5 we will interpret these dynamics to their emergence in organizations:

- **Fluctuation dynamics**: Ever-increasing injections of energy create an 'adaptive tension' (shifting mind-maps) that pushes the system out of equilibrium into a disequilibrium state. Sustaining this disequilibrium state for an extended period is said to be a prerequisite aspect of emergent order creation (Lichtenstein, 2000). 'Order through fluctuation' is central to the dynamics.
- **Positive feedback dynamics**: Once in disequilibrium state, small actions can be amplified through positive feedback loops and a cycle of self-reinforcement potentially leading to a 'scaffold of emergence' (Holland, 1995). Despite the absence of a central controller, the system's components 'communicate' as they are connected in a web.
- **Recombination dynamics**: The emerging new order of dissipative structures implies that some of the existing elements of the system must be

reconstituted to generate a new combination through a key dynamic known as recombination, a dynamic that helps us understand how self-organizing systems evolve and how novelty and variety are generated.

● **Stabilization dynamics**: Stabilization dynamics and mechanisms play an important role in moving the system into a new order or configuration. Stabilization is not as much about equilibrium but about the deep structure, principles, values and basic social rules, about the framework that facilitates a collective mind, shapes novelties and guides choices in a way consistent with the system's accumulated history and learning, preserving the system's identity and core behavioral patterns.

According to Lichtenstein (2014) and Plowman et al. (2017), these are the four dynamics that are recognized in whatever process of emergence. They are the characteristic dynamics that should be taken care of when trying to influence emergence in complex innovation eco-systems as for example when trying to transform the value-creating logic of an organization from industrial towards networked logic.

Non-linearity

By saying that complex systems are non-linear, complexity scientists mean something very specific: it means that small changes can have big effects, while sometimes big changes in the system don't have much effect at all. Complex systems exhibit, therefore, a fundamental disproportionality between cause and effect. This is one of the fundamental principles in which simple machines and complex systems differ. In a simple machine small changes generally have small effects, while big interventions have big effects.

3.4   Implications for management and leadership

To see organizations as CASs and to evaluate their status as evolving products of evolution, constitutes a major revolution in thinking about management and leadership. It questions the management know-how so far, which was thought to be 'objective truth about eternal natural laws governing unchanging systems' (Allen et al., 2011:2). Seeing organizations as CASs means that managerial issues shift on four basic assumptions underlying non-linear dynamic systems (West, 1985/2013):

● from maintaining control to supporting the emergence of new order;
● from analytical, reductionist approaches to integral approaches;
● from aiming for equilibrium to bringing the system slightly out of its equilibrium; and
● from cause–effect reasoning to think and act in terms of small but well-designed interventions.

This shift leads to a new focus, new principles, new skills and new tools.

3.4.1 A new focus: from hero to host

As the focus of management shifts from effectuating change to generating (new) order, the management responsibility shifts from seeking and articulating answers towards making sense of situations in dialogical processes (from managing people to managing words); from being oriented to entities and results towards being oriented to relational processes and dynamics, from predicting and forecasting the future towards designing the future direction in an inspiring way based on collective aspiration; from finding the ultimate organization structure towards keeping the structure fluid and adaptive; from being blinded by the limits of the organization towards unleashing the dynamic and creative potential of the broader system.

3.4.2 New principles for leadership: humility and the space between

As emergence and self-organization are essential concepts in complexity, leadership, seen through the complexity lens, means 'facilitating the emergence of novelty – in other words, creativity – within communities of practice' (Hutchins, 2016). Complexity leaders are like gardeners that create the conditions in which living systems can flourish. One of the key leaderships elements is the capacity to influence others and this can happen by everybody, anywhere and at any time. 'This means that leadership is not so much about the quality "in" someone, as it is about the quality of the "space between" individuals, reflecting networks of interactions' (McKenzie, 2014:8).

From the complexity perspective it makes more sense for leaders to 'nurture' new ideas and to empower people than to try to 'plan' or 'construct' new ideas and instruct people. Leaders should be humble catalyzers that generate the conditions for emergence through their own specific actions and behaviors. They disrupt existing patterns, encourage and empower others in self-organizing processes of rich interaction, stimulate reflection and experimentation, and support collective action.

3.4.3 New skills and tools: Systems Thinking and systems mapping

In the face of complexity, traditional linear frameworks (where a+b=c) and reductionist mental models no longer make sense. An alternative approach called 'Systems Thinking' will play an increasingly important role in making sense of this complex, changing world. Systems Thinking helps us to step back and, with the help of complexity metaphors and principles, identify underlying patterns and mental models that influence the overall performance of the system. According to Peter Senge (2006:69):

> Systems thinking is a discipline for seeing wholes. It is a framework for seeing interrelationships rather than things, for seeing patterns of change rather than static 'snapshots'[. . .] Perhaps for the first time in history, humankind has the capacity to create far more information than anyone can absorb, to foster far

greater interdependence than anyone can manage, and to accelerate change far faster than anyone's ability to keep pace.

Therefore we need new skills and new tools such as systems mapping.

Systems today are so extended and intertwined that it is no longer possible for any single person to have a complete understanding of the system as a whole. Mapping these interactions (and the nature of relationships, structures, processes and resources governing them) together with other actors in the system can help to understand the way the system works and to see points of leverage for transformative change or emergence. 'Mapping' can be an interesting tool not just to get a better understanding of the systems but, maybe even more important, to get a better collective understanding of the system. Mapping is a tool that stimulates the dialogue and the understanding of perspectives and processes in the system. More than visualizing the system, maps can help as dialogical instruments. Further new skills and tools such as the skill of Imagineering, are discussed in the chapters that follow.

3.4.4 The pervasiveness of the 'mechanistic lens'

Much of the problems we face today such as the financial crisis are a consequence of the fact that we use mechanistic approaches such as standardization, more prediction and control in coping with complex situations. Where the world is emergent and complex, it makes little sense to try harder to control. But this is exactly what happens when managers and politicians know but one lens, the mechanistic lens: they try harder. This tension between wishes and expectations on the one hand and ineffectiveness of actions in reality on the other can be a source of considerable stress and even despair.

According to the complexity scholars Boulton et al. (2015:2), as a consequence of the pervasiveness of the mechanistic lens there is a tendency towards polarization in management and policy thinking:

> On the one hand, there is an increasing focus, for organizations, on defining detailed rules, standardizing methods, evidencing and measuring outcomes. The intention is to make the hospital, school, or firm work as an efficient, optimized, well-oiled machine. The belief is that if we tell people exactly what to do and check they do it exactly, then standards and efficiency will improve. On the other hand, [. . .] there is increasing deregulation and laissez-faire [. . .] to lead to optimal outcomes. Yet [. . .] also here with the implicit assumption that the future can be predicted, that policies can be designed and optimized to control the future. What is remarkable is that these beliefs seem to harden and become ever-more entrenched despite the repeating crises facing our economies, ecologies, and societies. [. . .] if ever there were a need for fresh thinking and questioning underlying assumptions, we are seeing it now.

It becomes more evident every day: Complexity fits our time. 'It is what practitioners and researchers need to learn to cope with' (Tsoukas and Dooley,

2011:734) to become more effective innovators. But to get these insights implemented in our systems, it is of most importance that our leaders and politicians get inspired by complex Systems Thinking and acting (and not just employees, administrators and students in general), as they are the ones that have the legitimacy and authority to act systemically.

3.5 Implications for whole system innovation

As already mentioned, according to complexity scholars such as Lichtenstein (2014) and Dougherty (2017), we should approach the phenomenon of complex innovation eco-systems in terms of emergence, as the analogy between order creation in dissipative structures in nature and in organizations is commonly taken for granted. The lens of complex living systems then indeed does provide us with a fundamental shift in our understanding of innovation as a process of generative emergence and its dynamics. It offers a dynamic perspective to rethink central assumptions and to open the black box of complex invention and innovating processes. Understanding this perspective and these dynamic processes makes it possible that managers and leaders can make better choices on:

- how to foster innovation in terms of emergence;
- who should be involved both within and outside the organization;
- how to foster creative relations and interactions; and
- why integrate diverse voices and experiences.

As in the next chapter we will focus on designing for emergence, in this section we try to truly understand how these processes of innovating take shape as seen through the lens of complexity. How do these processes unfold? We illustrate the theoretical argument with examples of emerging innovation processes out of the field of healthcare.

3.5.1 Opening the 'black box' of the journey of emergent innovation

Mintzberg's (2005:362) statement that in management 'we are often compelled to provide a linear account of a nonlinear world' definitely counts for innovation. Conventionally innovation is articulated as a sequential process of a few phases: the perception of a problem or an incomplete pattern, setting the stage or articulating the brief, an act of insight or prototyping and, finally, a critical revision or implementation. According to Lane et al. (2009), it is this positivist mechanistic and analytic, scientific perspective of describing phenomena only and mostly even 'a posteriori' that is most probably one of the major reasons for the bad innovation figures. Besides the fact that this mechanistic perspective leaves the generation of an invention completely out of focus (relegating it to the domain of personal creativity), it also limits the study of how an invention is adopted and spreads throughout a population. 'Complexity lens', on the contrary, is a lens much more suitable for studying the emerging phenomena of inventing, changing and innovating than the conventional mechanistic lens.

In contrast to a sequential or synoptic view, Garud et al. (2016:456) present a performative view of innovation processes which conceives of invention and innovation 'as being implicated in the sayings and doings of the various actors involved'. The performative perspective acknowledges the indeterminacy and openness of an ongoing process in which the context is not given but negotiated and reconceived while acting. The innovation journey is here conceptualized as involving translation instead of diffusion (Garud et al., 2016:460). Novelty emerges through 'a non-linear recombination of already existing ideas in complex adaptive processes' or 'complex responsive processes', as Stacey (2003) calls them: large numbers of entities or actors interact, whose actions are driven by simple rules. Doing so the performative perspective of the innovation journey confirms the dissipative structures interpretation of the complexity scientists.

The overall process is one of accumulation of many small acts of insights of individuals, a process of going back and forth, a process of 'finding future utility from past efforts' (Garud et al., 2016:458). Innovation from this perspective is an ongoing, unfinished, never ending story of collective creativity in which (as we already mentioned in Chapter 1, Potts, 2007) generative creativity (new ideas), adaptive creativity (new processes) and retentive creativity (new institutionalizations) manifest themselves. Such a process cannot and should not be managed in traditional ways. This then is the fundamental paradox of innovation: 'That our efforts to manage the process of innovation "in traditional ways" may diminish the very possibilities of accomplishing innovation! To resolve this paradox, we must view innovation as process in and of itself' (Garud et al., 2016:461), processes of emergence that don't start all by themselves but that should be designed for, consciously or unconsciously. In the next chapter we present therefore the Systemic Design Approach of Imagineering, an approach to install innovation as a continuing, never-ending process of collective creation.

According to Lichtenstein (2014:176) two outcomes are endemic to dissipative structures: first, that emergence leads to a new level of order, a new tangible layer of systemic activity that is distinct from its components (for example co-creation that was never present in the system) and, second, it generates greater capacity for the system to do its work (as co-creation is definitely meant to do). As such Nijs (2014) has argued that the transformation of the enterprise logic from the industrial archetype of value exchange to the networked archetype of value co-creation can be approached as a matter of emergence: in this case an adaptive tension engine (which we prefer to call a 'Creative Tension Engine' as the design of one is never just meant for adaptation but for the creation of a new, collectively desired future) is designed to generate the emergence from the industrial, closed organization of the networked, open organization that is more capable of flourishing in a more complex environment.

3.5.2   Industry spotlight: Healthcare

Countries around the world are struggling with similar healthcare issues – increases in expenditures (also because of aging populations in Western countries) are often not commensurate with health outcomes: lack of quality, lack of access to care, lack of transparency of information, and a growing dissatisfaction among both patients and caregivers. With no reforms underway that would affect the fundamental drivers of healthcare expenditures, the World Economic Forum (2014) reports, that by 2040, total expenditures could grow by another 50–100 percent. The topic of 'healthcare reform' is a pressing issue for most countries, as required investments in this field adversely impact the ability to invest in other priority fields such as education, infrastructure and social welfare. In the first case we show how the design of a CTE generated a new, collectively desired reality and in the second case we illustrate how the design of one simple, appealing and evident rule can cause the fluctuation needed to generate new order, at least as long as it is possible to keep the actors in the system, acting on this rule.

Buurtzorg.NL

In many countries around the world, the complexity-inspired 'Buurtzorg' model (a new startup founded in 2006 by Jos de Block in the Netherlands) is now studied as a model that has the potential to permanently change the landscape of healthcare. Driven by the simple rule 'Humanity over Bureaucracy', de Block reintroduced the concept of district (community) nursing. Care is organized in and around teams of 12 nurses that manage themselves and their work, performing all the tasks necessary to provide care for 50 to 60 patients. According to complexity scientists in healthcare Kreitzer et al. (2015:41) 'the microscale of Buurtzorg neighborhood-focused teams makes it possible to know and use the local resources, build and support formal and informal networks, and initiate prevention activities that enhance health and wellbeing.' Launched in 2007 with one team, as of 2014, there are more than 700 teams employing more than 7,000 nurses, providing care to about 55,000 clients.

'Bring your heart to work' at Lakeland Health, Michigan

The next case is a less studied one but one that illustrates whole system innovation in a long existing healthcare system, 'Lakeland Health', a system in the southwest corner of Michigan that encompasses several hospitals, medical practices and clinics, employing 4,000 associates and taking in nearly $500 million per year. The case was presented by Gary Hamel in *Harvard Business Review*, June 12, 2015 with the title: 'Innovation starts from the heart, not from the head'. The case tells how Lakeland Health succeeded in innovating itself from laggard, with satisfaction scores between the 25th and 50th percentile, to leader with scores getting to the 90th percentile in just 90 days. The case tells how this evolution was effectuated by bringing in the simple rule of 'Bring your heart to work' and making people act upon it.

To invite and inspire all actors of the internal system to start acting on this simple rule, the case tells that the CEO asked his team to rent cinemas in the region and that he scheduled more than 20 kick-off events. Nearly all staff showed up at one of the events. The CEO's message was simple, unexpected and daunting:

'None of us aspire to work in an organization that frequently lets down its customers. We can and must do better than this. So let's set a goal of *getting to the 90th percentile in 90 days*. [. . .] We're going to raise our scores by touching the hearts of our patients – by making sure they know not only how well we care *for* them, but how much we care *about* them. We're going to learn to be more loving. To do that,' he said, 'I want to challenge you to bring your heart to work in new and creative ways. [. . .] For nurses an intervention can be a routine but for patients, the experience is anything but [. . .] For patients an intervention is something that is remembered for years afterwards.'

At the events, the hospital visit (the patient's journey) was presented as a drama in three acts: the admission, the phase of patient care, and the phase of discharge. Using role-playing the CEO himself demonstrated how each stage offers opportunities to create loving connections. He didn't offer a script or training program but challenged staff to say in every interaction with a patient *who* you are, *what* you are doing and then share a heartfelt *why*. The heartfelt *why* needed to be stated in a way that put the patient's hopes and fears at the center of the interaction.

Over the next 90 days, the CEO 'rounded' 120 times. He showed up in every department, on every shift, in every facility. 'How's it going?' he'd ask. 'Have you made any heartfelt connections? If so, tell me about it. If not, let's role-play right now. Let me be the patient.' Initially, many of his associates struggled to come up with a 'heartfelt' why. Despite all the caring that goes on in healthcare, making it personal doesn't always come naturally. It takes practice.

Over the ensuing months two things became apparent. First, success required that everyone, every day, opened their hearts to those they were caring for. One person with a bad attitude could undo the heartfelt efforts of a dozen colleagues. Not surprisingly, frontline employees and their managers started to become less tolerant of colleagues with crappy attitudes. In the end, more than a few of the curmudgeons were asked to leave. Lesson 1: Organization or system innovation is a matter of 'every-one or no-one'. And, second, though the focus of the CEO's initiative wasn't on call-light response times, pain management or discharge planning, patient scores on all these conventional metrics started to climb as the heart-to-heart message took hold. 'The lesson: love someone better, and they'll extend you grace on all the less important things. [. . .] A whole systems approach gets a whole systems answer!'

American management expert Gary Hamel reflects:

I often worry about just how de-humanized our organizations have become. Listen to the speech of a typical CEO, or scroll through an employee-oriented website, and notice the words that keep cropping up – words like execution, solution, advantage, focus, differentiation and superiority. There's nothing wrong with these words, but they're not the ones that inspire human hearts. And that's a problem – because if you want to innovate, you need to be inspired, your colleagues need to be inspired, and ultimately, your customers need to be inspired.

The lesson learned: we need to adapt our words to 're-enchant the world'.

These two healthcare cases illustrate the core thesis of this book. They illustrate how approaching a situation as a complex (adaptive) issue (bringing things together instead of fragmenting them) and using an inspiring whole systems approach can result in a fast creation (Buurtzorg.NL) or fast innovation of a whole system (Lakeland Health) if the conditions for a whole systems approach are in place: designing one simple rule that sets the stage for all actors to collectively and creatively make come true a new more desired reality and managing it . . . according to the principles and processes of complex, living systems. For those who wonder what happens when the CEO is no longer showing up everywhere, it is our experience that integrating the simple rule in the identity of the system, such as the logo, has a comparable, sustaining effect on the innovation efforts. Setting the stage for a longer period of time to make the emergence of whole system innovation possible is experienced as a crucial mechanism for whole system innovation the complex way.

3.5.3   A note on innovating by modeling and simulating

Finally, I would like to make a remark on the following: so far, the academic world has often perceived computational and agent-based modeling as the only, or at least the most important way to explore order creation in complex systems. The academic modeling community is one of the fastest growing communities at this very moment. They study complex phenomena with a positivist, mechanistic and analytic perspective as to understand these phenomena and to try to distill insights that can help optimize problematic issues of human complex systems. Their work results in major breakthrough applications in many scientific fields at this very moment. Modeling, however, works not just with emergence but to an important degree with choices made by the designer–modeler. According to Lichtenstein (2014:8) this dominant view is also clear 'in the scholarly reviews of complexity in organization science, which treat the study of complex systems and emergence as a computational issue'.

The group of complexity scientists that work with complexity principles and metaphors so as to try to influence the future of systems is much smaller. According to complexity scholar Lichtenstein (2014), this group, which uses the complexity lens to influence emerging processes by design, judges the dissipative structures theory as a very good alternative to computational modeling. The Imagineering design approach that we will discuss in the next chapter is aligned with this thinking. Imagineers try to influence systems for the better by making use of the complexity lens.

3.6   Conclusion: two kinds of sciences leading to two kinds of innovation policy

This chapter answered the question: How can complex thinking make us more effective complex innovators? It articulated how the complex systems lens enables us to think of leaders in terms of hosts instead of heroes and how it enables us to see complex innovation as an unfolding journey of people acting differently leading to a more competent organization able to flourish under more complex circumstances. It enables us to see the innovation journey as a process of large numbers of actors acting and interacting anew driven by simple rules. To be effective, such a process should not be managed 'in traditional ways', but it should be approached as a continuing, never ending story of collective creation.

At the end of this chapter, we now have two complementary lenses based on two kind of sciences, a mechanistic lens based on an equilibrium science of forces (as begun by Newton) that is ideally suited to coping with complicated issues (or else: technologically complex issues) and an ecological, systems lens based on a complexity science of rules (Potts, 2017:22) that is ideally suited to coping with complex innovation eco-systems (also called social complex issues). These two lenses lead to different thinking and acting concerning innovation. Being able to use them both besides one another, complementary, will make us more effective innovators. In the case of the city centers, for example, we now can think of two complementary kinds of policy: policy in terms of infrastructure and in terms of taxes and the like, and policy in terms of reframing the meaning of the city center for all actors, which asks for Imagineering, designing a generative image that enables a new reality to be generated by tapping into the imagination of all actors involved in the system. Even while these are complementary innovation policies, it will already be evident that, to be most effective, the second kind of policy should be dominant on the former. How to design for processes of generative emergence, then, is the subject of the next chapter.

Coming to the end of this chapter on the big shift in lenses, we would still like to make one important remark: if the use of both lenses in a complementary way can indeed make us more effective innovators, one can question why the use of two lenses is not yet more popular. There are several reasons for this. Besides the pervasiveness of the mechanistic lens, using two lenses alongside one another is not evident. Most often, one knows only one lens and thinks to understand the whole of the world from that perspective. On top of this, the mechanistic lens has its short-term advantages, as it works in terms of predicting and controlling. When actions are not evaluated on their effectiveness, the mechanistic lens definitely has its advantages. Using the complex systems lens, on the contrary, asks for quite some maturity. It asks for choosing effectiveness in the long term over actionability in the short term. And it asks for taking more time to think longer before acting to then gain time in the long term.

In the next chapter we will show how two kind of sciences not only lead to two kind of innovation policies but also to two kinds of design: conventional design that is based on the equilibrium science of forces and the Systemic Design Approach of Imagineering that is based on a complexity science of rules.

References

Allen, P., Maguire, S., and McKelvey, B. (2011). *The Sage handbook of complexity and management*. Sage Publications.

Barzelay, M. (1992). *Breaking through bureaucracy: A new vision for managing in government*. University of California Press.

Boulton, J. G., Allen, P. M., and Bowman, C. (2015). *Embracing complexity: Strategic perspectives for an age of turbulence*. Oxford University Press (UK).

Capra, F., and Luisi, P. L. (2014). *The systems view of life: A unifying vision*. Cambridge University Press.

Cavaleri, S., and Obłój, K. (1993). *Management systems: A global perspective*. Wadsworth.

Chapman, J. (2002). *System failure: Why governments must learn to think differently*. Demos.

Díaz, C. J. D. (2007). Complexity and environmental education. In: Capra, F., Juarerro, A., Sotolongo, P., and van Uden, J. (eds.) *Reframing complexity: Perspectives from North and South*. ISCE Publishing, pp. 47–58.

Dougherty, D. (2017). Taking advantage of emergence for complex innovation eco-systems. *Journal of Open Innovation: Technology, Market, and Complexity*, 3(1), 14.

Garud, R., Gehman, J., Kumaraswamy, A., and Tuertscher, P. (2016). From the process of innovation to innovation as process. In: Langley, A., and Tsoukas, H. (eds.) *The Sage handbook of process organization studies*. Sage Publications, pp. 451–466.

Hamel, G. (2015, June 12). Innovation starts with the heart, not the head. *Harvard Business Review*. At: https://hbr.org/2015/06/you-innovate-with-your-heart-not-your-head (accessed June 16, 2015).

Heinzen, T. E. (1994). Situational affect: Proactive and reactive creativity. In: Shaw, M. P., and Runco, M. A. (eds.) *Creativity and affect*. Ablex Publishing Corp., pp. 127–146.

Holland, J. H. (1995). *Hidden order: how adaptation builds complexity*. Addison-Wesley.

Hutchins, G. (2016, January 26). Embracing systemic thinking for our firms of the future (Interview with F. Capri). *TriplePundit*. At: https://www.triplepundit.com/2016/01/embracing-systemic-thinking-firms-future/ (accessed October 12, 2018).

Kreitzer, M. J., Monsen, K. A., Nandram, S., and De Blok, J. (2015). Buurtzorg Nederland: A global model of social innovation, change, and whole-systems healing. *Global Advances in Health and Medicine*, 4(1), 40–44.

Kuhn, L. (2007). Why utilize complexity principles in social inquiry? *World Futures*, 63(3–4), 156–175.

Lane, D., Pumain, D., van der Leeuw, S. E., and West, G. (eds.). (2009). *Complexity perspectives in innovation and social change* (Vol. 7). Springer Science & Business Media.

Lichtenstein, B. B. (2014). *Generative emergence: A new discipline of organizational, entrepreneurial, and social innovation*. Oxford University Press (UK).

Lichtenstein, B. B. (2000). Emergence as a process of self-organizing – new assumptions and insights from the study of non-linear dynamic systems. *Journal of Organizational Change Management, 13*(6), 526–544.

Mathews, K. M., White, M. C., and Long, R. G. (1999). Why study the complexity sciences in the social sciences? *Human Relations, 52*(4), 439–462.

McKenzie, F. (2014). Complex adaptive systems. Implications for leaders, organisations, government and citizens. Policy Brief No. I, Australian Future Project, La Trobe University, Melbourne, May.

McMillan, E. (2008). *Complexity, management and the dynamics of change: Challenges for practice.* Routledge.

Mintzberg, H. (2005). Developing theory about the development of theory. In: Smith, K. G., and Hitt, M. A. (eds.) *Great minds in management: The process of theory development.* Oxford University Press (UK), pp. 355–372.

Mitleton-Kelly, E. (2003). *Complex systems and evolutionary perspectives on organisations: the application of complexity theory to organisations.* Elsevier Science.

Morin, E. (2008). *On complexity.* Hampton Press.

Nijs, D. E. L. W. (2014). *Imagineering the butterfly effect.* Eleven International Publishing.

Obolensky, N. (2008). Who needs leaders? At: https://www.youtube.com/watch?v=41QKeKQ2O3E (accessed October 9, 2018).

Plowman, D. A., Baker, L. T., Beck, T. E., Kulkarni, M., Solansky, S. T., and Travis, D. V. (2007). Radical change accidentally: The emergence and amplification of small change. *Academy of Management Journal, 50*(3), 515–543.

Potts, J. (2017). Complexity, economics, and innovation policy: How two kinds of science lead to two kinds of economics and two kinds of policy. *Complexity, Governance & Networks,* (1), 22–34.

Potts, J. (2007). Art and innovation: An evolutionary view of the creative industries. *UNESCO Observatory, 1*(1), 1–18.

Prigogine, I. (1955). *Introduction to thermodynamics of irreversible processes.* Thomas, Springfield.

Senge, P. M. (2006). *The fifth discipline. The art and practice of the learning organization.* Rev. ed. New York, London: Currency Doubleday.

Senge, P. M. (1991). The fifth discipline, the art and practice of the learning organization. *Performance Improvement, 30*(5), 37–37.

Stacey, R. (2003). *Complex responsive processes in organizations: Learning and knowledge creation.* Routledge.

Stevenson, H., and Harmeling, S. (1990). Entrepreneurial management's need for a more 'chaotic' theory. *Journal of Business Venturing, 5*(1), 1–14.

Tsoukas, H., and Dooley, K. J. (2011). Introduction to the special issue: Towards the ecological style: Embracing complexity in organizational research. *Organization Studies, 32,* 729–735.

West, B. J. (1985/2013). *An essay on the importance of being nonlinear* (Vol. 62). Springer Science & Business Media.

World Economic Forum (2014). Sustainable health systems, visions, strategies, critical uncertainties and scenarios. A report from the World Economic Forum prepared in collaboration with McKinsey & Company. At: http://www3.weforum.org/docs/WEF_SustainableHealthSystems_Report_2013.pdf (accessed November 13, 2014).

4

LOGIC: a big shift in design – Imagineering, beyond conventional Design Thinking

Diane Nijs

4.1   Introduction: the 'Age of Design'

According to Conklin (1996:10) we are now in the 'Age of Design': 'The job of humanity is now shifting from understanding our world [which was central in the previous 'Age of Science'] to being conscious about creating it – that is, designing it.' While in the previous epoch we could manage well with the logic of predicting and controlling, individuals working separately, using linear processes, to come up with the right answers, in the networked world we have to turn to the logic of design: using language not just to describe but also to create, realizing that coping with complex issues is first and foremost a social process of emergence. Instead of searching for the one 'right' answer, in many societal issues today the challenge is to gain ownership and shared understanding of the collectively desired direction so as to enable collective creativity. Instead of thinking solutions, we have to learn to think and act in terms of evolution.

Shifting from the 'Age of Science' to the 'Age of Design', the design profession went through a whole evolution. While design as craft was known since the dawn of humanity, as a profession industrial design emerged during the Industrial Revolution. With the coming of the internet, the industrial design competency got extended in the experience direction: First with User Experience (UX) design for designing digital products, later with service design and customer experience design as customers asked no longer for just good products but particularly for great services. In the experience economy however, augmenting value creation is no longer about designers staging experiences to sell goods but about CEOs designing a strategic experience vision as the starting point for all value creation. Strategic experience design guides the branding efforts, the customer experience and the employee experience (Sontag and Puchert in Szostek, 2018). Herewith the focus in the design profession is shifting towards delivering means rather than ends.

Leading design scholar and practitioner Sanders (2006:28) articulates the shift in the design profession as follows: 'designers will learn to use their own creativity to amplify the creativity of everyday people'. So far design has not served people. Design has served markets. Design has served the needs of companies and not the needs of people. This has led to overconsumption but not to more happiness and sustainability. 'Everyday people want to be creators as well.' Just look at the emergence of personal websites and blogs to have a first impression of the unmet needs for creativity. All people have aspirations and most of them want to put their creativity to use 'in caring for and about others' (Ivan Illich in Sanders, 2006:30). This then is the crucial challenge that designers face today: How to enable the (collective) creativity of all actors in the system so as to generate new (collectively more desired) order in a system? The big shift in society and the big shift in science then leads to a big shift in design too.

Building on the former chapters about the big shift in the value creating landscape and the big shift in science, in this chapter we articulate our vision on the big shift in design. To do so, we first introduce you to the two modes of thought as articulated by cognitive psychologist Bruner (1986): the logico-scientific mode of thought and the narrative mode of thought. Then we introduce you to 'High Concept Thinking', a very popular way of designing (in the narrative mode) in the creative industries. We then turn to conventional Design Thinking and Systems Thinking (in the ratio-scientific mode) to show you how the narrative mode of designing naturally fits complex design thinking and doing. This then forms the bridge to presenting you Imagineering and the Systemic Design Approach of Imagineering (Nijs, 2014). We finish the chapter with a reflection on skills in the Age of Design to position Imagineering in the management toolbox of tomorrow.

4.2   Two modes of thought

According to cognitive psychologist Bruner (1986:11), human beings have 'two modes of cognitive functioning, two modes of thought, each providing distinctive ways of ordering experience, of constructing reality': the paradigmatic or the ratio-scientific mode of functioning and the narrative mode of functioning. 'The two (though complementary) are irreducible to one another. Efforts to reduce one mode to the other or to ignore one at the expense of the other inevitably fail to capture the rich diversity of thought.' For a very long time in history the logical, causal mode of thought has been dominant. The 'serious' industrial and the traditional academic world 'neglected' or 'limited' the narrative, non-linear mode of thought.

The more complex the world becomes, the more we realize that we do not achieve our mastery of social reality by acting only as 'scientists', 'logicians' or 'mathematicians' (Pink, 2005). Narratives have several characteristics which make them remarkably well suited for coping with complexity (Greenhalgh et al., 2005). 'Through dialogue and storytelling, strategic leaders shape the evolution of agent interactions and construct shared meanings that provide the rationale by which the past, the present, and the future of the organization coalesce'

(Boal and Schultz, 2007:411). Innovation narratives are 'cultural mechanisms' that address coordination requirements, by enabling and sustaining translation and interpretation, processes that are key to all generative emergence (Bartel and Garud, 2009:107).

The match between complexity and the narrative mode has been articulated by organizational scientists such as MacLean (2017) and Tsoukas and Hatch (2001). The latter argue that 'complexity is not only a feature of the systems that we study, [but that] it is also a matter of the way in which we organize our thinking about those systems'. They claim that complexity theory itself indicates and supports the use of the narrative mode. In his later work Tsoukas (2017) furthers that we shouldn't simplify our thinking in organization and management studies but that, on the contrary, we should complexify our thinking. He argues that 'a complex system of picturing' consisting of an open-world ontology, a performative epistemology, and a poetic praxeology', provides a more effective alternative to study organizational complexity than the hitherto dominant style of conventional thinking.

4.3   Two modes of designing

These two modes of thinking make possible two modes of designing: designing in the rational–scientific mode and designing in the narrative mode. While conventional Design Thinking happens in the former mode, we argue that this mode is limiting our ability to cope with social complexity. To become more effective we present the Systemic Design Approach of Imagineering, which is developed on the base of 'High Concept Thinking' and designing in the narrative mode, a way of designing that is core to all design work in the creative industries. First, I will introduce this thinking, then explain conventional Design Thinking, and finally explore the Systemic Design Approach of Imagineering.

4.3.1   High Concept Thinking in the creative industries

The creative industries design in the narrative mode – the mode of poetry and daily language as opposed to the linear, rational mode of talking and thinking that we use in business and science (Bruner, 1986) – which has several properties that set High Concept Thinking apart from conventional thinking. In the arts, the narrative mode is used as an end in itself, to stimulate collective creativity. The narrative mode is core to the creative business, as it has heuristic and holistic properties which are ideally suited to make people 'wonder'. Holistic properties means that this language enables the imagination to approach issues with a whole systems perspective. It is a process that emphasizes the importance of the whole and the interdependence of its parts. Heuristic (from the Greek 'heuriskein' meaning 'to discover') properties means that the narrative mode of reasoning 'pertains to the process of gaining knowledge or some desired result by intelligent guesswork rather than by following some pre-established formula' (Rouse, 2009).

High Concept

'High Concept' (HC) is 'a short, easy to communicate narrative which links the aesthetic and the commercial potential' (Wyatt, 1994:8) to bring forth a (fascinating) new perspective in society. Imagine the title of a song, a movie or a theatre play: that short narrative, sometimes only a few words sometimes a bit more, enables lots of people (players, producers of all kind and marketers) to start creating together. An HC is designed to set the stage for unlocking collective creativity in the whole of the system, as much externally as internally, and, as such, it can be said that an HC – different from conventional marketing concepts – is 'two-sided': It steers as well the creation as the marketing.

In some cases, the HC can result in years of work for many people. But the design of the HC itself can also take years and not all designed concepts will make it to a movie. To give a concrete example, the film *Ratatouille*: 'A rat that wants to be a chef in Paris.' At the Disney Company the Imagineering department is the core of the business and core to that department is the development of HCs. One of the major challenges for that department is stopping the development of concepts (and all the creative engagement that goes with this) that won't make it. The HC here is not just 'Ratatouille' but that one extra phrase: 'A rat that wants to be a chef in Paris.' These words make it possible for everyone to have an image in mind; they make it possible for everyone to start dreaming of what might happen with the rat. Concepts that can be creative but miss the associative power to emerge in good business should be recognized early, as they don't appeal to the imagination. But what is imagination and what are richly associating, imaginative narratives and what is collective creativity?

Imagination

Imagination is the generative ability, the ability that has the power or function of generating, originating, producing, or reproducing, to see things other than as they are. It is the unique capability of forging new ideas while staying within the confines of what is useful. Imagination is

'the capacity to transcend the actual and to construct the possible [. . .] and the impossible. It is a habit of mind that is marked by the joint conditions of the actual and the possible, the usual and the novel, the cognitive and the emotional, the logical and the extra-logical. It is a source of creativity and invention. And it is a quality that is highly desired, if not for ourselves, for our children' (Liljedahl, 2009:446).

What makes the imagination extremely powerful is the fact that the imagination is not just a cognitive phenomenon but that it is also strongly linked to the emotions. Liljedahl (2009:448) writes:

In fact, within the imagination, cognition and emotion are inseparable and complementary domains. When we imagine we reach out, not only with our thoughts but also with our emotions. We feel our way forward into new realities, and once there, we navigate the possibilities with our feelings. It is these emotions that engage us, that inspire us to imagine and to keep imagining. It is the emotional engagement that sustains the cognitive engagement. Without these the imagination would be not much more than novel musings.

To explain the concept of imagination *Merriam-Webster's Dictionary of Synonyms* (1984:415) compares it with the concept of fancy. 'Imagination can be understood as an ability to conceive of something, seen only fragmentarily or superficially, as a complete, perfected, and integral whole.' Fancy, on the contrary, refers to 'the power of inventing the novel and unreal by recombining the elements found in reality'. As Weick (2006:448) puts it: 'Imagination is a shaping or modifying power. Fancy is an aggregative and associative power.'

To illustrate the concept of fancy: Pegasus is a fancy construct as it is only a combination of two real, existing elements: a horse and wings and doesn't evoke (or even allow) another meaning or association in any direction (Weick, 2006). The construct misses the flexibility and the heuristic power of imaginative constructs. Many creative constructs are fancy constructs and not imaginative constructs. They don't open the imagination of other stakeholders to come up with their own interpretation (their own deductive reasoning) to, eventually, realize synergetic efforts with the broader organization. Fancy concepts have limited associative, shaping and modifying power. They have a limited 'flexibility'. It is not possible to give an interpretation which is different in every context and, as a consequence, the construct is limited 'actionable' in terms of innovation.

Collective creativity

For a very long time, creativity has been studied predominantly by psychologists as a variable of the 'creative personality' that can even be measured (Csikszentmihalyi, 1999). Creativity then has been defined as 'the generation or production of ideas that are both novel and useful' (George, 2007:441). Thus, outlandish, wild ideas are not considered creative when they are not useful novelties. Effective problem solving, in its turn, is not considered creative when the solutions are not new. Recently, however, interest is growing in what Hargadon and Bechky (2006) have come to call 'collective creativity', the creativity that emerges from interactive ideas of diverse people rather than from the mind of any given individual (Marion, 2012). In collective creativity, no single insight by itself is responsible for solving the problem, but the problem gets solved in unique and emergent ways.

The concept of collective creativity converges with the ideas of the systems approach ('two-sided': internal and external) to creativity. The *Dictionary of Creativity* (Gorny, 2007) defines the systems approach to creativity as 'a process at the intersection of individual, social and cultural factors' (Amabile, 1983, 1996; Csikszentmihalyi, 1988, 1996, 1999; Simonton, 1988; Woodman and Schoenfeld, 1989). Seeing creativity as a systemic or collective process brings into play an artifact (or infrastructure) that enables and inspires such processes (Nijs, 2014:181). According to Hargadon and Bechky (2006), there is still little understanding of collective creativity and the mechanisms that might trigger it, but it is obvious that the internet is a significant mediating infrastructure. Let us get back to the conventional design field to explore how the narrative mode can enrich this logic.

4.3.2 Conventional Design Thinking and Systems Thinking

According to Nobel Laureate and engineer Herbert Simon (1969), to design is to devise courses of action aimed at changing existing situations into preferred ones. DT then has been defined by Lockwood (2009:xi) as 'essentially a human-centered innovation process that emphasizes observation, collaboration, fast learning, visualization of ideas, rapid concept prototyping, and concurrent business analysis, which ultimately influences innovation and business strategy'. DT now generally refers to applying a designer's sensibility and methods to problem solving (Pourdehnad et al., 2011), no matter whether the problem is complicated or complex.

Recently, DT got quite some interest in management to complement the decision thinking attitude, as conventional practice is ever more failing. Management simply was and is in crisis and DT was and is perceived as a complementary view in the pursuit of more managerial effectiveness (Boland and Collopy, 2004; Dunne and Martin, 2006; Kimbell, 2012; Johansson-Sköldberg et al., 2013; Kolko, 2015). According to Liedtka (2018:74) design thinking is a social technology that 'has the potential to do for innovation exactly what Total Quality Management did for manufacturing: unleash people's full creative energies, win their commitment, and radically improve processes'. By offering clear process steps (inspiration, ideation and implementation) that enable engagement, dialogue and learning, design thinking gets around the counterproductive human tendencies that time and again block innovation.

Just like DT, ST is not new at all. It has been around for decades as 'Systemic Thinking', which is a simple technique for gaining a systems-wide focus (Bartlett, 2001). It is a way of mentally framing what we see in the world, looking at the whole first before looking at the parts or constituent elements. For a systems thinker, relationships and the structures that enable them are more important than the individual events that might be observed. Systems thinkers focus more on movements, processes, patterns, relationships and dynamics than on static entities and individual events. ST can be as effective for coping with complicated issues as complex issues, but in both situations we should base our thinking on the appropriate scientific framework.

To illustrate conventional ST, which is based on the Newtonian scientific framework: when designing a sports car, for example, the engineer considers the whole system and makes decisions on parts based on their role in the total picture. For example: the weight of the breaks will be related to the weight of the whole car to make the car as light as is most effective for the races. Here, linear thinking in terms of calculating cause-and-effect relationships, is the best thinking one can use.

4.3.3   Complex Systems Thinking and complex Design Thinking

Something new occurs when executing DT with complex ST in mind, ST executed with the scientific framework of living systems in mind. Complex ST brings to attention two key concepts: emergence and leverage points. Emergent properties arise only in living systems as totality. A duck, for example, is no longer a living duck when the heart or another crucial part is taken out. Emergent properties are not present in the disparate components, making it necessary to look at the whole picture to understand a living system. Besides that, the focus of the designer–intervener is on 'finding potential leverage points': rather than trying to design a wholly new, perfect solution, the focus is on finding an area where a small change can lead to significant revitalization of the system – a small intervention having potentially a big effect. Complex ST is a way of exploring real life rather than trying to represent it (Morgan, 2005).

The problem with using conventional (complicated or technical) DT in coping with social complex issues is that conventional DT (often) 'destroys the most critical aspects of human systems, e.g. the interconnections amongst and between the parts. [. . .] It encourages fragmentation and isolation and has an undue concern with individual events. We are becoming 'micro-smart' and 'macro-dumb'. We are losing the capability to make sense of how and why things work' (Morgan, 2005:6). Yet most innovation policy is still dominated by quantitative data collection and analytical methods based on a reductionist, cause–effect way of thinking and designing, by exerting control over people and processes.

The emergence of new design spaces and approaches does not mean that the traditional design spaces and approaches will disappear, but it means that all these design spaces will coexist over time. This extension implies a significant shift in the way we design and educate designers as well as in who we educate as 'new' designers (Friedman, 2016). Complex design thinkers generally aim to do something today to enable the system to improve itself tomorrow the self-organizing way.

This consideration brought organizational complexity scientist Hazy (2011:528) to the suggestion that the word 'design' itself can have a blinding effect as it implies a 'false certainty'. A design might be completed, but a complex system and a process of emergence is never finished. Using a new, complementary word such as Imagineering might have an eye-opening effect for 'saying and seeing' this new phenomenon of 'designing for emergence'. We hope that using another word might have an Imagineering effect in the design world itself: generating a new, more desired design-reality under growing complexity (Table 4.1).

4.4   The Systemic Design Approach of Imagineering

Aligned with the philosophical thinking of organizational complexity scholars such as Tsoukas (2017), Tsoukas and Hatch (2001) and MacLean (2017), the 'big shift' in society brought us to experiment in practice with HC thinking in coping with complex innovation eco-systems, leading to what we present here as the Systemic Design Approach of Imagineering (Nijs, 2014), designing for generative emergence.

Table 4.1 Relating conventional Design Thinking and the Systemic Design Approach of Imagineering

The three phases of any design process	DESIGN THINKING Solution thinking and doing	IMAGINEERING Evolution thinking and doing	
Inspiration	Empathize	Think like a System	A-ppreciating
	Define		B-reathing
Ideation	Ideate	Act like an	C-reating a CTE
	Prototype	Entrepreneur	D-eveloping
Implementation	Test	(Conway et al., 2017)	E-nabling
			F-lourishing

Just as DT and ST, HC thinking, thinking in the narrative mode and using 'two-sided' concepts, outside the creative industries is not new at all. Just think about the pitch for the Apple I-phone: '1,000 songs in your pocket.' This was designed to (re-)frame the existing mental models of the developers and creators, as well as the consumer market. But this is not yet an example of what is called 'generative emergence'. A design intervention has generated generative emergence when it enables the system to flourish more effectively under more complex circumstances. The evolution of the enterprise logic from a closed, profit and shareholder oriented logic to an open, co-creative, purpose- and stakeholder-oriented logic, according to us, can be a process of 'generative emergence' when it succeeds in making the system more flourishing in the face of growing complexity.

Let's first present the different contexts in which Imagineering has presented itself so far before then turning to defining the concept and presenting the design approach.

4.4.1 Imagineering

The word 'Imagineering' is a *portmanteau* word, a linguistic blend or fusion of two words, with the first part –'imagination' being fused with the last part –'engineering.' The resultant blend partakes of both original meanings to enable the 'saying' of a 'new' phenomenon: designing to generate a new reality by tapping into the imagination of the many involved actors. Or to put it in complexity language: designing a CTE (analogous to an HC in the creative industries) to generate new order in the system, so as to make it possible for the system to function effectively under growing complexity. As such, Imagineering is a design approach to cope with complex issues such as whole system, social, entrepreneurial or public innovation.

The origin of the word 'Imagineering' dates from 1942 at the engineering company ALCOA – Aluminum Corporation America. While producing war-materials was no longer seen as a sufficiently sustainable business proposition for the future, the company needed strategic innovation (reinventing the corporate future) besides 'just' product innovation. New markets and new directions should come into perspective instead of doing more, and better, of the same. For that reason the company introduced an integral approach, an approach in which all people of the organization and even the broader system was invited to participate creatively, not just the engineers but also other employees and even potential customers. To make this project an integral and sustained effort, the company was introducing an 'Imagineering' project that was also communicated externally (ALCOA's advertisement in *Time*, 16 February 1942, p. 59). Imagineering, as a new word, was used as a CTE to reframe the existing mental models concerning the identity of the engineering-system called 'Alcoa': a reframing of the identity from an engineering company to an Imagineering company.

One of the first new customers of ALCOA was Disney Studios, which was thinking about translating its movie figures into an attractive, live context for families in their leisure time. Used to working with HCs, Disney 'recognized' the word Imagineering as an interesting word for what 'they were doing all the time': engineering with imagination to appeal to the imagination. Disney made Imagineering the name of their core department: the Imagineering department, the department where they create the magic: from designing HCs to the translation of these HCs into fascinating productions with lots of creative employees working collectively together to make new fascinating worlds emerge. It was because of this 'HC way of working' with its 'collective creation' that the department became known as the Imagineering department.

In the meantime the word appears in academic fields as diverse as collaborative democracy, urban development and evolutionary economy. In the field of collaborative democracy Tom Atlee (2014:214–215), Founder and Director of the Co-Intelligence Institute (a non-profit organization facilitating and researching self-organization, collective intelligence, participatory modes of governance and collaborative democracy), defines Imagineering as the process that 'embraces any use of imaginative narrative to realize, create, or catalyze in real life the potentials we are imagining'.

In the field of urban development Ratcliffe (Ratcliffe and Krawczyk, 2011) defines Imagineering as a way to build future scenarios to inspire collectives in their planning efforts. In that same field Suitner (2015:13) recently published his doctoral research, *Imagineering Cultural Vienna*, in which he defines Imagineering as 'the discursive construction of an imaginary, i.e. a simplistic logic of planning, which might be powerful enough to influence the development paths of a city'. In this work, Suitner acknowledges the deep links between practice and discourse, between materiality and meaning in urban space and its development. Imagineering is seen in this field as generating and using (simple) 'cultural' images that shape the dialogue so as to make it possible to handle the complexity of urban development with lots of stakeholders.

In the field of evolutionary economy Wentzel (2006) defines Imagineering as being on the crossroads between cognition (mental shifts) and economics. Imagineering is about creating new connections in the economic system. This view relates to the perspective of Potts (2011, 2017), the evolutionary economist and complexity scientist we discussed in Chapter 1. Potts argues that 'the arts, the cultural and creative industries drive, facilitate and engender the origination, adoption and retention of new ideas (the innovation process) into the socio-cultural and economic system' (Potts, 2011:2). In this book we argue that the CTE fulfills that same, infrastructural role at the micro-level of a system. In evolutionary economics Imagineering is seen as creating mental shifts/new meanings that, by causing new connections and by acting as an infrastructure that keeps these processes going, can generate economic development and economic evolution.

Now that we know where the word comes from, how it was evidently adopted in the creative industries while linked with 'High Concept' Thinking, and now that we know how the concept is also used in several academic disciplines, we can define the concept more properly.

An academic definition

Imagineering is designing for emergence. It is a complexity-inspired design approach to cope with complex issues by unleashing collective creativity and collective action in a strategic desired direction.

- **Emergence** is the coming into being of a new, dynamic state.
- **Complexity-inspired**: Imagineering is based on the scientific framework of the living systems in which the primary focus is on 'generating (new) order in CAS (complex adaptive systems)'. (See Chapter 3 for an initial introduction to CAS.)
- **Design approach**: Design is defined as 'changing existing situations into preferred ones' (Simon, 1969:111). Design is also seen as 'a process by which an artifact is brought into existence' (Khella, 2009). Imagineering is an approach in which a CTE (or: strategic generative image) is designed in order to innovate an existing situation for the better. In the creative industries such a strategic generative image is called a 'High Concept,' and in complexity science such an image is called 'a Creative Tension Engine'.
- **Complex issues**: Complex issues are issues in which everything is related to everything else, which makes it impossible to discover clear cause-and-effect relationships. As a consequence, complex issues cannot be 'solved'. The best one can do is to try to influence the evolution of the system in a more desirable direction.

To finish with a practical definition:

Imagineering is a design approach that shifts the collective focus from reactive problem solving to pro-active future co-creation. By designing a creative tension engine the collective creativity is liberated to enable the co-evolution of an organization and its environment towards a more human, participative and productive future.

4.4.2   The design approach of Imagineering

The design approach of Imagineering consists of mainly two stages:

1. Designing the CTE (comparable to the HC) to shift the collective focus from reactive problem-solving to pro-active future co-creation and set the stage for generative conversations and processes of collective creativity in a desired strategic direction.
2. Managing the emerging processes the generative way.

Let us explain two essential elements more in that first step, mental model and CTE, before articulating the design approach itself in detail.

Mental model

To innovate more effectively under complexity, Senge (1990; Senge et al. 2015) argues that organizations need to discover how to tap into people's commitment and capacity to learn and create together at all levels of the organization. According to Senge, this is a matter of a fundamental shift of mind among all the members of the system. Designing for generative emergence is a matter of framing or reframing mental models in such a way that both internal and external actors start to act upon it creatively. What then is a mental model that a CTE should try to alter? And how do we design such a CTE?

According to Peter Senge (1990:8) mental models are the 'deeply ingrained assumptions, generalizations, or even pictures and images that influence how we understand the world and how we take action'. They are formed by our experiences, beliefs, and values and they determine the way we perceive life.

Remember the concepts of the Goods Dominant Logic (GDL), Service Dominant Logic (SDL) and Experience Dominant Logic (EDL), that we discussed in Chapter 2. These constructs are articulations of different mental models that people use when acting in the market. People with a GDL mental model think and act in terms of 'exchange', in terms of producers and consumers and in terms of material goods dominating business. People with an SDL logic think and act in terms of 'co-creation', in terms of suppliers seeing consumers as co-creators of value and in terms of service being dominant over eventual goods that can be sold under that service umbrella. People with an EDL mental model think and act in terms of creating meaningful things for society at large in which all people, internal as well as external, can and in which many are willing to join forces; think, for example, of Wikipedia.

As becomes evident from the previous example: mental models can facilitate or hinder the effectiveness of operating of an individual. Managers acting with a mental model based on the GDL have tough times in the networked world, while managers with an SDL or an EDL interpret that same business reality more often as full of opportunities. The problem with mental models is not that they are not 'right'. All mental models are by definition simplifications. But the core problem, according to Senge (1990), is that mental models are often not articulated. They are the silent, unconscious, hidden models with which people either flourish when their models fit their context, or struggle with when their models no longer fit their context. The design approach of Imagineering tries to reframe an existing, problematic (because outdated) mental model into a more updated, relevant mental model, using an appealing, narrative format to enable pro-active collective creativity. Integrating the designed CTE into the identity of the system (for example, in the logo and in the human resource management (HRM) instruments) is meant to enable and sustain the much-needed systemic shift in the existing mental model.

Creative Tension Engine

A CTE is a verbal construct that shifts a GDL mental model of 'exchange' into a more EDL mental model of 'collective creation' – in an aspirational direction, a direction that makes the system more flourishing. The shift from profit to purpose in society definitely creates this context for Imagineering, in favor of designing collective creativity in the purposeful direction. Senge (1990, 2014; Senge et al., 2015) defines creative tension as the gap between the current reality and the aspirational future, a gap that creates energy and that exists as much in situations of 1G expert innovation as in 5G experience innovation. In 1G situations, engineers or economists can make a plan to bridge the gap. In situations of 5G innovation – such as the gap between a profit orientation and a purpose orientation – a well-designed CTE can act as an 'engine' that catalyzes 'emergent, experience innovation'. Nijs (2014) calls this design discipline Imagineering: designing and using a CTE to catalyze innovation as collective creation.

A CTE articulated as an HC in the narrative mode can infuse realities with the heuristic and holistic properties of the narrative language to create flexibility for interpretation, invention and innovation of existing systems. In Chapter 1 we illustrated how the 'first national park in Belgium' and 'Arnhem Fashion Quarter' act as a CTE, making it possible to use nature conservation in the former and fashion design in the latter as a catalyzer to effectuate a more flourishing eco-system in regions that were earlier deteriorated. We also pointed to the fact that designing a CTE is definitely simple in hindsight (effective CTEs are very simple by nature), but tough in foresight, as it asks for complexity thinking! We suggested that this might be what is meant by the statement: Simplicity at the other side of complexity: it is the simple idea (not a simplistic idea!) that makes people act and interact engaged, collectively and creatively in a new, more desired direction. The CTE is the simple articulated idea that can ignite a systemic process that physicist Doyne Farmer observed, 'It is not magic [. . .] but it feels like magic' (in Waldrop and Gleick, 1992:279). Nijs (2014) articulated many more illustrations of CTEs that reframe existing mental models (on the identity of the city of Antwerp and the Belgian retail chain Veritas).

At first glance, CTEs (or: strategic generative images) have nothing in common. But a deep unity lies beneath the variety. Effective strategic generative images share five common traits:

- **Ambiguous**: they are ambiguous, and need to be interpreted time and again before acting.
- **Relevant**: they are tailored to a specific systems aspiration, influencing action in a strategic direction.
- **Strategic**: they are created on the generative power of an organization (strategic direction).
- **Actionable**: they provide clear and flexible guidance for innovative action.
- **Systemic**: they are integrated in the identity of the system so as to influence all actors' behavior, internal actors as well as external actors.

Some further explanation of these five common traits:

- To evoke 'ambiguity' we will shift from rational, business language to daily language or poetic language so as to create metaphorical language that doesn't tell you what to do exactly but that deliberately evokes first interpretation in context.
- On 'relevance', people internally and definitely externally will only be inspired to action when what is asked for makes more sense than what they are routinely used to do.
- 'Strategic' is a trait that is directly linked with the complexity of a system. To 'liberate' a complex system to function more effectively it is only possible to unlock the complexity with one simple rule/guiding principle, otherwise the system becomes even more complex. Therefore, the simple rule should be built on the generative, relevant power of the system for society at large.
- 'Actionable' – the simple strategic guiding principle or rule should be articulated in a way that people can evidently join forces by acting/relating differently.
- 'Systemic', then, is a very simple trait whose importance is often underestimated. It means that the strategic generative image has to be integrated in the identity of the system *and* explicitly articulated in the broader system. If not, external stakeholders definitely won't understand the intentions of the internal stakeholders, which prevents the necessary 'co-evolution' of the system.

Relating Design Thinking and Imagineering

In this section we won't sketch the whole evolution of the thinking on design approaches that grew aligned with the evolution of innovation models from 1G to 5G. Nevertheless, we will start with a very short introduction to the basics of a design process and an articulation of where the thinking on design processes is right now so as to be able to show where and how Imagineering adds to this thinking and where and how it makes a difference. For this quick scan we will limit ourselves to the published work of two leading thinkers: Brown (CEO of IDEO) and Martin (Former Dean of the Rotman School of Management), as they are recognized as operating on the edge of both science and practice.

All design approaches ultimately pass through three spaces, which Brown (2008:4) articulates as:

- **Inspiration**: the process of understanding the problem by empathizing so as to frame or reframe the original problem the commissioner started with, to enable the next phase.
- **Ideation**: the process of generating, developing, and testing ideas that may lead to solutions. Core to this space is rapid prototyping to get often and early feedback until the user is delighted.
- **Implementation**: the charting of a path to the market and keeping an eye on feedback mechanisms so as to be able to intervene when things tend to go in undesired directions.

As with growing connectivity and growing openness design, just like innovation, evolved beyond the world of products towards services, processes, strategies and systems. With this evolution, 'its tools have been adapted and extended into a distinct new discipline: design thinking' (Brown and Martin, 2015:58). With the growing complexity of what has to be designed or redesigned, the design process becomes also more complex: instead of focusing primarily on the design of an artifact, a carefully designed 'intervention' becomes even more critical to success than the design of the artifacts themselves.

The more immaterial the innovation at stake and the more actors involved in the eco-system that needs improvement, the more the interactions, the dialogues, the empowerment and the adoption of innovative new ideas and experiences have to be designed for. Brown and Martin (2015) illustrate this scenario with nothing less than the case of 'Designing a New Peru'. They illustrate how a banker's ambition to help transform Peru's economy by building up its middle class depended on the thoughtful design of many artifacts: a leading-edge bank, an innovative school system and businesses adapted for frontier towns across Peru; and at the same time it depended on designing interventions to empower people so as to be able to introduce these new artifacts into the status quo.

Traditionally, design approaches are founded on the materiality of artifacts instead of being organized around human experiences such as learning and creating, healing or living (Sanders, 2006). Imagineering, on the contrary, is a design approach organized around human experiences. The one central artifact that is designed in this process is a dialogical artifact meant to catalyze the intervention.

Imagineering infuses the practice and theory of design approaches with organizational know-how stemming from complex living systems. This leads to a fundamentally different implementation of the conventional design phases and spaces as illustrated in Table 4.2.

The design approach of Imagineering covers two broad aspects that fit seamlessly together:

- Designing the CTE (A–B–C activities) to unlock collective creativity in a strategic way; and
- Managing the (eventual) emerging processes accordingly (D–E–F).

These two aspects are approached as a cycle of activities that contains three design phases or spaces 'rather than a predefined series of orderly steps. The spaces demarcate different sorts of related activities that together form the continuum of innovation' (Brown, 2008:4). The designer, or even better the design team, should realize that starting the design approach is at the same time starting the innovation process.

The three key spaces and the six key activities of the Imagineering design approach, summarized in Table 4.2, are articulated in an 'A–B–C–D–E–F format'.

Step/Space 1: Inspiration   Discover the generative core of the entrepreneurial activity most relevant to society at large by taking a bigger picture approach.

> **Appreciative analysis**: to take care of the sensitivity of initial conditions and to prevent the emergence of resistance against innovation and change (as is often the case), the Imagineering design team will take an appreciative stance from the very beginning of the process of intervening. The team will engage key actors in the system in a broad set of deep dialogues about the most meaningful things in the organization and the most inspiring actions happening in the industry. This is a matter of zooming in.
>
> **Breathing on the system**: reflecting on the 'bigger picture' of what is at stake is a matter of zooming out and discovering crucial relationships and crucial patterns of interaction. This activity can be explored by designing stakeholder maps and a business model canvas. Both instruments can help in reflecting on the difference it makes doing both with a profit orientation and a purpose orientation.

Step/Space 2: Ideation   Design the desired behavioral change in a CTE/HC and translate it in an experiential world.

> **Creating the vision and HC/CTE** that will make the system wonder. This is the activity that should reframe the existing mental model in an inspiring way towards a new mental model of operating. As an example, consider the effect on co-creation as to whether we know 'Mark's company' as 'The Zuckerberg Corporation' or as 'Facebook'.
>
> **Designing the experiential world**: the HC then is translated into very concrete experiences and values to give the value creating system a first materialization and according stabilization in all its openness. This very concrete 'translation' work can be experimented with using 'designerly' tools such as personas or customer journey mapping. A 'Declaration of Corporate Values' should be part of the ideation phase as it is an essential instrument that enables decentralized decision making.

Step/Space 3: Implementation   Enable the co-creation of value and managing the dynamics of dissipative structures.

> **Enabling**: co-creation by building the Enabling platform (physical and digital): designing touch-points that enable the co-creation of stakeholders;

Table 4.2 The Systemic Design Approach of Imagineering

Design space	Core activity	Core question	Core objective	Organizational resource and/or core instrument	Complexity principle
Inspiration	A-ppre-ciating	What kind of (inter)action are we proud of?	I try to understand a (problematic) situation in an appreciative way.	Appreciative interviewing (Based on Appreciative Inquiry)	Sensitivity of initial conditions
	B-reathing	What good (inter)actions could make the system more flourishing?	I try to put my understanding in a bigger perspective for society and I explore.	(Complex) ST and systems mapping	CAS or complex co-evolving systems
Ideation	C-reating	What core (inter)actions can shift outcomes?	I create a working principle for the experience and I give it an inspiring name: CTE.	Designing a CTE as a dialogical instrument using 'poetic' language (Relational)	Fluctuation
	D-evelo-ping	What elements can support these new, creative (inter)actions?	I translate the working principle in very concrete experience(s) and design for them.	Experience design and articulating values	Stabilization
Implementation	E-nabling	How can we enable actors to join forces in the desired direction?	I connect the experience platform with involved stakeholders in an engaging way.	Creating physical or virtual platforms for rich interactions	Taking care for recombination and positive feedback
	F-louri-shing	How can we keep the movement going and, eventually, growing?	I nurture the system for sustainable flourishing.	Coming up with sequentially new chapters sustaining fluctuation	Managing dynamics of dissipative structures

the organization of co-creation with internal (across departments) and external stakeholders.

Feeding flourishing futures: Contrary to material worlds, experiential worlds lose their magic when not managed dynamically. Therefore, leaders reflect on how to keep the magic and the engagement going. When the motion fades away, leaders should come with new 'chapters', new interpretations of the CTE that cause new fluctuations. This again would lead all actors in the system to re-combine things in new ways as to generate ever more the collectively desired reality. This activity is about managing the dynamics of dissipative structures (*fluctuation, re-combination, stabilization* and *positive feedback*) (see Chapter 3, Section 3.3.2).

Each application of the Imagineering design approach is different and each is designed to meet the unique challenges of the organization or system involved. The purpose of the application decides on the implementation of all the activities. The design approach can be applied on a central corporate level but it can also be started at a lower tactical level in the organization. From there it mostly will spread to the whole of the system, as most people like to be creative when there is an evident opportunity.

4.4.3   An illustration: how poetic language can innovate bureaucracies (Nijs, 2018)

In the previous chapter we introduced you to the challenges in healthcare in Western countries and we discussed the CTE of Buurtzorg as a new startup in the Netherlands and the case of 'Bring your heart to work' as a CTE that helped Lakeland Health in Michigan to evolve from laggard to leader in just 90 days. In this section we report on one of our own design research experiments to illustrate how poetic language can innovate bureaucracies making them creative. The organization at hand is a healthcare organization (Surplus) in the south of the Netherlands, an organization that has already existed for more than one hundred years and works with 3,000 employees and 3,000 volunteers. This organization is one of the four core organizations in an experiment with the Ministry of Health Care to learn how healthcare can evolve from rules to relations, an evolution that entails a whole system innovation.

Going through the A–B–C activities of the Imagineering design cycle, the core design team of the organization, a team in which also the Board of Directors participated, came to design the CTE of 'See Me' as the simple rule to reconsider actions in the system by all actors. It is an invitation to all kinds of actors to look anew at one another in their daily activities: managers to nurses, nurses to patients, managers to patients, patients to nurses, patients to managers, nurses to managers, family to actors in the healthcare organization and healthcare actors to the family members of the patients and also the administrators of the ministry to the health organization and administrators of the health organization to those of the ministry.

This CTE sets the stage (creates the 'infrastructural' context) for relevant new connections to cope more 'relation-wise' with an organization that was suffering from too many rules. This CTE was then illustrated with some core experiences such as the conventional 'intake talk' for an elderly person in a home for the elderly. That important moment was redesigned from an 'intake talk' into a 'welcome talk' to make that very first moment of going to a home for the elderly much more human (remember the importance of the sensitivity of initial conditions in living systems (Chapter 3)). The elderly person was asked to bring some pictures from his or her life to the welcome talk and, instead of just filling in forms, they took the time to have a nice chat to get to know one another and to fill in the forms at the end. They also created the possibility of organizing a house-warming party for family and friends so as to lower the threshold for visiting the elderly person afterwards.

What came forth in the months after is that the CTE of 'See Me' set the stage for three types of creativity: generative creativity – new ideas, adoptive creativity – new processes, and retentive creativity – new institutionalizations. We give one example of each. With regard to generative creativity, soon after the introduction of the CTE, students invented a kind of make-a-wish activity in which the elderly people were invited to dream of one thing in life they would love to do once more. This became a yearly activity on every location and the implementation of these wishes brought lots of enthusiasm and pride during the year. For adoptive creativity, at one location the nurses decided to no longer report on every person with every shift of nurses. This was a tough experiment that brought a lot of discussion between the nurses. But finally they discovered that this was acceptable for all and it made quite some time free that now became available for spending time with the elderly people. After this experiment in one location, it was spread to more locations. With regard to retentive creativity: the organization created an internal digital platform on which small movies and messages about new creations became visible for the whole of the organization. This became a source of inspiration and interaction that invited the different locations to make lots of creative fun to show the others their collective creativity.

At the moment it is still too early to talk about measurable results, but it is reported recently that absence figures are structurally going down in the departments that are already working with the CTE of 'See Me'. What is definitely emerging in these departments is 'beauty'. Different locations (nurses, elderly people and administrators) find themselves in the meantime a bunch of very creative people that make good fun. And one of the family members reported that 'it feels as if we get our mother back!' These are just three examples of the hundreds of collective creations that are taking place daily. No one can change a system on his or her own, but together it shows that we can! Box 4.1 gives another powerful illustration of how innovators can become much more effective by integrating the complexity, living systems perspective in their design initiatives.

4.5   A reflection on skills in the 'Age of Design'

According to management consultant Conklin (2009), we are now in the midst of a shift from the Age of Science to the Age of Design: in the Age of Conventional

IMAGINEERING SNAPSHOT: HELPING TROUBLED FAMILIES

On October 18, BBC News (2016) reported that the troubled family scheme, a governmental initiative at a cost of £448 million set up following the 2011 riots in English cities to help the most disadvantaged families, had made 'no significant impact' on school attendance, employment or behavior. The National Institute of Economic and Social Research showed that the conventional (mechanistic) approach of 'targeted interventions', with families getting dedicated workers who help with everyday tasks and teach, for example, better household management and control of children's behavior, had 'no significant impact'.

Realizing that the costs of ineffective interventions are sky high, in Australia TACSI, The Australian Center for Social Innovation, designed the CTE of 'Family by Family' based on complexity insights of living systems (TACSI Creation, 2018). It is a new model that empowers families to thrive instead of just survive. It is a peer-to-peer program that draws on the experience and resilience within communities – they find and train families who have been through tough times (Sharing Families), match them with families who want things to change (Seeking Families), and coach the families to grow and change together.

The biggest difference is that families are primarily supported by other families, rather than professionals. Family by Family activates a largely untapped resource – the strengths and experiences of families that have 'been there, done that' – and at the same time builds community capability and strengthens connections. One of the real strengths of this model is that families don't work nine to five, Monday to Friday – they're there to support each other 24 hours a day.

One professional Family Coach works with 15 Sharing Families, who in turn work with 40 Seeking Families, reaching up to 100 children at risk. With just one professional for every 100 children, it's extremely cost-effective. The program has an unprecedented cost–benefit ratio of 1:7 – a huge saving for governments in keeping children out of state care and other child protection and crisis services.

While there are other programs that use a 'mentoring' or 'peer-to-peer' model, the key difference with Family by Family is its firm focus on behavior change. It's not only about offering support and encouragement (although that is valuable), it's about families setting their own goals and being coached and guided to make a lasting change in their lives – from ending drug and alcohol abuse, to spending more time together as a family. The change journey has been very intentionally designed into the program, leading to a much higher likelihood of success.

It's not only families 'in crisis' who benefit. TACSI believes any family that wants to create change and improve their lives should be given support to do so. Working with all types of families also helps avoid the stigma that the program is only for 'disadvantaged' families, which too often can discourage families from taking part.

Science, describing, predicting, planning and controlling made sense. 'Facts' legitimized decisions, people worked separately in silos and the problem definition was clear (build a bridge across the widest river in the world). The goal was to find the right answers for complicated issues involving sometimes hundreds of people and years of effort. Those days are gone. In the emerging paradigm, the Age of Design, we seem to be confronted mainly with complex problems and chaos. The problem solving process is now social and we base our shared understanding on stories that give us a more coherent sense of meaning. The focus of our activities shifts from description to experimenting, learning, creating and innovating together. Today, leaders, not in the least public sector professionals, are countries' most important designers. It is their collective design decisions that affect millions of people and involve billions of euros.

Up to now the toolbox of managers as designers has been limited. With Imagineering we are enthused about adding a powerful design approach to this toolbox.

As already explained elaborately, to become more effective managers and politicians, a first step is making the distinction between complicated issues and complex issues. Once this distinction is understood, it is our experience that relaxation and even compassion emerges. When a collective can take a step back to have a complex systems view on the issue, people start to see that 'the issue is not whose fault the mess is – the issue is our collective failure to recognize the recurring and inevitable dynamics of the mess' (Conklin, 2009:20). People start to realize that both issues require a different style of leadership and a different type of design: designing for evolution instead of designing solutions – or, to use the words of Garud and his colleagues (2008): designing for incompleteness instead of designing for completeness, the former illustrating with the 'new' concepts of Wikipedia and Linux, names we tagged as 'poetic or daily language'. We need leaders that practice what Colander and Kupers (2014) call 'Laissez-faire activism': leaders that are able to design and manage an eco-structure in which the system can re-order itself and we need designing for evolution instead of designing solutions. Designing for incompleteness leads to a better 'fit' to environments characterized by continual change and openness.

'This is the new frontier in which we find ourselves. Problems are ill-defined, preferences are fluid and solutions emerge in action. In such situations, an emphasis on completeness is likely to result in the creation of designs that forclose future options' (Garud et al., 2008:352). In such an environment governance mechanisms need to be underspecified (Weick and Quinn 1999) or semi-structured (Eisenhardt and Brown, 1997); that is, they possess minimum critical specifications (Emery, 1980) to keep the design in a state that is neither too fluid nor too crystallized (Gehry, 2004).

In this chapter we have argued that the Imagineering perspective is an essential design perspective for the business and management school to complement conventional DT. To implement this Systemic Design Approach of Imagineering, new skills are needed: the skill of (complex) ST (see Chapter 6), the skill of appreciative thinking (Chapter 5) and using liberating structures that help people interacting informally as, for example, World Cafés. Also, the skill to organize learning cycles to reflect on our own actions to prevent ourselves from harming the system (Chapters 6 and 10), and, finally, the skill to think in terms of experiences (Chapter 8) and interactions (Chapter 9), and the skill to articulate 'strategic thinking' in strategic, poetic narratives that have holistic and heuristic value (Chapter 7). In the second part of this book we will discover these new skills or competencies step-by-step, from A to F.

References

Amabile, T. M. (1996). *Creativity in context: Update to the social psychology of creativity.* Hachette UK.

Amabile, T. M. (1983). The social psychology of creativity: A componential conceptualization. *Journal of personality and social psychology, 45*(2), 357–376.

Atlee, T. (2014). *The Tao of democracy: Using co-intelligence to create a world that works for all.* North Atlantic Books.

Bartel, C. A., and Garud, R. (2009). The role of narratives in sustaining organizational innovation. *Organization Science, 20*(1), 107–117.

Bartlett, G. (2001). Systemic Thinking, a simple thinking technique for gaining systemic focus. Paper presented at the 5th International Conference on Thinking, Leuven, Belgium.

BBC News (2016). Troubled families scheme has made 'no significant impact'. At: http://www.bbc.com/news/uk-politics-37686888 (accessed April 10, 2018).

Boal, K. B., and Schultz, P. L. (2007). Storytelling, time, and evolution: The role of strategic leadership in complex adaptive systems. *The leadership quarterly, 18*(4), 411–428.

Boland, R., and Collopy, F. (eds.) (2004). *Managing as designing.* Stanford Business Books.

Brown, T., and Martin, R. (2015). Design for action. *Harvard Business Review, 93*(9), 57–64.

Brown, T. (2008, June). Design thinking. *Harvard Business Review, 86*(6), 1–10.

Bruner, J. (1986). *Actual minds, possible worlds.* The Jerusalem–Harvard lectures. Harvard University Press.

Colander, D. and Kupers, R. (2014). *Complexity and the art of public policy: Solving society's problems from the bottom up.* Princeton University Press.

Conklin, J. (2009). Building shared understanding of wicked problems. At: http://www.cognexus.org/Rotman-interview_SharedUnderstanding.pdf (accessed October 9, 2018).

Conklin, J. (1996). *The Age of Design.* White paper. CogNexus Institute.

Conway, R., Masters, J., and Thorold, J. (2017). *From design thinking to systems change: How to invest in innovation for social impact.* RSA Action and Research Centre.

Csikszentmihalyi, M. (1999). 16 implications of a systems perspective for the study of creativity. In: Sternberg, R. (ed.) *Handbook of creativity.* Cambridge University Press, pp. 313–328.

Csikszentmihalyi, M. (1996). The creative personality. *Psychology today, 29*(4), 36–40.

Csikszentmihalyi, M. (1988). The flow experience and its significance for human psychology. In: Csikszentmihalyi, M., and Csikszentmihalyi, I. S. (eds.) *Optimal experience: Psychological studies of flow in consciousness.* Cambridge University Press, pp. 15–35.

Dunne, D., and Martin, R. (2006). Design thinking and how it will change management education: An interview and discussion. *Academy of Management Learning & Education, 5*(4), 512–523.

Eisenhardt, K. M., and Brown, S. L. (1997). The art of continuous change: Linking complexity theory and time-paced evolution in relentlessly shifting organizations. *Administrative science quarterly, 42*(1), 1–34.

Emery, F. (1980). Designing socio-technical systems for 'greenfield' sites. *Journal of Occupational Behaviour, 1*(1), 19–27.

Friedman, K. (2016). New challenges for design. *She Ji: The Journal of Design, Economics, and Innovation,* Open access. Available: https://www.sciencedirect.com/science/article/pii/S2405872617300825 (accessed April 10, 2018).

Garud, R., Jain, S., and Tuertscher, P. (2008). Incomplete by design and designing for incompleteness. *Organization Studies, 29*(03), 351–371.

Gehry, F. O. (2004). Reflections on designing and architectural practice. In: Boland, R. J., and Collopy, F. (eds.) *Managing as designing.* Stanford University Press, pp. 19–35.

George, J. M. (2007). 9 Creativity in Organizations. *The academy of management annals, 1*(1), 439–477.

Gorny, J. (2007). *A dictionary of creativity: Terms, concepts, theories & findings in creativity research.* Viitattu 24.10.2013. At: http://creativity.netslova.ru/ (accessed October 12, 2018).

Greenhalgh, T., Russell, J., and Swinglehurst, D. (2005). Narrative methods in quality improvement research. *BMJ Quality & Safety, 14*(6), 443–449.

Hargadon, A. B., and Bechky, B. A. (2006). When collections of creatives become creative collectives: A field study of problem solving at work. *Organization Science, 17*(4), 484–500.

Hazy, J. K. (2011). More than a metaphor: Complexity and the new rules of management. In: Allen, P., Maguire, S., and McKelvey, B. (eds.) *Sage handbook of complexity and management.* Sage Publications, pp. 524–539.

Johansson-Sköldberg, U., Woodilla, J., and Çetinkaya, M. (2013). Design thinking: past, present and possible futures. *Creativity and innovation management, 22*(2), 121–146.

Khella, A. (2009). Design thinking for startups. At: https://www.slideshare.net/akhella/design-thinking-for-startups-1971227 (accessed October 9, 2018).

Kimbell, L. (2012). Rethinking Design Thinking: Part II. *Design and Culture, 4*(2), 129–148.

Kolko, J. (2015). Design thinking comes of age. *Harvard Business Review, 93*(9), 66–71.

Liedtka, J. (2018). Why design thinking works. *Harvard Business Review, 96*(5), 72–79.

Liljedahl, P. (2009). Imagination. In: Kerr, B. (ed.) *Encyclopedia of giftedness, creativity and talent.* Sage Publications, pp. 446–448.

Lockwood, T. (2009). *Design thinking: Integrating innovation, customer experience, and brand value.* Skyhorse Publishing, Inc.

MacLean, D. (2017). Dynamic capabilities, creative action, and poetics. *Revista de Administração de Empresas, 57*(3), 264–272.

Marion, R. (2012). Leadership of creativity: Entity-based, relational, and complexity perspectives. In: Mumford, M. D. (ed.) *Handbook of organizational creativity.* Elsevier, pp. 457–479.

Merriam-Webster's dictionary of synonyms. (1984). Merriam-Webster.

Morgan, P. (2005). *The idea and practice of systems thinking and their relevance for capacity development.* Maastricht: European Centre for Development Policy Management.

Nijs, D. E. L. W. (2018). How poetic language can innovate bureaucracies. At: https://vimeo.com/253845875/33fca8f3a0 (accessed October 9, 2018).

Nijs, D. E. L. W. (2014). *Imagineering the butterfly effect.* Eleven International Publishing.

Pink, D. H. (2005). *A whole new mind: Moving from the information age to the conceptual age.* Riverhead Books.

Potts, J. (2017). Complexity, economics, and innovation policy: How two kinds of science lead to two kinds of economics and two kinds of policy. *Complexity, Governance & Networks,* (1), 22–34.

Potts, J. (2011). *Creative industries and economic evolution.* Edward Elgar Publishing.

Pourdehnad, J., Wexler, E. R., and Wilson, D. V. (2011). Integrating Systems Thinking and Design Thinking. *The Systems Thinker, 22*(9), 11–15.

Ratcliffe, J., and Krawczyk, E. (2011). Imagineering city futures: The use of prospective through scenarios in urban planning. *Futures, 43*(7), 642–653.

Rouse, M. (2009). Heuristic. At: http://whatis.techtarget.com/definition/heuristic (accessed October 9, 2018).

Sanders, E. B. (2006). Design serving people. In: Salmi, E., and Anusionwu, L. (eds.) *Cumulus 19.* Working Papers. Copenhagen, University of Art and Design, pp. 28–33.

Senge, P., Hamilton, H., and Kania, J. (2015). The dawn of system leadership. *Stanford Social Innovation Review, 13*(1), 27–33.

Senge, P. M. (2014). *The fifth discipline fieldbook: Strategies and tools for building a learning organization.* Crown Business.

Senge, P. (1990). *The fifth discipline: The art and science of the learning organization.* Currency Doubleday.

Simon, H. A. (1969). *The sciences of the artificial.* The MIT Press.

Simonton, D. K. (1988). *Scientific genius: A psychology of science.* Cambridge University Press.

Suitner, J. (2015). *Imagineering cultural Vienna: On the semiotic regulation of Vienna's culture-led urban transformation.* Transcript Verlag.

Szostek, A. (2018). Where is the difference between UX, CX and Service Design? At: https://uxdesign.cc/where-is-the-difference-between-ux-cx-and-service-design-8ce0b8654a43 (accessed December 7, 2018).

TACSI Creation. (2018). Family by family. At: http://tacsi.org.au/project/family-by-family/ (accessed April 10, 2018).

Tsoukas, H. (2017). Don't simplify, complexify: From disjunctive to conjunctive theorizing in organization and management studies. *Journal of Management Studies, 54*(2), 132–153.

Tsoukas, H., and Hatch, M. J. (2001). Complex thinking, complex practice: The case for a narrative approach to organizational complexity. *Human relations, 54*(8), 979–1013.

Waldrop, M. M., and Gleick, J. (1992). *Complexity: The emerging science at the edge of order and chaos.* Viking.

Weick, K. E. (2006). The role of imagination in the organizing of knowledge. *European Journal of Information Systems, 15*(5), 446–452.

Weick, K. E., and Quinn, R. E. (1999). Organizational change and development. *Annual review of psychology, 50*(1), 361–386.

Wentzel, A. (2006). 2. Conjectures, constructs and conflicts: A framework for understanding Imagineering. In: Pyka, A., and Hanusch, H. (eds.) *Applied evolutionary economics and the knowledge-based economy.* Edward Elgar Publishing, pp. 13–39.

Woodman, R. W., and Schoenfeld, L. F. (1989). Individual differences in creativity: An interactionist perspective. In: Glover, J. A., Ronning, R. R., and Reynolds, C. R. (eds.), *Handbook of creativity.* Plenum Press, pp. 77–92.

Wyatt, J. (1994). *High concept: Movies and marketing in Hollywood.* University of Texas Press.

Part II

The Systemic Design
Approach of Imagineering

Introduction to Part II

As we already stated in the Preface to this book: rather than a management problem, according to Paul Hawken in *The Ecology of Commerce* (Hawken and Shah, 1993) today we have a design problem. We must learn to design systems 'where doing good is like falling off a log, where the natural, everyday acts of work and life accumulate into a better world as a matter of course, not a matter of conscious altruism'. We have to learn to redesign our systems in a radical way so as to unleash and harness innovation as collective creation. We have to learn to design for evolution instead of designing (material) solutions and this is a matter of learning to design for empowering the many in a creative way.

Recently, the concept of Design Thinking is rising in management, both as academic and policy focus. But in much of today's management practice and education it remains still overlooked and oversimplified as a process of empathizing and rapid prototyping in relation to products and services with the Newtonian scientific framework in mind. This often results in an add-on to the more important managerial decision thinking. To be effective in coping with social complex managerial issues such as organizational, public, entrepreneurial or social innovation, we have argued in Part I of this book that conventional 'Newtonian' Design Thinking should be extended with complex systems Design Thinking. We have argued that 'High Concept Thinking' is such an extension. Just like a High Concept can set the stage for a whole bunch of people to start creating a new movie or a new theatre play in the creative industries, a Creative Tension Engine (CTE), if well designed and properly managed, can set the stage for collective creation (think, for example, of the 'first national park' in Belgium (Chapter 1)) or collective innovation (think, for example, of 'See Me' in the healthcare organization of Surplus).

In today's networked world managers have to learn to set the stage to make something possible that feels like magic: a small intervention that generates an important, big effect. As already mentioned: no one can innovate a system on its own, but together we have a pretty good chance to change a system if only the people in charge of the system design it to unleash that self-organizing process of re-ordering the system in a more desired way. They have to learn to set the stage for 'innovation as collective creation'. They are the ones that can make it possible that 'people create something together which has beauty, power and life' (Senge, 2005:217). Therefore management education has to develop its own 'design thinking toolbox'.

This second part of the book is meant as a resource for your actions as an Imagineer. It offers practical inspiration for the entrepreneurial people that are intending to generate a new reality or to revitalize an existing reality by tapping into the imagination of the many involved actors. Think of the creation of a new event, a new business or the re-generation or re-vitalization of an existing system such as a retail-chain or whatever governmental or commercial organization. Innovating whole systems is a matter of innovating with lots of people together starting to act anew in the envisioned direction. It is a process of collective creativity leading to many new actions in line with one another. Such a process can be unleashed by the design of a High Concept (Imagineering as applied in the creative industries) or a CTE (advanced Imagineering as applied outside the creative industries and as presented in this book) that sets the stage for new engaged action. Innovation as collective creation is a matter of liberating the collective creativity in an integral way. It is by creating strategically the conditions in which people can interact creatively for a longer period of time that a new reality can emerge.

This second part is built according to the three design phases (Inspiration, Ideation and Implementation) and the six design activities or steps as articulated in the A–B–C–D–E–F model: A-ppreciating, B-reathing, C-reating, D-eveloping, E-nabling and F-lourishing futures. Each chapter has been written by a colleague specialist on the issue at stake. Each chapter articulates models, tools, methods and techniques that might be used in each specific step toward the co-creation of a flourishing system. As several tools and techniques such as actor mapping, customer journey mapping or business canvas modeling are used predominantly to ignite and enrich the dialogue in the direction of collective creativity, most tools and techniques can be used in several steps during the Imagineering Design Approach (IDA). However, to limit the number of pages to read, we have decided to articulate every tool and technique in one chapter only and to refer to the eventual applicability of a tool or technique in other chapters. The reader should keep this in mind when using the different chapters as a source of inspiration to effectuate great design work.

The reader should also keep in mind that no two IDAs are alike. Just like other design approaches, Imagineering is never a matter of filling in a form or following a recipe but always a matter of genuine thinking, doing and reflecting on feedback given by involved actors. Each IDA is designed to address a unique strategic systemic challenge faced by the organization or an entrepreneur. Each is designed to guide an organization or community in the process of (re)framing the (corporate) identity and developing the organization or community toward a more humane, participative, and productive future in the networked society. This means, in essence, that every IDA is always a search for the generative core of the human activities so as to set the stage for collective creativity and action. Every IDA is aiming at harnessing the creative power of an eco-system, and this can only be liberated collectively when it is focused on a greater good, on a 'better' future for the envisioned actors in the eco-system.

The basic architecture of an Imagineering Design Approach

The basic architecture of an emergent process of system creation or innovation is threefold (Inspiration, Ideation, Implementation – see Table 4.1) and acts more like a scaffolding than as a solid structure. In the Inspiration and Ideation phase, it goes each time from an activity of divergence to an activity of convergence. The Implementation phase then is an emergent phase, a phase of continuous further innovation. Depending on the context, the two first phases can work with participatory methodologies and there are, of course, very good reasons to implement those phases as such unless it is not possible to do so for one reason or another. The participatory dimension is of such importance today, that it is even said that it is more important to have lots of co-creators backing you than to have a bank doing so.

Core to the first phase of inspiration in every IDA is the discovery of the generativity of the eco-system. To have a clear idea of what generativity of an eco-system means, the next quote can once more be revealing:

> It's common to say that trees come from seeds. But how can a tiny seed create a huge tree? Seeds do not contain the resources needed to grow a tree. These must come from the medium or environment within which the tree grows. But the seed does provide something that is crucial: a place where the whole of the tree starts to form. As resources such as water and nutrients are drawn in, the seed organizes the process that generates growth. In a sense, the seed is a gateway through which the future possibility of the living tree emerges. (Senge et al., 2004:2)

Discovering the generative core of a living system such as an organization, and taking care of that in the long run, is the essence of Imagineering. Talking about the generativity of living systems such as trees, we are not yet talking about the generativity in human systems in which the unique human capability of the imagination can get ignited. It is clear that when it comes to tools for working with the generative core, we are still in our infancy. Time and again, however, you will discover that when working with human systems, even with systems that are in the worst conditions one can imagine (and maybe even especially well in those 'terminal' situations) systems start to flourish again when their generative core gets liberated. It is the generative core that energizes the system, that makes it possible that co-creation with other actors in the system becomes possible, that the business model can evolve continuously and that the system can arrive in a positive evolutionary perspective of continuous innovation. The translation of the generative core in the narrative mode (poetic or daily language) in the Ideation phase then makes it possible that internal as well as external actors can join the process of emergence.

This means that even while no two IDAs are alike, the focus in every IDA is the same: a deep search for the generative core and how to unlock the value creating system from that perspective, also with a long-term perspective in mind. In the chapters of this part of the book, we provide some deeper explanation with tools and techniques for use in every activity of the Imagineering design process.

Preparing for the journey

The construction of an Imagineering design team: 'the ID team'

Design is people business and in Imagineering this is an even more important truth. Imagineering is a complexity-based design approach the application of which asks for a basic understanding of the science of the living systems. It is a matter of reframing the deep logic about change, innovation or transformation in terms of emergence, as has been articulated in Chapters 1 and 3. And even while it is not necessary to have a good theoretical grasp of complexity science, it is important for the people at the head of entrepreneurial processes, including the Board and C-suite (i.e. the chief officers, typically considered the most powerful and influential members of an organization), in general, to have a good grasp of the phenomenon of emergence and the basic principles and concepts of the living systems so that they are able to see the potential of an IDA that is in many ways in opposition to conventional business administration thinking concerning change and conventional innovation. The risk that the generative core is treated with a mechanistic mindset as window-dressing instead of being treated as an authentic starting point of all value creation is even more dangerous than staying oriented toward the creation of shareholder value (profit only) in today's transparent society.

Ideally an Imagineering Design Team (IDT) will be composed of diverse functions and all levels out of the organization. Nine to 16 people from over the whole company and maybe also stakeholders from the broader system will take the lead in the process. After every session these team members take care for their own inner circle to distribute knowledge, insights and competencies and to absorb necessary input and reflections from their circle. After the Ideation phase, at the moment that the CTE is 'installed' in the core identity of the system (logo, human resources management (HRM)-cycle, interaction platform), the ID team stays the one responsible for taking care of orchestration, reflection and evaluation of the implementation of the creative ideas that are delivered continuously to the team from all over the eco-system.

The appointment and the decoration of an ID room or an ID corner

Approaching innovation as collective creation with an IDA makes the design competency central to the whole organization. From now onwards, this competency should never leave the organization. The future is about innovating continuously, not only in products and services for customers/participants but also in systems, procedures and institutionalizations with as well internal and external actors. Therefore a physical room or corner as well as a digital platform can act as an important, visual instrument catalyzing the process. If installed, the ID room or corner should be decorated to enable this crucial activity to continue in the longer term. The room should facilitate, for example, continuous business modeling (for example, one of the walls can be decorated with the business model canvas of Alexander Osterwalder) or experience journey mapping and it should also facilitate showcasing: exhibiting (the wall of fame) the recent new creations and their results (positive feedback of realizations in the strategic direction) to inform and inspire all stakeholders on the central orientation of the organization – continuous innovation by design. This showcasing has the explicit intention of making people want to participate in the continuous creative jamming of the organization for the good of society.

After having set the context, ID team and ID lab, let's go now to the design process with the activities themselves as they are articulated in the following chapters:

Inspiration
  Chapter 5: A-ppreciating
  Chapter 6: B-reathing
Ideation
  Chapter 7: C-reating
  Chapter 8: D-eveloping
Implementation
  Chapter 9: E-nabling
  Chapter 10: F-lourishing.

References

Hawken, P., and Shah, K. (1993). *The ecology of commerce: A declaration of sustainability* (No. HD60. H39 199). HarperBusiness.

Senge, P. (2005). Afterword: Discovering the magic of collective creativity. In: Brown, J., and Isaacs, D. *The world café: Shaping our futures through conversations that matter.* Berrett Koehler, Inc, pp. 217–220.

Senge, P., Scharmer, O., Jaworski, J., and Flowers, B. S. (2004). *Presence: An exploration of profound change in people, organizations, and society.* Currency Doubleday.

5

A-ppreciating: how to discover the generative core

Celiane Camargo-Borges

5.1 Introduction

This chapter concerns the first phase of Imagineering design, where you will embrace an appreciative mindset that will lead to generative processes and outcomes. Appreciative and generative are the two core concepts in this phase and they are highly connected to one other. You will come to realize that an appreciative point of view will enable you to examine well-established conventions and traditional assumptions in fresh new ways.

In the Appreciative phase you will be surprised and inspired by the research you do. We will present a number of creative tools that you can use to collect data in this phase. The many insights you gather will form the basis of the B-phase.

The ultimate goal of the A-phase is to gain an understanding of the current situation of the system you are investigating/working with and to provide the basis for opportunities that will unfold in the rest of the Imagineering design process.

5.1.1 Appreciating . . .

The A-phase stands for analysis as well as appreciating, emphasizing an appreciative attitude, defined by Whitney and Trosten-Bloom as "the study of what gives life to human systems when they function at their best" (Whitney and Trosten-Bloom, 2010:1). This attitude underlines a strengths-based approach that focuses on assets, capabilities and resources of organizations, communities and people that can be leveraged and encouraged (Cooperrider and Whitney, 2005).

5.2 What does being appreciative really mean?

The appreciative attitude comes from the Appreciative Inquiry approach, which is based on the theory of social constructionism with the fundamental concept that language does not represent the world but creates it (Gergen, 2015). According to Gergen (Gergen and Gergen, 2004) meaning arises from what people do together and not from an individual's mind. Language is fundamental to the creation of meaning, which in turn creates action and action will create new realities (Gergen, 2015).

The way we talk when we interact with others, the way we choose our words and how we relate together drives our actions, our behaviors and our way of living. This suggests that we always move in the direction of what we choose to focus on and that we create new meaning by the questions we ask. So the best way to generate positivity is to study it.

Generativity is closely related to the Appreciative Inquiry approach and also part of the A-phase, examining well-established conventions and meanings, and challenging traditional assumptions about life, the organization, and so forth. The focus of generativity is on the capacity to look at these conventions, meanings and assumptions in fresh new ways (Gergen, 2014). The generative approach provokes examination and reflection in order to (re)consider what is taken for granted, and aspires to (re-)create new ways of being and acting (Bushe, 2013).

This is exactly what A-phase is about: embracing an appreciative mindset that will lead to generative processes and outcomes.

You are often faced as a practitioner/researcher with the traditional problem-solving attitude of finding out what is wrong, rationally explaining it and then fixing it. The focus here is always on identifying mistakes and ways to repair them.

Appreciative analysis, on the other hand, invites us to examine a system beyond its constraints, to focus on what gives life to this specific system, and to view it generatively. Remember that generativity is the ability to see things with new eyes, to co-create new understanding and to make innovative constructs. The appreciative mode stimulates a generative stance towards a system by inquiring through affirmation. It invites us to consider the best elements of "what it is" and to picture "what it might become". We illustrate this below with a description of two oppositional approaches to food management.

A traditional project on food management would likely start with an analysis of the heart of the problem (i.e. food waste) to prepare for the next phase, which is finding solutions. Thus, you would first collect information from the usual sources, such as food service and management, food production and product developments, supermarkets and other distribution channels, restaurants, hotels and all kinds of industry representatives. You would talk to the people in these areas asking them: "What is wrong? How do you deal with the problem of food waste here?" You would then search around the food legislation concerning production, regulation, inspection and distribution and you would ask: "How can we manage people better? How can we manage things better? Why is this causing such disputes concerning small farming and consumption at the end of the chain?" This type of analysis already sets the stage for a focus on food waste as the reason for such inequalities and the hunger in the world. The logical next step after this analysis would be to raise awareness of food waste and to invest in education to bring about change. However, this focus may very well create resistance among those responsible for food waste, since they would tend to see themselves as not good enough and in need of education.

Embracing an appreciative analysis, the investigation would start by trying to understand what is working well in this realm, what are the best achievements in food management? This does not mean that you will not see the problems, but you will instead focus on elements that unite people rather than separate them (i.e. food sharing). This focus brings energy rather than resistance.

The underlying principle is that food belongs to all of us. From this starting point you can "flip" the meaning from food waste to food sharing. This small alteration changes the perspective from "who is to blame?" to "we are all involved". It has suddenly become a global system in which we are all responsible for taking action. This second perspective engages stakeholders and brings inspiration for something new rather than fixing what is wrong. It also takes the analysis in the direction of exploring advocacy and social causes. A good example on this topic is the slow food movement (http://www.slowfood.com (accessed October 12, 2018)), which is all about valuing local food resources, taking the time to appreciate them and preserving the ecosystem; another one is the "from farm to table" movement (http://fromfarmtotable.ca (accessed October 12, 2018)), which promotes the direct acquisition of food from the producer; and the ozharvest project, which is a perishable food rescue organization in Australia that collects food that would not otherwise be used and delivers it free of charge to charities (http://www.ozharvest.org (accessed October 12, 2018)).

The idea of sharing is an appreciative idea. It started with the same topic (i.e. food management), but the approach and the outcome are completely different.

Food waste calls for a more individualistic, rational and hierarchical attitude to solving the problem. Food sharing involves the whole system and everyone in it. It is about relational and ethical responsibility (McNamee, 2017) where everybody is responsible for making it happen.

This illustrative example shows how the appreciative component in the A-phase can lead to discovering the generative potential of the endeavor.

The paths chosen and the questions asked will make a vast difference to the way information is provided. In turn, it will determine the direction taken and the findings uncovered. Working in an appreciative and generative way will lead to more opportunities and open up new paths for possibilities. Moreover, the findings will generate other (positive) ways to look at the issue.

It is important to note that the way we communicate, either explicitly or implicitly, will give rise to specific meanings, which in turn will bring forth certain actions and, ultimately, create the reality we live in (McNamee and Hosking, 2012).

A language of promise and opportunity is much more likely to create a reality filled with possibilities for your project. A language of trouble and challenge is more likely to create a reality of a nest of problems (Cooperrider and Whitney, 2005). In other words, when we choose to focus on best practice, promise, possibility and opportunity, these very phenomena tend to flourish.

What does this approach mean in practice? The search is for what is really valuable in a system (by which we mean an organization, a community, a school, or any other kind of institution). The aim is to discover the magic of the system in order to help it grow, rather than focusing too deeply on problematic issues.

All the aspects of the topic should be an inspiration for understanding the elements involved and the larger context in which the topic exists.

This phase is the first step towards articulating the generative core of the system. It prepares for the creation of the High Concept (the generative image) in the later phases of the Imagineering process. This phase will harness the collective imagination to generate new action in a more desirable direction. In this A-phase, you will collect data using some of the tools described below. The many insights revealed using the tools will form the basis of the B-phase.

5.3   The classical dimensions of organization analysis

A well-established way of investigating and understanding a system and its context (such as an organization) is through classical supply and demand dimensions. This can be a good initial way of approaching your topic and to start mapping what you need to cover in your analysis. The supply dimension relates to the organization itself and its surroundings. It explains what it is and what it offers. Take a piece of paper and describe your system both internally and externally. Then dig into the system by asking follow-up questions such as: What is the focus of the organization? How does it function? What is its purpose? You might consider doing some field research using these questions too. You should also take a look at the values, successes, dreams and cultural elements of the organization in order to better understand the whole system. In other words, identify the habits of the organization, how individuals relate to each other and their everyday way of talking, behaving and making decisions. Try to discover pivotal moments in the history of the organization when key changes and transformations took place. You might find these in books or reports or simply by talking to people.

Finally, explore the relationships with external environments and how the organization positions itself. A good place to start is to examine the original vision that the founders or pioneers had when the organization (company, school, community, etc.) started. Then look at how the organization has developed since then. Dig around for the special stories they have celebrated. These can be especially illuminating in helping to understand the historic values and how they play a role in the present.

Once you have organized and described all these elements in the supply dimension, it is time to move on to the demand dimension, which is related to the customers and the target group. In this dimension you ask the questions: Who are the stakeholders or the community that is involved? Why do they use the products and services? What drives them to do so (i.e. what is the value to them as customers)? What are the other segments outside the organizations that are key? Who else is connected in some way to your topic? Who else could have an impact on the system?

The target audience of your organization (i.e. customers) is an important aspect of the demand dimension. An empathy map (Gray et al., 2010) is a creative way to investigate this group. In particular, this tool helps you understand how the target group perceives the world and how they relate to the organization you are investigating. It helps you to pinpoint what your target audience really needs.

To use this map put yourself in the shoes of your target audience and consider what they think and feel, what they hear and see, and what they say and do. Then determine what their pain and gains are.

Explore each quadrant one at a time. The questions you ask should be a mixture of concrete, objective questions and more general, subjective questions. Here are some examples of questions that you might ask for each quadrant:

- **Think and feel**: This section is about understanding what matters most to the target audience. How do they feel about this topic? What do they wonder about in their daily life? Is your target audience stressed or relaxed? Do they enjoy what they do? What do they think about the organization you are investigating? Do they feel connected to it? How?
- **Hear and see**: This section covers the influences that impact the customers. What are music, movies, advertisements they watch and listen to? What "self talk" goes through their heads on this topic? In general are they more visual? Do they search for innovative stories or more traditional ones? How do they see the organization in general?
- **Say and do**: This section helps to understand the attitudes customers have towards others. What do they communicate about with others? How do they communicate? Do they talk about this organization at all? If so, what do they say about it? What are their day-to-day behaviors and actions? What do they say to each other? What are their cultural habits?
- **Pain and gain**: This section identifies obstacles that customers face as well as the things they are hoping for (i.e. that represent success for them). What frustrates them about their current situation? What annoys them? Where would they like to be? What would they like to be doing? What encourages them? What are the good things about the organization in question? And what are the bad things?

The empathy map is highly effective when completed with stakeholders working as a team to answer the questions.

5.4   Don't forget about values

Values are a key part of all levels and dimensions of the A-phase. Indeed, values play a role in every single phase of the Imagineering Design Approach, as you will see in the forthcoming chapters.

Values are those qualities that are considered worthwhile by people and organizations (Rounds and Armstrong, 2005). They represent the highest priority and they are the underlying driving force of a system. Values can be understood from the perspective of cultural values, personal values and/or consumption values. Values are more stable and lasting than needs, which are fluid and can evolve fast. Values, however, are much more deeply engrained into a specific culture and society. Values are all about what organizations and customers believe in and how that affects their behavior. Understanding values is a fundamental part of a business strategy (Desarbo et al., 2001).

Nevertheless, it is not always easy to grasp exactly what the values of an organization and the customers are. Values are often written down in statements and they manifest themselves in behaviors. The challenge is to see beyond the statements and to translate the behaviors into the real underlying values. Note that, although values tend to be more or less constant, they are context-related. Values may change when you change places and relationships. This is something to consider at the end of your Imagineering process if you conclude that values need to be changed.

One way to better recognize and understand values is to look at them in two categories: terminal and instrumental (Rokeach, 1973). Terminal values are the views of people that represent their ultimate goals in life and their opinions and beliefs about those goals. For example: how do they fulfill themselves? How do they enjoy life, friendship, etc.?

Instrumental values are "value tools" that people use to support their terminal values. They are the beliefs that people have about how they should act in order to achieve their terminal values, for example: going out to meet more people, or changing jobs, or visiting friends, or buying a nice house. Terminal values are more abstract (e.g. happiness, equality, harmony) and can be generalized more easily than instrumental values, which are often specific to an individual.

There are many ways to uncover the values of organizations and customers. You can observe an organization's website – its colors, what kind of language is used, the pictures that are posted – but always reflecting upon what kind of values they might represent. You can also observe the behavior of people, for instance by interviewing them or even by reading their comments about the organization (see also Box 5.1).

Values show the deeper level of what drives people and organizations. All systems are value driven even if those values are not obvious. Some values are

---

BOX 5.1

TWO EXAMPLES OF DETERMINING VALUES

1. You visit an organization (or their website) and they tell you that their priority is to be transparent with their clients by showing all their processes, services and production clearly. They also tell you that they motivate their employees to express themselves, not to lie and to be direct to their capacity and positions. From this you can deduce that the underlying values of this organization are honesty and respect.

2. You are working with a community and in order to understand it better you decide to walk around the neighborhood and observe how people live and behave. By being there you can see people in action. You see them separating garbage before placing it into the trash bin. You also see some people recycling materials in their garden. From these behaviors you deduce that one important value of this community is sustainability.

material in nature (e.g. products you use, logos and so forth), while others are immaterial (e.g. ways of speaking, actions, etc.). Either way, values always influence the way people behave, how they judge things, the choices they make, and what they need in order to lead their lives. It follows that by understanding the values and making them very explicit, you will be able to determine the purpose of a system. This, in turn, will allow you to create meaningful value for the system. As already explained in Chapter 2 ('Landscape'), there is a shift in value creation that moves from mechanistic logic towards a more networked generative logic. The Imagineering Design Approach will help to transform the enterprise logic by tapping into these values in a systemic way. A new value co-creation frame of reference can be put in place by examining the values of all those involved in a system. This will provide mutually beneficial relationships in which creative collaborators will participate and become involved in the process.

5.5   Trends and best practices

Another dimension that you need to take into consideration in your A-phase is Trends and the Best Practices. What are the trends of the industry and in society and what are the best practices in the field? You must look for relevant cutting edge developments and identify similar organizations that might already be working in the desired new direction. Search for related organizations and examine their best practices. Discover who is developing something new or different from what is already out there. These may or may not be competitors to the organization you are studying.

Try to determine what makes the trends so promising. Work out what makes the best practice organizations so successful. Look for how the organization you are working with could learn from the trends and best practices. Searching for the new and innovative developments helps you understand your topic better and opens up a vision for the future.

Don't get stuck on "facts and figures", on "what is" and leave space for "what can be". The focus here is on human systems and emerging potentials, and not simply fixing problems.

5.6   Next step: resources for exploration

In your A-phase you are searching for the generative core of the organization you are investigating. The ultimate goals of this phase are to gain an understanding of the current situation of the system you are working with and to identify opportunities that will unfold further in the next phases. We have already discussed above the dimensions and components that you will need to cover. It is important to consider these elements at all levels of the system in question. We find it helpful to consider each of the following three levels for every system: the micro (e.g. the individual), the meso (e.g. the organization, target group, etc.), and the macro (e.g. society).

You should look at the internal state of affairs and ask questions such as: what do these people do well? Try to make the internal context clear as well as the relationships in place there. It is also about understanding the complexity and contradictions around your topic. You must know who the major players are, who all the stakeholders are. Consider also the environments that affect the organization/system you are working with, while embracing all the interconnected variables.

You can obtain more information using creative tools and approaches that inspire participants to interact, talk and co-create new ideas on the topic.

We offer below some tools for you by way of inspiration to get you started. There are many other resources you can use (Rooijackers et al., 2016).

Most of the tools below are interactive. It is highly recommended that you talk to people in the A-phase – people who experience on a daily basis what you are trying to understand. Try to make use of every informal conversation, every phone call, and even talk to people in the street if you can. You should try not to behave as a passive researcher, simply listening to the content and absorbing it. Be active and connect to people, trying to see when people are energized or enthusiastic or proud about a topic. This is important information for the Imagineering design process and these tools will help you uncover it.

5.6.1 Desk research

This method concerns the secondary, steady, linear information that you can find online and in books. You can use desk research investigation on all three levels: micro, meso and macro.

The micro level is about understanding the internal affairs. If you are working with an organization, you might start by looking at their website. If you are working with a community, you could search the website of the municipality as well as comments online about it. Try to find some documents written by them and about them.

The meso-layer research looks for what other companies or communities are doing (related to your topic) and how people are involved. Look at reviews and commercials as well.

The macro layer concerns how your topic plays a role in society. What has been written about it? What are the latest publications on this topic? Who is writing about it? What is the situation right now with this topic? What kind of research and practices are happening around your topic? Look also for the trends.

Finally, try to identify the core values that emerge from your desk research data. Can you discern values from the language that is used to talk or write about the organization? Can you see the values from the images they use? Or from the colors?

5.6.2 Appreciative interviews

The appreciative interview is about embracing an appreciative attitude by asking questions that invite people to share personal stories as well as images of their organization when it is working at its best. Through stories and images, you help your interviewees not only to expand their descriptions of what the organization is, but also to start dreaming about what it could be. The idea here is to move away from purely rational questions that usually invite pre-fabricated answers, and instead to inspire novelty. We are not suggesting that facts and figures are not important – of course they are –but it is of utmost importance to uncover what drives people, discovering the stories behind the actions they take in their daily working lives. You can use appreciative interviews with all stakeholders in the study in order to understand the community you are working with or employees of the organization you are studying. You can also select some participants from the macro level to try to better understand trends and the societal aspects.

How to do appreciative interviews – tips and tricks

Preparation is fundamental here. In addition to preparing for the interview yourself, you should also prepare the interviewee, explaining the type of questions you plan to ask because they may be different from what they are used to. Indeed, an appreciative interview may sometimes be a little awkward for the person you are interviewing, as they do not expect such questions.

The purpose of the interview is to focus on the generative core, on what keeps the system vibrant and alive. However, be prepared, as you may find you are interviewing someone who does not like what they do or where they work. In this case it is important that they feel free to talk; you do not want them thinking that they do not have permission to talk about problems. Nevertheless, you should endeavor as interviewer to turn their negative comments around by asking, for example: what would be an ideal situation? What are some ideas you have that would change things for the better? What would you recommend differently?

Another way to be prepared is to pay attention to the interview rhythm as well as keeping the flow of the conversation. A good way to create an engaging and empathic rhythm is to bring an inspiring story to start the interview with. Engage your interviewees in the story if you can, valuing the best in them. Try to avoid acting as an expert with protocols to follow. On the contrary, be a learner and make clear that you are there to learn from what they know.

Stories are a good way for you to learn about the organization, and at the same time they engage your interviewee. Invite them to share stories and do not try to analyze them as they tell them. You can extract the specific insights you need after the interview has finished. Try not to ask systematically for each piece of information you need from them, but have patience and wait for the stories to come.

Confidentiality is key, especially when working with delicate issues. It is important that your participants know that they are safe talking to you. Make this explicit.

Below are some examples of appreciative questions that invite storytelling:

● Can you tell me a story or image about your system/organization? What was the impact that this story/image had on you? What makes it so powerful?

- Can you give an example of a recent story that gives you a sense of hope and opens up new possibilities? What speaks to you most in this story?
- What is your dream for this system/organization? What would be your story for the world? What is your image for something we could do better or smarter?
- Why is this organization alive despite all the struggles? What are the meaningful things that this organization offers to you and your co-workers? What does the organization offer for society at large?

These questions all invite a focus on what is working well and not on what is wrong. By emphasizing the generative core in this way (i.e. by concentrating on what keeps the system alive), we can better understand what these people do well.

Helpful phrases to keep the conversation flowing:

- Tell me more about this story . . .
- What makes you really proud in this story?
- Why do you feel that way? Can you explain further?
- Why was that important to you?
- How did this situation affect you?
- What was your contribution in this story?
- What was the organization doing that helped you do this?
- What really made this work?
- How has it changed you?

Participant observation

In this research method you become part of the situation to experience how others really feel in the system and to understand better how they perceive it. This method is useful for the micro and meso levels. You as researcher become an insider by taking on a role and participating for a limited period of time, a day for instance. The nature of your involvement will depend on your topic. You might try to be a customer for a day, or a visitor, for example. The most important thing for you is to understand what it is like for people to be in that specific situation. You will find that immersing yourself in other people's reality gives you a kind of emotional energy. However, this is a challenging method because you must find a balance between diving into their world and yet keeping some distance so that you can observe and analyze later. You will find that it is helpful to cross check results obtained from interviews and your desk research.

Cultural probes

This is a design research technique that generates genuinely new ideas, and reveals preferences, worries, interests and wishes. It is an approach that values uncertainty, play and imagination in order to provide alternative ideas about how people behave, how they interact and what their thoughts are.

Cultural probes are artifacts that stimulate inspirational responses from participants. These can be a map, a postcard, a photo album or any other object that could inspire the participant in some way. The participants can be given a task related to a probe that they work on themselves or the probe can be an initiator of a dialogue between the researcher and the participant.

The goal of the probes is not simply to collect data but to provoke the emergence of unique and creative designs. The probes aim to encourage autonomous action from the participants. This is very different from the controlling methods that researchers traditionally use (Gaver et al., 2004). Here you will have minimal influence on how participants act, which is precisely the point since you want to gather information by stimulating innovative thinking.

Although this is an open-ended and creative research method, there are some steps to take by way of preparation in order to ensure that it is successful. They are described below:

- **Intentionality**: it is very important to have clear goals on what you want to achieve for the activity since it is a very open and unstructured tool. What are you trying to understand with this method? When this is clear then you can proceed to the next step.
- **Selecting participants**: who are the best people to involve? Who are the best participants for the session? Furthermore, think about an appealing way to invite them.
- **Defining the activity and the probe-kit**: you will choose the materials based what on what you are investigating and who is participating. In any event, the kit should be imaginative. You might consider stickers, postcards, metaphor cards, notebooks as well as cameras, voice recorders, and so forth. Cultural probes can be anything that will help the participants to produce, gather and report information in a creative way. They should be user-centered and context-related.
- **Briefing participants**: make sure at the beginning of the activity that there is a good balance between providing information to the participants and leaving it open enough for creativity to emerge. Be clear but not too concrete. Leave space for imagination and creation. Questions such as "Tell me about an experience that was memorable?" are better than ones like "Do you think this topic is applicable? And why?" Questions that invite rational answers tend to stop creativity.

An example of the use of cultural probes to understand and inspire has been provided by Gaver et al. (2004). They describe the use of cultural probes in their research on domestic technology developments. They wanted to overcome stereotypes on how people live at home and how families interact. They decided to expand their understanding of their target group by using cultural probes. They sent packages to houses where volunteers had agreed to work with the probe-kits. The package included (1) a camera with a list of inspiring requests for pictures of daily life and routine at home; (2) a map that the members of the house should complete by thinking of the many relationships they have and how they are related; and (3) a "dream recorder", which was a voice-recorder into which participants had ten seconds to talk about a dream they have.

The variety of these probes would encourage the participants to share stories about themselves in a different, metaphorical and inspiring way. The stories would show how they lived their daily lives and how they interacted in ways that an interview would likely never reveal. They would give the team of researchers an insider perspective.

The probes were returned after a month. The data collected resulted in a deep understanding of the domestic environment. It gave the researchers valuable insights into how people used technology in their daily life and how this was linked to their relationships. This research inspired design ideas for technologies that enriched people's lives in new and pleasurable ways.

Customer journey map

This visual technique is a graphic interpretation of the customer perspective and their relationship with an organization, service, product or brand. It is very helpful when used with the demand dimension at the micro and meso levels. The whole map is drawn from the customers' perspective. It emphasizes the important intersections between what is expected and the real experience. The fundamental components of any customer journey map are personas, timeline, emotion, touch points, and channels:

- **Personas**: this is the description of the main characters in your system and their goals, thoughts and expectations.
- **Timeline**: there must be a specific timeframe for the map; it could be a week or a year or whatever is relevant in your case. The timeline is used to describe the phases in which the customer goes through.
- **Emotion**: don't forget to add emotions to the map illustrating motivations, frustrations, and moments of anxiety and happiness.
- **Touch points**: how and when do the customers interact with the system? What is the customer is doing at these touch points?
- **Channels**: where do the customers and the organization interact? It could, for example, be a digital interaction through a website or an app. It could be through call centers or even face-to-face.

The customer journey map, which is sometimes called the customer experience map, is a tool that can be used in many different ways to achieve different goals. It can, for instance, be used to develop a marketing and communication strategy as well as for improving the service of an organization. However, the core purpose is always the same, namely to map in detail the actions of a specific customer before, during and after their interaction with the organization. (For a visual map, see https://www.behance.net/gallery/5217737/Lancom-brand-journey (accessed October 12, 2018).)

5.6.3   Last but not least: storytelling

Storytelling is an element that you can add to any dimension of your A-phase research. It is a narrative approach in words or images that you can use in many different formats and in many different situations. You can tell a story yourself to appeal to the imagination of your participants. You can ask for inspiring stories from your participants. You can analyze data and present it in a story format.

Storytelling helps you not only to communicate ideas but, more importantly, to connect people through the values embedded in those ideas. Stories are powerful because they engage people in a metaphorical way that encourages multiple interpretations. Good stories are always retold.

Storytelling has become useful in many different disciplines as well as in research as a way to explore different voices and diverse understandings of a topic (Leavy, 2017). Storytelling amplifies the perspectives of a subject and opens it up for new understanding.

Storytelling is used in research to comprehend a topic by describing how people are connected through stories. It is also used to communicate results in a more appealing way (McNamee and Hosking, 2012). Storytelling as an investigative tool allows the creation of open-ended and metaphorical descriptions of a situation, rather than a collection of facts and figures. Take a moment to reflect upon your research topic in this A-phase and see when and where stories would best fit for you.

The information gathered using the tools described above will expand your understanding of your organization and your topic. You will have gathered data from facts and figures to ideas. You will have viewpoints, stories, thoughts, maps, drawings and many metaphors as well. The next step is to organize all this data in a way that will help you envision challenges and opportunities and move onto the next phase. There are many ways to do this but in the Imagineering Design Approach we recommend using the **Golden Nuggets** process.

5.7   Finding the golden nuggets

Golden nuggets is an appreciative process that allows meaning to emerge as conclusions from the A-phase. They are inspired by the gold diggers of the 19th century. They would do extensive research to discover the best possible places to find gold. Nevertheless, the golden nuggets were still hidden from view. They had to sieve through a lot of sand, separating coarser from finer particles, until through careful observation they found their nuggets of gold. The metaphor of gold diggers was first articulated by Frank Ouwens as a way to invite researchers to look differently at the results of the Imagineering Appreciative analysis (Ouwens, 2017). Ouwens defined golden nuggets as: "Unique pieces of information that speak to the imagination and which could function as a starting point for new appreciative design processes" (Ouwens, 2017:33).

The appreciative analyst sifts through a great pile of information looking for pieces of imagination to use for the (creative) phases to come. The best pieces of imagination are your golden nuggets. Golden nuggets are not the same as key conclusions. Conclusions are an attempt to bring together and summarize the entire collection of data collected. Golden nuggets are the hidden details that fire your imagination. They are packets of insight that lead to new thoughts, new ideas, new directions, and new actions. Golden nuggets are what we as Imagineers are looking for when we study a system. Golden nuggets will provide you with the basis to create new insights and new starting points to design truly different experiences.

Golden nuggets can be anything you can create from your analysis. They could be a forgotten hero from the past, an amazing story that has been neglected, ignored facts that you managed to find, hidden and untold stories, a core quality that has been overlooked, a side product which actually is the star of the show, and so forth. Golden nuggets often emerge from the combination and recombination of different pieces of data. Golden nuggets are sources of inspiration and they trigger the imagination of those involved. They create space for creative exploration. And just like the diggers of the 19th century, you will know when you have struck gold.

At the end of the A-phase of the Imagineering Design Approach you will hopefully have a greater appreciation and understanding of your research topic, one that has the potential to engage all the stakeholders and to invite them to look at the issues differently. This is the phase in which the system (i.e. the organization or city/community) is placed at the very center of the analysis. The golden nuggets that you have discovered will now become the focus of the B-reathing phase and will help you towards a bigger picture perspective.

References

Bushe, G. R. (2013). Generative process, generative outcome: The transformational potential of Appreciative Inquiry. In: Cooperrider, D. L., Zandee, D. P., Godwin, L. N., Avital, M., and Boldan, B. (eds.) *Organizational generativity: The Appreciative Inquiry Summit and a scholarship of transformation* (Advances in Appreciative Inquiry, Vol. 4). Emerald Group Publishing, pp. 89–113.

Cooperrider, I. D., and Whitney, D. (2005). *Appreciative Inquiry: A positive revolution in change.* Berrett-Koehler Publishers.

Desarbo, W. S., Jedidi, K., and Sinha, I. (2001). Customer value analysis in a heterogeneous market. *Strategic Management Journal, 22,* 845–857.

Gaver, W., Boucher, A., Pennington, S., and Walker, B. (2004). Cultural probes and the value of uncertainty. *Interactions, 11*(5), 53–56. At: http://cms.gold.ac.uk/media/30gaveretal.probes+uncertainty.interactions04.pdf (accessed 2017).

Gergen, K. J. (2015). *An invitation to social construction,* 3rd edition. Sage.

Gergen, K. J. (2014). Pursuing excellence in qualitative inquiry. *Qualitative Psychology, 1*(1), 49–60.

Gergen, K., and Gergen, M. (2004). The drama of social construction. In: *Social construction: Entering the dialogue.* Taos Institute Publishing, pp. 7–23.

Gray, D., Brown, S., and Macanufo, J. (2010). *Gamestorming: A playbook for innovators, rulebreakers, and changemakers.* O'Reilly Media.

Leavy, P. (ed.) (2017). *Handbook of arts-based research*. Guilford Press.

McNamee, S. (2017, November). Far from "anything goes": Ethics as communally constructed. *Journal of Constructivist Psychology*. DOI: 10.1080/10 720537.2017.1384338.

McNamee, S., and Hosking, D. M. (2012). Inquiry as engaged unfolding. In: *Research and social change: A relational constructionist approach*. Routledge, pp. 63–86.

Ouwens, F. (2017). *From analysis to inspiration* (unpublished teaching material, 2nd year International Leisure Magement study, Academy for Leisure). Breda University of Applied Sciences.

Rokeach, M. (1973), *The nature of human values*. Free Press.

Rooijackers, M., Camargo-Borges, C., Marée, G., Weber, J., and Brink, H. (2016). *Toolkit for design research & interventions* (e-learning project). Breda University of Applied Sciences.

Rounds, J., and Armstrong, P. (2005). Assessment of needs and values. In: Brown, S. and Letn, R. (eds.) *Career development and counseling: Putting theory and research to work*. John Wiley and Sons, pp. 305–329.

Whitney, D., and Trosten-Bloom, A. (2010). *The power of appreciative inquiry* (2nd edition). Berrett-Koehler.

6

B-reathing: how to understand the bigger picture

Lilian Outtes Wanderley and Fabio Campos

6.1   Introduction

In the six steps of the Imagineering design process this is step B: Breathing. It is a moment to take a breath and to think before moving on to the Ideation phase. This step is designed to help you avoid jumping to what at first sight might look like a quick and easy way forward based on your Appreciative analysis. This is a potential pitfall in all complex situations.

This chapter describes situations that may be tempting to try to deal with in an easy or linear way. As you may know, there is risk in complex situations that apparently easy or linear actions can actually make the situation worse and take it in unwanted directions. Our task here is to raise awareness of this risk in order to reduce its likelihood. Let's take a breath.

Breathing is the second step in the Imagineering design process and it is based on Systems Thinking applied to complex situations. The starting point for Breathing is the Appreciating step that was described in the previous chapter.

Actor mapping is an important part of Breathing and it will be covered in some detail below including a brief look at an actor mapping tutorial. Before that we would like to discuss why Breathing is so important when you are faced with complexity. As you read further, however, it may be helpful to have the following questions already in the back of your mind:

- Are all the important actors considered?
- How the actors are interacting?
- Which opportunities we have for better interactions?
- Which interactions should be improved or better explored?

6.2   Linear thinking and the pitfalls of jumping to conclusions

Let us start with a well-known social project for emerging countries, namely the "One Laptop per Child" initiative. The idea was amazing at first sight: who could question the idea of giving a laptop to each child in the underdeveloped countries? Surely it would allow underprivileged children to bridge the digital divide? It would certainly improve the performance of these children at school.

It is easy to jump to conclusions like this. It is a good example of linear thinking. Neither the children nor the schools in underdeveloped countries have laptops; so let's solve this problem by giving a laptop to each child and teacher.

We have followed several projects like this in Brazil and the results were sadly far from the desired outcomes. In some cases the teachers and students chose to sell their new laptops in order to be able to buy things they needed more. In other cases they kept the laptops even though the software was inadequate. In another, no one was able to connect to the internet, and so on.

However, there are also several circumstances in which the "One Laptop per Child" project did work. These were the ones where it was designed with a whole systems approach. For a project like this to succeed you must consider all elements in all the systems involved (security, ownership, internet at school, internet outside school, support, software, training, and so forth). You must understand the interactions between all the elements and identify which ones can help the success of the project and which ones could be bottlenecks.

So the lesson here is to avoid using more traditional or linear thinking and jumping to conclusions for complex situations. Instead, you should consider all the systems and sub-systems as the context for the situation and understand the interactions between them. The mindset should be one of connections and networking.

However, identifying all the systems and sub-systems and their interactions is usually not as obvious nor as easy as you might first imagine. This is exactly why we need to Breathe.

6.3   Thinking beyond

Breathing helps you to break the linear flow of reasoning and gives you an opportunity to think beyond the obvious and to see a bigger picture. The idea is to zoom out in an attempt to grasp the complexity of the systems and networks involved.

We can distinguish two kinds of Breathing, namely passive and active.

6.3.1   Passive Breathing

We use passive Breathing to describe a process of taking a break from thinking about or working on your challenge (Cashman, 2012), which is actually harder than you might think! Breathing is based on mind innovation mechanisms that describe how the conscious mind is linked to conscious memories and the acknowledgement of the existence of an unconscious or subconscious mind (Dechaud-Ferbus, 2016; Dijksterhuis and Meurs, 2006).

The reasoning of our minds is based mainly on our memories. The conscious memory tends to store things by category and organized by similarity. You can think of it like a cabinet in which the drawers keep our memories organized by alikeness. If, for instance, you are thinking of a new solution for blind people to move safely in a city, your memory is likely to release all kinds of walking sticks, guide dogs, tactile pavements, braille signals, and all the other things you have consciously identified as being related and have stored in your blind mobility drawer. These ideas will not be innovative, of course; you are simply browsing through your repertoire of things you already know (Jacoby et al., 1993).

However, at the same time the conscious memory is storing data, the unconscious memory is doing the same but with one interesting difference. Instead of storing the data by similarity, it is associating it with sensory and emotional indexes. For instance, if the temperature is warm when you receive a particular piece of data, this will be used as an index. When you think of warm your memory might bring back this seemingly random piece of data; or at least it will seem random to your conscious mind.

Temperature is not the only index of course. Data will be associated by the unconscious mind with all kind of emotions (boredom, excitement, love, empathy, etc.) and other complex and simple sensory data (for example the perception of comfort or danger).

In summary, when we access our unconscious memory the data does not come organized by similarity; it comes organized by these emotional and sensorial indexes. Through this mechanism we are able to reason not only with what we already know as similar, but also on apparently unconnected or random data. This can lead to moments of insight and innovative ideas (De Bono, 2015a).

But there's a catch. It is not easy to access the unconscious memory through a conscious effort alone. Our conscious minds continually want to take us to our memories stored by similarity (De Bono, 2015b).

One of the techniques you can use to unlock this access is passive Breathing (Campos et al., 2010; De Bono, 1976). Take some time after the A-ppreciating step to think about or to do things that are totally disconnected from the topic you have been working on. You can do anything except something that is related in some way to your topic. Give your unconscious mind the chance to communicate with your conscious mind and let insights appear by themselves (De Bono, 1995; Vandervert et al., 2007). This is passive Breathing.

We cannot emphasize enough the need to avoid linear thinking and jumping to conclusions (De Bono, 1995) when applying Imagineering. Another technique to help you in this respect is active Breathing.

6.3.2 Active Breathing

Active Breathing is the mapping of actors, which we introduced briefly above (Zhou et al., 2011). This technique involves identifying the actors, understanding their perceptions and including them in the co-creation process. It is important to keep in mind that the network and interaction among the actors is an essential part of the solution process. Active Breathing therefore has a much more dialogic role than the observations and data collection you did in the A-ppreciating step. This dialogic process usually presents several hurdles that need to be overcome but that also point to areas for potential system improvements. For instance, it is not uncommon that the actors:

- aim for the same general goal (for example, better education) but this goal does not mean the same to all of them – for some in this example it could be reaching a median grade on an international survey, yet for others it could be that children are able to spell and do basic math;
- agree on the main goals and their attributes but do not agree on how to reach them, so the actors have the same intention but could work in divergent directions;
- do not know about the experiences of other actors and their lessons learned;
- do not know (or think that they are already doing everything they can) about what is missing or what can be improved in their interactions with others;
- have never stopped to think or talk about the networking and interaction possibilities; and
- did not know (or have ever taken in account) a different point of view brought by someone else.

Active Breathing has a purpose that reaches beyond representing and capturing the perception of the actors. The overriding objective is to promote dialog and reflection, and to improve the networking and interaction. This in turn makes it possible for small and simple actions to deliver big results.

Interestingly, the dynamic of the interactions within a network brings with it the power to heal the system, often in surprising ways. A social project in the backwoods of the Brazilian state of Pernambuco gives us a real-world example of this healing power. The aim of the project is to help economically vulnerable communities become self-sustainable. The situation here is highly complex with a mix of "physical" systems (such as basic infrastructure like water and electric power, transportation, security, and so on) and non-physical ones (such as cultural and traditional beliefs, education, culture, and so on) (Campos et al., 2015). The complexity of these systems and the interactions between them called for a design based on a co-creation process that involved all the mapped actors (Lichtner et al., 2010).

In one of the communities the only economic activity was a very basic level of cotton cultivation. Co-creation led to the plan to install a machine to process cotton and a computer space. Selling processed cotton instead of in natura cotton would make the community economically self-sustainable. The computer space (similar to an internet café) was intended to connect the community to other similar communities and to enable remote consulting support. The children from the community were among the first to use the computers after they were installed and connected. They used them to communicate online and play games. However, one of the children did not join in and just stood looking at the others. When asked why he wasn't on a computer, he unexpectedly revealed a profound truth:

> I work in the cotton fields from the time the sun rises to the time the sun goes down. It is the same with all my family, at least the ones who are still alive. I left school after learning how to sign my name and how to do sums because it is all I thought I would need for my life in the fields. I don't want to play now with the computers, but for me it was already worthwhile (to be here today). Now I understand why I should return to school – to be able to use these computers someday.

This story also illustrates the power of engaging the actors. We tend to assume that actors will speak up naturally but this is not always the case. People sometimes need a sort of trigger to be able to see beyond their own reality and to comment on it. This should not be too surprising in fact since we all see our experiences through the lens of our own life-experiences and personal paradigms. This is why it is so important to include actors in the co-creation process instead of assembling a team of experts.

Another example of system healing is a project commissioned by the government of a different Brazilian state called Minas Gerais (PlugMinas, 2014). The main objective of the project is to improve the school performance of at-risk populations in order to stop them ending up working for drug dealers or falling prey to other criminal activity. The co-creation design process led to the development of a set of units that involves youngsters and helps them to express themselves. So there is a unit teaching circus skills, another teaching foreign languages, one for dance, one for photography, and so forth. There are even some that you might not consider as ways of self-expression such as game design, programming, and entrepreneurship (Campos et al., 2013). The project is redesigned from time to time in order to stay up to date. It was during one of these redesigns that one young user of the project said to us:

> Before entering this project I thought I had the best job of the world: I transported drugs for a big drug dealer from a point to another point of the slum. So, I wasn't really doing something too bad; I wasn't consuming drugs, I wasn't selling them; and I didn't need to rob people because I was earning more than enough. Now I don't have a job, but I am satisfied since, because of this project, I am able to imagine, for the first time in my life, a real possibility of a life outside the slums.

As our society evolves, it becomes an increasingly complex system of intertwined sub-systems. You can think of it as a house of cards in the sense that moving a wrong card can cause a catastrophic collapse; yet, at the same time, with care and an appreciation of the whole structure we can continuously improve the castle. Sometimes we have to zoom out to be able to understand a system, which is the subject of the next section.

6.4   Zooming out for complex Systems Thinking

How do you differentiate between simple and complex issues? It is widely accepted that simple situations are those we have some experience of and, to a greater or lesser extent, we know how they work. We can make safe assumptions about the expected results and goals are almost always successfully reached. Think, for instance, of watching online videos on a modern smartphone. We connect via wi-fi or the cellphone network, choose a video app and play a video. You may possibly need someone to show you the first time you do it, but after that it's simple. Most people would say that it's basic phone functionality nowadays.

But when do we characterize a situation as complex? Many have tried to answer this question but it has proved remarkably elusive. Experts in the field acknowledge the limitation of traditional reasoning and suggest that a Systems Thinking approach would be helpful. It is clear that complex situations are unique and what is eventually found to work in one system can rarely be applied to another system, however similar it appears at first sight. There is also a mounting body of evidence to show that collaborative creativity can be helpful in dealing with uncertain outcomes. It can reduce risks and improve the chances of success.

Reflect for a moment on a situation where a region or community lacks education. It is easy to see that schools are missing, but it is misguided to jump to the obvious conclusion: let's build schools! This simple and only apparent solution has failed many times all over the world. Why? The situation is much more complex than it appears. There are hidden factors and interactions that drive the lack of education.

Let us go back to Brazil for an example. A recent project there concerns the lack of access to basic education (Arrastão, 2014). Active Breathing revealed that parents forbid their children to go to school after a certain age. They believe that once children have learned how to sign their name and do basic math there is no additional benefit to attending school. It is better for family survival to send their children out onto the streets to beg for money.

You could build as many new schools as you wish, but the children will not come. Instead the chosen approach was to establish a social project to show parents and their children what they could achieve though education. However, even this had to be done with care. Active Breathing also showed that parents struggle to believe in attaining anything beyond their actual lives in their limited social context. So it was very important to show them what was realistically achievable through education in their context rather than, say, how great it would be to be an astronaut!

The mindset of the parents and children changed in astounding ways during the project. For the first time they were able to see beyond their social context. They began to support their children's education in new and surprising ways.

This is yet another example of how the dialog that is inherent in active Breathing can uncover previously hidden insights. These insights can not only contribute to system healing but also help to surpass the original goals of the designed interventions. It is the live dynamic nature of networks that makes this possible. We will take a closer look at Breathing and insights in the next section.

6.5   Breathing as a trigger to insights

Let us take a moment to reflect on why we are so keen to look for fast and hurried solutions. This could be related to the strong desire to build our ego through helping others. Or perhaps there is a tremendous satisfaction in helping to solve something that others have struggled with and failed, not to mention the appreciation we would receive for doing so. The question is whether rushed solutions ever make a lasting impact. In most cases we would argue that they do not. Rushed solutions usually fail to anticipate the likely (negative) consequences of our actions.

This is most evident in solutions that are thought of as being simple common sense. They are so obviously a good idea why even bother to think through how they might go? Of course it'll work, it's just common sense! This type of solution is most often found coming from an individual at the top of an organization who is known in leadership literature as a "savior". This is a traditional style of leader who sees it as their role and is expected to provide solutions. How often do such solutions prove ineffective and how risky is it to depend on the vision of a single individual, however smart they are (Weisberg, 1986)?

Hopefully the advantages of combining passive and active Breathing are starting to become clear to you. Complex and incompletely specified problems usually require innovative solutions. The passive Breathing concept has taught us that it takes time and technique to unlock the power of the unconscious mind to come up with innovative ideas. However, passive Breathing alone would lead to a kind of trial-and-error, linear approach. We would have an idea, test it, reject it, have another idea, test it, and so forth. However, if we use active Breathing to map the actors and create dialog between them our ideas stimulate their ideas in an endless loop of creativity that releases hidden insights. In other words, by applying both kinds of Breathing we catalyze the emergence of insights.

Emergence is a key concept in complexity thinking. It is all about allowing the participants to raise initiatives that can contribute to the desired situation. In other words everyone in a community is aiming to make improvements or to change for the better. It is helpful to openly state the desire to change for the better because it raises awareness that a negative or worsening situation could happen despite our best intentions. In this way, a community can try to foresee potentially undesirable consequences. The fact is that bad things can get worse and it is our responsibility as Imagineers to do everything we can to raise awareness of this and try to reduce the chance it happens.

Having just read the paragraph above, you might begin to doubt just how effective you can ever be as an Imagineer or as a leader of change in an organization. We would urge you to embrace this doubt by acknowledging that for each action there is a reaction. It is often called a boomerang effect. We would encourage you to be reflective and to open your mind to dialog with all the actors in order to discover a diverse spectrum of possibilities. In short, we appeal to you to be open to emergence. You will find that listening is the most helpful skill in this respect. Help others to do the same, to listen and to make an effort to understand different perspectives without blocking any ideas.

Each person has their own opinions, of course, and most people want their point of view to "win". Allowing time to reflect on the ideas and to recognize an emergent perspective taking shape can mitigate this.

We hope you can begin to see why a one-size-fits-all approach is not going to work in co-creating a better world. Continuous collaborative learning is the way forward.

You can think of active Breathing as a time to break for reflection – eventually it will become a continuous and repeating action. You will find that you will learn to focus better when you listen to your environment. You can think of it as being like yoga – by concentrating on your breathing in and out, you gain focus in your mind.

Be aware that your social reality will also likely change during Breathing and this will be felt by all participants, directly and indirectly. Similarly, any actions you take will be felt by all and perhaps not always positively. Or, more likely, your actions are perceived positively by some participants but not at all by others. Moreover, change in activated dynamic networks can happen exponentially.

It is, therefore, always worth thinking through potential actions. Be wary of solutions that are seemingly easy or obvious. Think of different possible scenarios and their potential impact on the proposed actions. Try to learn from other initiatives avoiding commonly made mistakes as you test new ones. Remember these are all heuristic techniques; nothing will be perfect!

We will end this section with one final example from Brazil. It involves a community that for quite some time had been demanding a set of services from the municipality in support of their youth (CRJ-BH, 2018). The municipality finally agreed to build a Youth Center. Fortunately, a systems design process including passive and active Breathing was undertaken before building actually started. It turned out that what the community really wanted was to be taken seriously by the municipality. They wanted political representation and a say in the municipality decision. Indeed, it became clear that unless there was a public hearing the new Youth Center would not be accepted and used by the community. The municipality accepted this situation and agreed to a redesign of the Youth Center, which the community enthusiastically supported.

Interestingly, the redesign in the end involved only minor changes compared to the original design. They may have been only minor but it made the difference between success and failure for this project. It is useful to reflect that small, subtle factors such as this can have a big impact. It is comforting to know that such factors emerge during Breathing.

6.6   Actor mapping

We mentioned "actor mapping" earlier in this chapter. It is time now to go into this in more detail.

Actor mapping is a key element for a successful outcome in the Imagineering design process. It is important that you keep in mind that its main purpose in this process is as a dialogic tool. This is worth noting, since you might be thinking that an actor map is simply a way to document the actors involved, their perceptions and interactions. The whole point of the actor map in Imagineering is that it supports the expression of the actors through dialog. It is especially useful in uncovering potential bottlenecks and for identifying ways to improve interactions among the actors. In other words, the actor map shows us the weak links that need attention to create better connections, and the strong points that can be leveraged to drive the decision making. The actor map also gives you a broader view of the whole system. This helps you to see the inspiring new possibilities that can build from what is already in the system. It also helps you to recognize the key elements of the generative emergence of desired changes.

Gopal and Clarke (2015) describe actor mapping in three stages: Prepare; Facilitate; and Refine/Revise. These stages appear to be sequential but more often than not you will need to do them in multiple, repeating cycles. The underlying concepts are logical and sensible, although they are not so easily absorbed, grasped, applied, or even believed by the actors involved (Campos et al., 2014). In order to deal with this, the Refine/Revise step is frequently used as a way of cycling back to the actor map following a first (pilot) deployment of an innovative solution.

Take, for example, a project that was undertaken for a multinational telecoms company with the objective of developing smartphone apps. A linear thinking approach would be to hire and manage teams of app developers to design and code the apps. However, the Imagineering design process, which included an actor mapping, led to a co-created plan to offer a course in app development in a format similar to a medical residency. The aim was to develop the apps at the same time as a group of developers was trained. This would lead to greater capacity for app development in the company.

Although this seemed to be a good solution, some of the actors from the company were not fully convinced. As a result we chose to start with a small-scale version of the plans to prove their feasibility and worthiness. The idea was to do several such courses after validating the results of the first one.

However, during this validation someone suggested that they should use the same methodology for the design of the apps themselves. In other words develop the apps as co-creation projects with the involved actors (i.e. the company staff, customers, users etc.). This proposal again met with a lot of internal resistance from staff who said that they already knew their customer and user needs. Nevertheless, they went ahead and developed a series of co-created apps. The results were so good that the company ported the new apps into more than a dozen different languages and made them available worldwide.

6.7   An actor mapping practical tutorial

There are many ways of doing actor mapping. What is important for all of them is that you somehow stimulate a dialog between all the actors. This can be done very informally in collaborative sessions. However, there are a number of structured frameworks that you may prefer to use for actor mapping (Bourne and Walker, 2005). In this section, we will highlight a common framework that is used by FSG (FSG, 2018).

You can also find free detailed tutorials online (FSG, 2018) and there are even specialist software tools to help you draw the map (Kumu, 2018, for example). We tend to recommend you just use your favorite mind-mapping tool.

We will use a fictitious example of a project to design better services for a neighborhood of the provincial city of Breda in the Netherlands. There are four steps: Feasibility Assessment; Preparation; Facilitation; and Revising and Refining.

6.7.1 Feasibility assessment

The aim of this first step is to identify if the actor mapping tool is suitable for the particular situation you are in. If it is, do you have the means and the time to prepare and execute it?

The actor map tool is suitable when you know who will make use of the complete map or who will benefit from the mapping of the system. Moreover, there must be agreement on the scope and boundaries of this system.

As a general guide, it will take about two hours to execute the Facilitation phase and about eight to ten hours to prepare it. Besides a space to run a session, you will need materials such as colored pens, sticky notes, colored adhesive dots, paper, flip charts, and so forth.

6.7.2 Preparation of the Facilitation phase

The first action of this step is to decide who the facilitator will be. The facilitator is then responsible for preparing the session using the following checklist:

(a) Clearly identify the topic, the "who" of the actor map.
(b) Set the boundaries of the actor map by determining the geographic reach and segmentation of the actors.
(c) Make the system frame. This is made up of the main beneficiaries and sub-systems that influence the system.
  1. Place the main beneficiary inside a circle in the middle of the map.
  2. Place the related sub-systems around the circle and trace radial lines dividing the region of each sub-system around the map.
     Figure 6.1 shows an example of a system frame for designing better services for a neighborhood in Breda, NL with postcode 4811 TC.
(d) Identify an initial set of key actors and, optionally, populate them on the system frame (Figure 6.2). Obviously, if you opted to populate the map you should share this with the participants at the beginning of the Facilitation phase.

6.7.3 Facilitation

Once prepared, you are ready for the actor mapping group session. The ideal number of participants for this session is between 10 and 25 people. It is important that the group is made up of actors with diverse points of view,

Figure 6.1 System frame for better services at Neighborhood 4811 TC

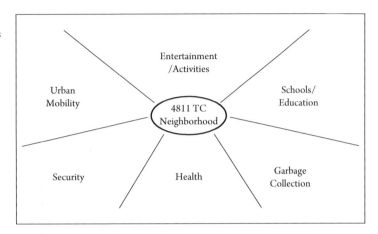

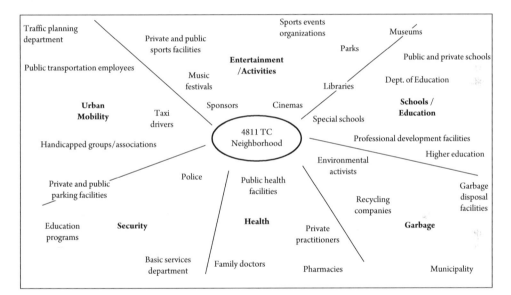

Figure 6.2 System frame populated with some actors

life-experiences and levels of specific knowledge. It should take between one and a half and two hours to run.

A session like this will usually proceed as follows:

a. Divide the group in sub-groups of about five to eight people.
b. Decide whether each sub-group will work on the whole map or only on a region of the map.
c. Provide the work materials to each sub-group (sticky notes, colored pens, colored adhesive dots, paper, flip charts, etc.).
d. Introduction: explain to the sub-groups what the problem is, what they will have to do and in what timeframe. Show the draft actor map if you opted to pre-populate it.

e. If you did not pre-populate the map with actors they will need 15–20 minutes to do this.

f. If you did pre-populate the map they will need 15–20 minutes to refine the actors on the map.

g. After the map is populated with actors, the sub-groups will have 15 minutes to map the levels of engagement, relationships, and connections among the actors. The idea is to mark the most important or strongest actors. This can be done using a sliding scale of importance (e.g. strong, moderate, weak, or no engagement) or by simply marking the most important actors (the colored adhesive dots are good for this).

h. The sub-groups then have a further 15 minutes to identify and map momentum, blockages, and opportunities for each of the most important actors identified in the previous step. They should indicate whether they have a positive (momentum, opportunity) impact on the goals of the main beneficiary or a negative impact (blockage, challenge or gap). The colored adhesive dots can be useful here too.

When this step has been completed, you should allow the group some time to reflect upon which actors or clusters of actors could be a potential target for leverage or influence.

i. The mapping itself is almost finished now and it is time to discuss the implications of the map and to draw conclusions. This can take anywhere from 15 to 45 minutes. It is recommended that the groups reflect upon questions such as: Which actors are ready to act? Which ones are engaged? What opportunities does the map reveal? What other actor or actors should be mobilized into action?

j. The last step is to agree the next steps.

6.7.4 Refining and Revising

It can be very useful to refine and revise the actor map. Systems are changing all the time, as are the perspectives of the actors themselves. To do this, simply repeat the process starting at Facilitation, step f.

We cannot emphasize enough that the goal of the group sessions is dialog between the actors in the system. The dialog is the key to the convergence of intents and actions. It is essential for system healing. Dialog aids the improvement of the network and it allows the emergence of insights. Consequently, the focus should always be on the dialog. What people say to each other is much more valuable for a network than any documentation.

6.8 Conclusion

At first sight it seems logical to jump directly to apparently simple solutions. Indeed, this linear way of solving problems can work for some situations. However, many of today's problems are complex. They are composed of networks of sub-systems all interacting with each other. A Systems Thinking approach is much better suited to tackling this class of problem.

The Imagineering design process is a Systems Thinking approach that can cope with complex and incompletely specified situations. It is made up of six steps, A–B–C–D–E–F. The Breathing step is a moment to reflect on the findings from A-ppreciating before proceeding to the Creating step. Breathing stops you jumping to conclusions by helping you zoom out to see the big picture.

The two kinds of Breathing, passive and active, work in different ways. Passive Breathing is all about giving your unconscious mind the chance to communicate with your conscious mind. Passive Breathing reveals hitherto hidden insights and lets innovative ideas flow freely.

Active Breathing is a dialogic process that uses the actor mapping tool. The aim is to improve the interactions in the network through co-creative dialog. This not only reveals insights but it can also lead to system healing.

Now that you have mastered Breathing, it is time in the next chapter to think about the vision of your project and what concept might ignite the system to move towards this vision. This is the C-reating step.

References

Arrastão (2014). Website. At: http://www.arrastao.org.br/ (accessed 26 March 2018).

Bourne, L., and Walker, D. H. T. (2005). Visualising and mapping stakeholder influence. *Management Decision*, 43(5), 649–660. At: https://doi.org/10.1108/00251740510597680 (accessed October 1, 2018).

Campos, F., Soares, M. M., Correia, W., Ferreira, R., Melo, E. V. V. de, and Correia, A. (2010). The effects of explicit alternative generation techniques in consumer product design. In: Kaber, D. B., and Boy, G. (eds.) *Advances in cognitive ergonomics*. CRC Press – Taylor & Francis, pp. 336–345.

Campos, F., Peres, F., Neves, M., and Correia, W. (2013). Using a digital game in teacher training and training courses for young adults from low-income communities in Brazil. In: *Proceedings of SITE 2013*, March 25, New Orleans, LA. Association for the Advancement of Computing in Education (AACE).

Campos, F., Figueirôa, D., Neves, M., Correia, W. F., and Soares, M. M. (2014). Data gathering for ergonomic and design evaluations: Issues and pitfalls. In: *5th AHFE – International Conference on Applied Human Factors and Ergonomics*, Kraków. AHFE International.

Campos, F., Neves, M., Cavalcante, S., and Correia, W. (2015). Improving design methods by the incorporation of consumer behavior principles. *Procedia Manufacturing*, 3, 5670–5676.

Cashman, K. (2012). *The pause principle: Step back to lead forward*. Berrett-Koehler Publishers.

CRJ-BH – Centro de Referência da Juventude de Belo Horizonte [Youth Reference Centre of Belo Horizonte]. (2018). https://www.facebook.com/crjbh/ Latest access 30/11/2018.

De Bono, E. (1976). *Practical thinking*. Peng.

De Bono, E. (1995). Serious creativity. *The Journal for Quality and Participation*, *18*(5), 12–18.

De Bono, E. (2015a). *Serious creativity: How to be creative under pressure and turn ideas into action*. Random House.

De Bono, E. (2015b). *The mechanism of mind: Understand how your mind works to maximise memory and creative potential*. Random House.

Dechaud-Ferbus, M. (2016). Perception et relaxation analytique: une pause créatrice. *Revue française de psychosomatique*, *49*(1), 147–162. At: https://www.cairn.info/revue-francaise-de-psychosomatique-2016-1-p-147.htm (accessed October 12, 2018).

Dijksterhuis, A., and Meurs, T. (2006). Where creativity resides: The generative power of unconscious thought. *Consciousness and Cognition*, *15*(1), 135–146.

FSG (2018). Website. At: http://www.FSG.org (accessed 26 March 2018).

Gopal, S., and Clarke, T. (2015). *System mapping: A guide to developing actor maps*. FSG.

Jacoby, L. L., Toth, J. P., and Yonelinas, A. P. (1993). Separating conscious and unconscious influences of memory: Measuring recollection. *Journal of Experimental Psychology: General*, *122*(2), 139–154.

Kumu (2018). Clarity begins with Kumu. At: https://www.kumu.io (accessed October 1, 2018).

Lichtner, V., Petrakaki, D., Hibberd, R., Venters, W., Cornford, A., and Barber, N. (2010). Mapping stakeholders for system evaluation – the case of the Electronic Prescription Service in England. In: *Proceedings of MEDINFO 2010*, 12–15 September, Cape Town, South Africa.

PlugMinas (2014). Website. http://www.plugminas.mg.gov.br (accessed 26 March 2018).

Vandervert, L. R., Schimpf, P. H., and Liu, H. (2007). How working memory and the cerebellum collaborate to produce creativity and innovation. *Creativity Research Journal*, *19*(1), 1–18. DOI: 10.1080/10400410709336873.

Weisberg, R. (1986). *A series of books in psychology. Creativity: Genius and other myths*. W. H. Freeman/Times Books/Henry Holt & Co.

Zhou, F., Xu, Q., and Jiao, R. J. (2011). Fundamentals of product ecosystem design for user experience. *Research in Engineering Design*, *22*(1): 43–61.

7

C-reating: how to define vision and concept/Creative Tension Engine

Frank Ouwens

7.1   Introduction

The basic premise of this book should be becoming clear to you now. Creative organizations should approach innovation from the experience perspective. In other words, their starting point for innovation should be a better ideology rather than a better technology. It is ideology that adds meaning for people and in doing so engages and mobilizes them to innovate and to alter reality into an envisioned future. In this chapter you will work on ideology and learn how to express meaning in two ways that are essential for Imagineering: the 'vision' as a description of the aspirational desired future and the 'concept' as a way to work towards that future.

7.2   Vision

The vision is the first element you will define in the Creating step. The word vision itself comes from the Latin 'visio', which means 'to see, behold' or an 'idea or representation' (Van der Loo et al., 2007). This is a broad description that has spawned a multitude of interpretations over the years. Our observation is that, despite the fact that almost all organizations have a stated vision, only a few have a truly *desired* and *aspirational* vision that is formulated in an Imagineering way. We would like to emphasize that, throughout this book and the Imagineering design process, we use vision in this deeper, more meaningful context. But why do you need one anyway?

7.2.1   Why a vision?

In Chapter 1 we talked about 'creative tension' as a way to describe the gap between current reality and the aspirational future (Senge, 1990, 2014; Senge et al., 2015). This tension explains why aspirational visions are so important for experience design and experience innovation, since they appeal to our values and trigger emotions. Neurologist Donald Calne notes that: 'The essential difference between emotion and reason is that emotion leads to action while reason leads to conclusions' (in Roberts, 2006:42). Aspirational vision adds meaning, triggers emotions and gives you the drive to set things in motion. It is worth considering vision in some more detail.

7.2.2   Vision considerations

Beyond an organizational context

Vision is often developed in an *organizational context* with a purely *organizational relevance*. For Imagineers *aspirational vision* goes beyond the organization. Imagineering vision should inspire others beyond the limited business context. Moreover, anyone or any group in the system should be able to formulate their desired future image. In other words, vision in the Imagineering context does not limit thinking: it opens minds to emerging outcomes. Take, for example, the case of Ignace Schops and his friends that we described in Chapter 1. Their vision 'Making nature conservation sexy' led to the concept of 'the first national park in Belgium', which emerged into a sustainable movement in the region.

Long-term time frame

We argue, as do many authors on the topic of Imagineering (Van der Loo et al., 2007; Sinek, 2009; Collins and Porras, 1994), that aspirational vision has a long-term time frame. Some refer to this as 'dream scenarios'. A famous example of such a vision is Martin Luther King's 'I have a dream' speech in 1963. He described a desired future without racial segregation. This inspired his followers even though he did not say exactly what steps would be needed to achieve it. It was King's dream vision that further ignited the American civil rights movement and it is still working its magic today.

Collectively shared outlook

We would like you to think of vision from now on as a collectively shared view. It is the shared aspect that engages people in the system in unexpected ways. Note, however, that visions that were originally defined as personal views can spark a whole organization or movement. Martin Luther King is a clear example, of course, as is Mahatma Gandhi with his nonviolent civil disobedience movement or Jamie Oliver with his food revolution. In all these cases, inspiring personal visions became powerful collective visions.

Subjective character

You should also be aware of the subjective nature of vision. Vision always represents an opinion on how today's reality could be improved. It is a view, or a bundle of views, on a topic. In an organization context, vision provides a truth for those involved, i.e. management, employees, customers, followers and other stakeholders. These different groups may differ on the details, but cooperation is likely to fail if they disagree on a visionary level. Aspirational vision contains a truth for everyone involved.

To help you develop an aspirational vision for your project, we propose the following four steps:

Step 1: choose (the subject)
Step 2: formulate
Step 3: check
Step 4: share.

We will explain these four steps below.

7.2.3 Step 1: choose (the subject)

One of the first and most important questions to ask before you start is 'for what do we need a vision?' In other words, what is the subject? You should also consider the breadth of scope of the vision. Geursen (1994) argues that visions can be:

1. about life, human beings, Earth and the cohesion of all things; or
2. about a certain field/ industry/ sector or topic.

It is important to note that we do not define a vision on a product level. Products are tools that fulfill customer or user needs and as such they are interchangeable. A new technological development could make an individual product obsolete. If the vision was for the product it would then become obsolete too. Vision should be independent from products or technological developments and describe fundamental needs behind a product. Kodak is an often-quoted example of a company that failed to have a vision beyond their products. At their zenith they were the largest producer of camera film but they underestimated the emergence of digital photography, which led eventually to their catastrophic decline. The tragedy of their decline might have been avoided had Kodak been led by a vision on 'photography', or (even more abstract) 'reality captivation' instead of 'camera film'. Kodak now describe themselves as 'a technology company focused on imaging'. The lesson is clear: avoid defining your vision on a product level.

Each of Geursen's vision levels has their own advantages. For instance, it is far easier to create a meaningful and inspirational vision on a specific sector, field or industry since it is more narrowly defined. On the other hand, the more specific a vision is, the bigger the chance that a change in the external environment could render it irrelevant.

Organizations can and do switch between vision levels, especially when forced to do so when their *raison d'être* no longer fits reality. Indeed, many organizations today are re-evaluating their position as a result of the ever-increasing need for meaning and significance in society. Large corporations used to be unchallenged on global topics, but the complex systems they operate in and the increasing demand for transparency force them to take a stand and reconsider their role. Corporate Social Responsibility is evolving and, as we learned in Chapter 2, organizations are thinking more about their role in the world beyond making money for shareholders. As a consequence, we see a shift from a specific level of vision towards the overall life, Earth and cohesion level, as the following Nike example shows.

Nike has always had a very specific view on the world of sports, e.g. 'Bring Inspiration and Innovation to every athlete in the world', or 'If you have a body you're an athlete' (Nike, 2018). In recent years, however, you can see Nike beginning to express positions and opinions on topics beyond the world of sports. Community impact and sustainability have become major topics for them (Oregon Live, 2017). In 2017 Nike CEO Mark Parker published an employee statement reacting to US president Donald Trump's executive order banning citizens of seven Muslim countries from entering the USA. Parker stated: 'Nike believes in a world where everyone celebrates the power of diversity. Regardless of whether or how you worship, where you come from or who you love, everyone's individual experience is what makes us stronger as a whole' (www.oregonlive.com, 2017). This statement coincided with the release of a new advert entitled 'equality'. Together these make clear Nike's view of the immigration policy of the USA. Nike has moved from being a company that had a vision in the field of sports to one that has clear opinions on much broader human-related topics.

7.2.4   Step 2: formulate

The next step for you is to formulate the vision as a shared purpose through the P^3 model. It consists of three key components for a vision statement, namely:

1. Purpose
2. Principles
3. Promise.

Purpose is arguably the most important part of an aspirational vision. The purpose answers the 'why' question. For a system this might be: 'why is transformation needed?' For organizations it is: 'why do we exist, our reason being, our *raison d'être?*' or perhaps 'what is the one goal that we pursue for the long term?' The daily struggle to survive in a competitive world often keeps many companies and organizations from asking this crucial question. In other words, they are too engaged in 'what' they are doing to ask 'why' they are doing it. This is a fundamental error since the 'what' should always be a result of the 'why'. The ends should justify the means.

It is the purpose that adds *meaning* to what you do (Box 7.1). It is meaning that provides experience designers such as Imagineers with the fuel to light the fire. They plant the seed for a system to transform by articulating collective meaning. But how can you find and formulate a purpose?

BOX 7.1

SOME EXAMPLES OF PURPOSE FORMULATIONS

Walt Disney: 'To create happiness for people of all ages, everywhere'.

Starbucks: 'To inspire and nurture the human spirit, one person, one cup and one neighborhood at a time'.

Sources: Van der Loo et al. (2007); Starbucks (2018).

Collins and Porras (1994:228) use an interesting scenario in an organizational context to come to what they call the Core Purpose. They call it the 'Random Corporate Serial Killer' scenario as follows:

> It works like this; Suppose you could sell the company to an individual who would pay a price that everyone inside and outside the company agrees is more than fair, taking into account a very generous set of assumptions about the expected future cash flows of the company. Suppose further that the individual will guarantee stable employment at the same pay scale for all employees after the purchase, but with no guarantee that those jobs will be in the same industry. Finally, suppose the buyer plans to 'kill' the company after the purchase – its products or services will be discontinued, its operations will be shut down, its brand names will be shelved forever, and so on. The company will utterly and completely cease to exist, wiped completely from the face of the Earth.

What would be lost for the world if the company were indeed shut down? What could no longer be experienced? Why should the company continue, now and in the future? When faced with this scenario, executives start to think about bigger questions beyond shareholder value, employment and satisfying customers. They start to contemplate the very reason why they exist.

Principles describe the deeply rooted values that underpin the behavior and ways of working. Principles connect people and show them clearly *how to* do things. They provide ethical guidelines that direct action. As is the case with most successful guidelines, less is often more. Most authors (Van der Loo et al., 2007; Geursen, 1994; Collins and Porras, 1994) advise a total of three to six values. Too many values dilute the focus and are difficult to remember and abide by. Fewer, well-chosen values often lead to better results. In addition, although the principles say something about how you to do things, they should never be a straightjacket and frustrate collective creativity. Quite the reverse, principles should ignite collective creativity and create emergent action (Box 7.2).

Collins and Porras (1994) use an activity called 'Mars Group' to help discover principles (they call them 'Core Values'). Imagine the hypothetical situation that an organization is planning to open a new branch on Mars but they can only send a maximum of five to seven people to staff the new branch. Who would they send? Collins and Porras did this exercise with many top brands and organizations and they observed that most of them deliberately sent those who

---

BOX 7.2

EXAMPLES OF PRINCIPLES

Volvo
Safety
Quality
Environment.

Virgin
Providing heartfelt service,
being delightfully surprising,
red hot, and straight up,
while maintaining an insatiable curiosity
and creating smart disruption.

Sources: Volvo (2018a); Virgin (2018).

BOX 7.3

EXAMPLES OF PROMISES

Volvo

'Vision 2020 is about reducing the number of people that die or are seriously injured in road traffic accidents to zero. Protecting and caring for people is at the heart of Volvo Cars' philosophy and this is our commitment to saving lives.'

Nike

'Our mission is to double our business while cutting our environmental impact in half.'

Sources: Volvo (2018b); Nike (2018).

---

represented the organization at the principle or value level. In other words, they sent those people who understood what the organization stood for and who could start building based on the core values. They did not send those who were the most technically educated, nor the ones with detailed product or marketing knowledge.

Promise is all about the bold, daring goals we can set that will drive us towards the aspirational desired future. Promise is especially fitting in the Imagineering design methodology of appreciative and determinant interventions. Having defined the why (purpose), the how (principles), it is the promise that defines the 'what'. Promise puts purpose and principles into a more tangible perspective. Promise makes sure that all stakeholders are connected and directed towards an ambitious goal (Box 7.3).

The best-known example of a bold promise is probably John F. Kennedy's speech in Houston, Texas on September 12, 1962. It was the height of the

Cold War with the Soviet Union and the USA was the underdog in the space race. The Soviet Union had already put a man in space. Kennedy gave NASA and the American people a daring goal by promising to land a man on the Moon and return him safely to the Earth by the end of the decade. The latter part, putting a man into space is one thing, but bringing him home safely is an entirely different matter. Kennedy made this promise at a time when NASA was still very far off from being able to reach that goal and the American people were far from convinced that it was worth the huge investment. However, his speech in Houston resonated widely and it is still remembered. It gave a focused, specific goal to NASA and a daring promise to the American people. The rest is history.

You will find that the main challenge in articulating a promise is the ever-present tension between direction and inspiration. Too much direction and too little inspiration will make the promise feel more like orders to be followed. Too much inspiration and too little direction leaves us wandering aimlessly.

Imagineering seeks to stimulate joined-up, emergent innovation and we argue that we can ignite and facilitate this if it well designed. It is up to you as the Imagineer to facilitate a process for vision formulation that provides just enough direction yet leaves plenty of space for emergence. Balance is key.

7.2.5   Step 3: check

Once the vision is formulated through the 'P^3 model' (Purpose, Principles and Promise), you can check its strengths by considering the following eight characteristics for a strong vision:

Aspirational:	A good vision sets the bar high and functions as an ever-present guiding star. Easily achievable short-term visions do not exist.
Directive:	A good vision has the power to direct in pursuit of the desired outlook.
Distinguish:	A good vision is unique and different. It sets organizations apart from others.
Meaningful:	A good vision matters; it gives meaning to the organization.
Authentic:	A good vision is considered as real and worthy by those involved.
Generative:	A good vision brings the desired future into existence. It awakens energy.
Inspirational:	A good vision inspires all those involved.
Connect:	A good vision connects. It connects not only people but also activities. It connects stakeholders both inside and outside the organization. It is the glue that keeps things together in pursuit of the desired future.

These eight characteristics form an acrostic that spells out **ADD MAGIC**, which of course is the very goal of any vision.

7.2.6   Step 4: share

Your final challenge, having chosen the topic, developed the purpose, principles and promise, and checked your vision, is to make it come alive. There are two levels for you to consider here.

Materializing the vision

You need first to create an articulation of your visions that speaks to the imagination. All too often a poorly written vision becomes just another policy document that disappears into the files. Poetic language is needed to make it come alive, something that Collins and Porras (1994) call 'Vivid Descriptions'. The vision should be described in enough detail for those involved to have an idea of what the future they are aiming for might look like. On the other hand, the description should leave enough room for flexibility so it cannot become a 'fixed' representation. Think again of Dr. King's 'I have a dream' speech. He paints a vivid picture of the future but leaves plenty of room for the listeners to add their own examples.

Articulation through language is key, since it is usually through words that a vision is shared. However, there are other ways of making the vision come alive. Visual tools such as mood boards, key images, symbols, computer-generated images and video content can support a vision. You could create 3D objects, miniature worlds, games, and so forth – or choose a combination of all of these. The most important point is that the materialization inspires those involved. It should refer to their context and their world. It should use plain language that provides a clear path to follow.

Spread the wor(l)d

You have materialized your vision in an inspiring way and now it is time to spread the word. It is time to use communication to unleash the power of your vision and let it work its magic. Marketing instruments, social media, the built environment, employee events, the Human Resource Management (HRM) cycle, and so on, all are tools that can be used to create moments and methods to communicate the vision.

7.3   Concept

Now that you have your aspirational vision formulated, it is time for you to work on the second part of the Creating step, namely the concept.

7.3.1   Vision and concept

Before we continue it is important to define what we mean by a concept in Imagineering and experience innovation. We have already explained above that vision provides the aspirational outlook that deals with the *'why'* question. Concepts go one step deeper into the *'how'*. Concepts are inspired by the aspirational vision and provide a clear *approach* to achieving that vision. Concepts offer more concrete working principles or methods that help us move towards the vision.

The 'why' and the 'how' are closely related, of course. Indeed, they are intertwined since some components of the vision (principles) also say something about

---

BOX 7.4

IMAGINEERING SNAPSHOT: BURNING MAN

Larry Harvey and some friends founded the Burning Man Festival in Black Rock City, Nevada, USA in 1986 (Burning May, 1989–2018). Since then it has grown into a well-known and unique event. The goal for each event is the temporary realization of a community in which everybody is welcome and free to express themselves. Art, music and inclusion play key roles in this community. The event has been a huge success and has grown significantly over the years. In 2015, 70,000 people attended the Black Rock City festival. The people at a Burning Man event are called 'Burners' in order to represent their kinship with the Burning Man culture and community. Being a Burner is a way of being in the world. It is this that makes the festival fundamentally different from any other events. Burners do not visit the festival – they are the festival.

The free spirit, artistic and expressive culture is at the center of the concept and it has inspired many people since the start. They feel connected to the Burning Man culture, which has been formulated in Ten Principles. It is a reflection of the community's ethos that these principles have developed organically over time. The culture has also spread beyond Nevada. There are now over 100 local Burning Man communities all over the world, many of whom organize their own event. It has become a global cultural movement that is also supported by the Burning Man organization. They feed and facilitate the system, while safeguarding the essence of Burning Man.

Burning Man now has become a unique and distinctive culture rooted in the values expressed by their Ten Principles. This culture is manifested around the world through art, communal effort, and innumerable acts of individual self-expression. It has become a way of life for many.

Source: Wikipedia (n.d.).

---

organizations to become 'individuals' that represent something that you like and feel connected to. You share the same interests, values and beliefs with the organization as you would with another person. Values mobilize people to action to try to resolve the creative tension they feel. Remember that creative tension is the way that Imagineers describe the gap between current reality and the aspirational future. The gap between the way things are and the way we want them to be.

7.3.3 Concept scope

We saw earlier how concepts can be seen as a working principle. They are a formula, a method or approach to doing things. We would like to turn your attention now to the scope of concepts. In practice we see that while some concepts are detailed formulated approaches, others work on a more inspirational level, even overlapping with visions. In order to understand the variety

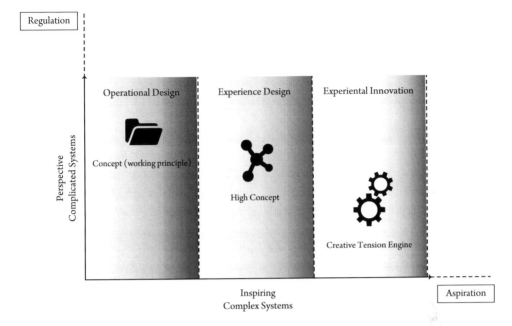

Figure 7.1 The Concept Continuum

of different concept approaches, we have developed the Concept Continuum. This shows the difference between three different types of concepts: Concepts; High Concepts for Experience Design (as used in the creative industries); and Creative Tension Engines (used as concepts for experiential system innovation). We position the three concept types according to their level of regulation and their degree of aspiration towards a vision (see Figure 7.1).

Concept

The continuum shows on the left a prescriptive concept with a set of working principles operating at the procedural level. The approach is worked out in detail and ensures that the design and execution is clear and widely reproducible. The working principles are key to making sure that everything runs as intended, especially for complicated problems in a technical design environment. For instance, in the automotive industry concepts are worked out in detail for each of the different parts of the car to ensure the car as whole functions as designed. The Double Tree Hilton hotel's famous chocolate chip cookies are an example from the hospitality industry that illustrates the reproducibility aspect. The recipe, smell, presentation, timing, location, etc. have all been thought through to create a unique recognizable experience wherever in the world the hotel is located.

High Concept

Prescriptive concepts as described above work very well to orchestrate regulated activities. However, this high level of detail and regulation make them less suitable for use as experience or organizational principles. The detail is too limiting and the different contexts are not well served by an exactly reproducible set of principles. Moreover, prescriptive concepts lack overarching, imaginative connecting elements.

The experience and creative industries (entertainment, film, hospitality, tourism, leisure, etc.) have realized that concepts for meaningful experiences require very different characteristics. They need to be less prescriptive, more encompassing, more meaningful and inspiring. We refer to these as High Concepts. You will recall from Chapter 1 that Wyatt (1994:8) describes a High Concept as: 'a short easy to communicate narrative which links the aesthetic and the commercial potential to bring forth a (fascinating) new perspective in society'.

High Concepts have a high degree of simplicity. In addition, they have an overarching and associative capacity that people feel connected too. This transforms them from simple internal working principles or prescribed regulations into principles that also inspire *external* stakeholders, such as customers. They have the power to generate, ignite and facilitate emergence of all kinds of initiatives. It is this feature of High Concepts (generative images) that requires a less detailed prescription balanced with just enough guidance to steer the generation of ideas. In other words, what they lack in detail, they make up for in inspiration for people to connect and become involved. High Concepts are aimed at unleashing creativity as a goal in and of itself.

These features make High Concepts especially relevant for organizations in Experience Design. High Concepts have the '*looks*' (visual potential), '*hooks*' (marketing potential) and '*books*' (storytelling potential) that lead to consistency for whole systems innovation.

Creative Tension Engine

High Concepts in the creative industries have proven their potential to enable collective creativity. Although companies and organizations drive and manage these High Concepts, they breathe imaginative power and they inspire many people to connect and participate. Take the example of Harley Davidson. The lifestyle the brand represents is much more than a corporate reality; it has become part of the identity of their customers.

There is a third type of concept shown in the Concept Continuum, one that is strongly related to High Concept but which is even less regulated and more aspirational. This is the Creative Tension Engine (CTE) in which the concept is specifically designed to ignite collective creativity in order to pursue an aspirational desired future. In simple terms High Concepts are created to fascinate, while CTEs are created to agitate. Where for High Concepts, creativity/inspiration and associative power are *goals* in themselves in order to create the experience, for CTEs creativity becomes a *tool*. CTEs also differ significantly from High Concepts in context, function, desired output and relation to the vision. Let us take a look at each of these aspects now.

Context   CTEs have a different context and much wider scope than High Concepts. Think, for example, of High Concepts such as Nike or Red Bull. These are designed to create unique organizational experiences with and for customers who share the same values. However, they still retain some kind of 'frame work' or context in which they are applied (i.e. the company). CTEs, in contrast, are designed primarily to change systems. They leave a tremendous amount of space for actors to become inspired and involved. Together they work towards the desired and shared vision in multiple co-creative ways. CTEs tend to be focused on aspiration without a clear prescription for how to make it happen. This gives a CTE a much stronger visionary and aspirational power than a High Concept.

Function   The function of the CTEs also differs from a High Concept. CTEs are not used for (organizational) Experience Design but are aimed at innovating complex systems *through* the experience. You have seen this already in the example of the first national park in Chapter 1 and the Family by Family example in Chapter 4. We call these types of concepts CTEs because of the 'imaginative tension' the concept should evoke in the system (Nijs, 2014).

Desired output   High Concepts leave plenty of room for interpretation but are nevertheless carefully monitored to make sure the intended experience is delivered. This is not the case in CTEs. Here the *catalyst effect* towards the shared visionary image is key, rather than the experience itself. The CTE ignites co-creation towards the desired future (vision). This is what makes CTEs fundamentally different from High Concepts.

Vision relation   The Concept Continuum shows that CTEs are low on the scale of regulation and high on the aspiration scale. This makes their relation to vision fundamentally different. High Concepts are somewhat regulated and require some further articulation of the desired future. This is not the case with CTEs. In High Concepts the *how* and the *why* are separate and distinct. CTEs fuse the *how* and the *why* into a single poetic articulation of the vision. It is purely the formulation of the CTE that activates the involvement of all kind of actors in the whole system.

CTEs are therefore instruments that ignite collective creativity in order to pursue aspirational and desired futures. You saw several examples of CTEs in Chapter 1 and you will have noted that these were often spontaneous rather than explicitly designed processes (think for instance of the Slow movement). Only in hindsight do you see the CTE that fueled it all. However, do not underestimate the power of CTEs to truly change (global) systems. There are many examples that have triggered collective creativity and led to entirely new industries and processes emerging. CTEs have had an impact not only in sectors such as health, leisure, gastronomy, holiday, work, and family but they have also had huge psychological, social, technological and economic impact too. There is a great potential for Imagineers to facilitate and design system innovation in the networked world once the power of CTEs is acknowledged (Box 7.5).

BOX 7.5

IMAGINEERING SNAPSHOT: THE CREATIVE TENSION ENGINE OF 'PEACE PARKS' IN SOUTH AFRICA

In 1997 President Nelson Mandela, Prince Bernhard of the Netherlands and Dr. Anton Rupert, a South African philanthropist and visionary, decided to reframe some of the dangerous trans-border areas around South Africa by using the CTE of 'Peace Parks'. The idea is that the border countries in each region manage Peace Parks. The transformation of a dangerous area into a peaceful one calls for many people in the system to change their behavior. In other words, it is a socially 'complex' innovation challenge; one that requires the imagination of actors involved to be triggered through the power of aspirational goals.

It was most probably pure intuition of the founders that led them to believe that the concept of Peace Parks would result in the border regions flourishing. It was hoped that it could bring together inhabitants from the neighboring territories and encourage inter-regional cooperation. One idea was for special education for people from disadvantaged backgrounds to become park rangers and professionals to spark the development of ecotourism.

On the face of it, reframing the name of a region with a 'generative image' such as 'Peace Parks' is a small intervention. Yet the results have been anything but small. The border region improved environmentally, economically and socially. The trans-border populations finally turned the page on civil war and started to cultivate the natural resources in the regions. The generative image of 'Peace Parks' created the conditions in which people could reinterpret their actions in the midst of all kind of actors, local as well as global, and begin to act in a new, collectively desired, direction. It is highly likely that nothing like this would have happened in this direction without the design of this dialogic concept.

Source: Nijs (2014) based on Hammill and Besancon (2007).

The reach of CTEs can be enormous. Their narrative power can travel the world in just a few clicks. They can mobilize a multitude of people to join forces and participate. CTEs can turn imagination into an instrument of mass transformation.

7.3.4 Characteristics of High Concepts and Creative Tension Engines

Powerful High Concepts and CTEs share some essential characteristics. We list ten of the most important ones below. Although they share these characteristics there is a difference in the way they are applied in each case. CTEs have a wider scope than High Concepts. They also have a much more 'open' character, are less directive, more inspirational, more generative and more meaningful with a clear visionary shared outlook.

Powerful High Concepts and CTEs are:

1. **Meaningful**: they should be connected to the vision and *mean something* for those involved. This is linked to a strong value-fit, which we described earlier.
2. **Distinctive**: they should set themselves apart from what already exists. They provide a new, reframed perspective that shakes things up.
3. **Enduring**: they have a long-time span. They go beyond trends and hypes and remain relevant for a long period. The concept of the Olympic Games (Fraternity through Sports) is an enduring working principle that is as relevant today as it was at the end of the 19th century when it was formulated. These types of concepts should last.
4. **Simple**: they are easy to communicate. There should be some simplicity to them, which makes them easy to understand and implement.
5. **Free of discipline**: they are an approach and a formula for how you can deal with things. They are free of discipline and function as a key principle, which can be applied to everything. This characteristic tends to apply only to High Concepts.
6. **Internally and externally relevant**: they are not specifically restricted to any internal organizational boundaries. They are not created for a narrowly defined internal group of people. They activate all those inspired to participate and join forces.
7. **Visionary**: they have a strong visionary character. Although they still deal with *how* to achieve the goal, a clear visionary perspective is present. After all, if the horizon presented to stakeholders is inspiring they are more likely to explore, get involved and to co-create towards that goal (e.g. the 'Peace Parks').
8. **Imaginative**: they speak to the imagination. This is the very essence of Imagineering. The idea and its linguistic translation should ignite associative powers of others and activate them to join forces. You could therefore say that they have some sort of a *contagious* character; once touched many want to be involved.
9. **Generative**: they are generative images, specifically designed to unlock and ignite *collaborative* creativity. Generative Power even goes one step beyond the imaginative power: it 'stretches' possibilities and opens up a *creation space* for others to continue co-creating based on the original working principle, thus multiplying the effect.
10. **Narrative**: they must be formulated in an inspiring way with narrative strength. As humans we use language to interpret the world we live in. If there is no word for it, it does not exist. And words do create worlds, change reality and innovate systems.

The last characteristic is central to Imagineering as value creation in the narrative mode. If you ever doubt the power of an inspiring narrative, consider Mindfulness for a moment. This term has opened up a huge creation space with its own mindset for dealing with the world and daily life. All over the world courses, apps, meals, holidays, training, workshops, etc. have been developed around this recent term. It has become a way of life for millions of people. This is the power of the narrative mode in action.

7.3.5 An instrument for High Concept and CTE design: the Molecule Principle

Now that you have an understanding of High Concepts and CTEs, one question remains: how to create one? Unfortunately, there is neither a magic formula nor any shortcuts. However, the Molecule Principle is a visual tool that you may find helpful in articulating the essence of High Concepts and CTEs.

First, however, you need an understanding of the nature of creativity. New ideas come to life when new connections are made that have not been created before. Arthur Koestler introduced this concept of 'bisociation' in his 1964 book *The Act of Creation*. Bisociation is the 'putting together of two previously unrelated elements through a process of comparison, abstraction and categorization' (Nielsen and Thurber, 2016:51). The ability to bisociate is not an inherited trait. Neurobiologists Benedek, Fink, Grabner and Neubauer have shown that people can actually be successfully trained in divergent thinking and bisociation. Bisociation enables us to create something new, including new working principles that trigger people (i.e. a concept).

The Molecule Principle is based on bisociation. It is an instrument that can be used to both recognize and dissect existing concepts as well as to develop new ones. As the name implies, it is a combination of atoms (essential elements) that together define the core of the matter (i.e. the molecule). For Imagineers the atoms of the Molecule Principle show the essence of the High Concept or CTE.

The Molecule Principle consists of three parts:

1. The **one-liner/title** that summarizes, emotionalizes and inspires through the narrative mode.
2. The **atoms** representing the essential elements that make up the working principle.
3. A **rationale** that further defines and explains the interpretation of the chosen atoms. It is a short narrative that summarizes the essence of the High Concept/CTE. It is a description of the working principle covering not more than half a sheet of A4 paper. Something 'you can hold in your hand', as Steven Spielberg refers to it (Spielberg in Wyatt, 1994:13). And formulation is key, after all, an exemplary term (= atom) such as 'light' can refer to weight, a light source, a mental state or scaled-down version of something. A rationale therefore is a description in more words to shortly explain the interpretation of, as well the relation with other atoms.

You will appreciate that these three parts are simply three different ways of expressing the same thing. They only differ in the prescribed detail. The more words you can use, the more detail you can specify. The less words you use, the more you leave room for interpretation. In a nutshell the Molecule Principle is a formulation in the narrative mode (the one-liner) of the summary (the atoms) of the concept description (the rationale).

The rationale and atoms tend to have an internal focus and as such provide guidelines for an organization and its employees. Hence, they are very useful for High Concepts. The rationale and atoms will help you to find the right balance between prescription and inspiration, between control and emergence, and between articulation and imagination. The one-liner expresses the concept in the narrative mode with the imaginative power to unleash collective creativity. The Nike one-liner 'Just do it' is a great example of a narrative expression of a strong High Concept. Although it represents certain key atoms/elements that define the 'Nike-way', it is this one-liner that speaks to the imagination of many.

The one-liner is the key element for CTEs, since this is part of the Molecule Principle that is focused on awakening external creative power. Its brevity provides room for interpretation. It generates a creation space and inspires actors to become involved in co-creative value creation. You should be aware that the descriptions of the atoms and rationale can sometimes hinder the imaginative possibilities of the one-liner, and therefore the strength of the CTE. On the other hand, they can also help you to make choices on the formulation of the one-liner.

Let us consider Red Bull as an example for the Molecule Principle, since their High Concept approach and working principles are clearly visible in all of their marketing (Figure 7.2). We have interpreted this and come up with the following atoms:

These atoms are the essence of Red Bull and recognizable in everything they do. For instance, all their events and marketing efforts are based on these same key ingredients whether it is Crashed Ice, X-Fighters, Stratos, Air Race or the

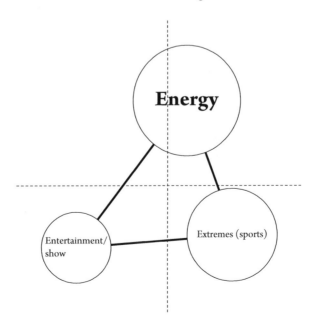

Source: Author interpretation.

Figure 7.2 Atoms of Molecule Principle applied to Red Bull

Formula 1 team. Combined as a molecule they define the 'Red Bull way' of doing things and a unique and recognizable working principle. The one-liner name Red Bull epitomizes and summarizes this essence. The visual image of two red bulls is a symbol of energy.

The Molecule Principle is a useful tool that will help you define the various levels of concept descriptions. It is not, however, a template that can be filled in easily. As an Imagineer you should carefully consider what type of concept you are developing and what level of description (and therefore freedom in interpretation) is needed for your desired outcome. Here are some tips that can help you successfully apply the Molecule Principle:

1. **Search for the right words, the atoms**: understand that words and language determine the imaginative power. Play with the words in order to find the right ones. Use synonyms, explore the richness of the term and do not be satisfied until you have found exactly the right words for what you need.
2. **Select atoms that are principles by themselves.**
3. **Select atoms that speak to the imagination.**
4. **Do not use too many atoms**: strong concepts are easily understood and easily communicated. So keep it simple. Molecules consist ideally of a minimum of two and a maximum of five atoms.
5. **Use the size of atoms to signify importance**: 'energy' is the key atom for the Red Bull molecule and is therefore the largest. The others further strengthen the molecule and give additional interpretations.
6. **Find inspiration in other areas**: successful Imagineering is based on creating new connections, most especially in the narrative mode. Literature, poetry, movies or song titles can certainly inspire you to associate freely, but other creative industries such as design and architecture can do so as well. Nature can also be a good source of new connections. Think of biomimicry for instance.
7. **Use values (e.g. brand essence or core values)**: a concept becomes much stronger when it represents truth or meaning.

References

Burning Man. (1989–2018). At: http://www.burningman.com (accessed July 22, 2018).

Collins, J., and Porras, J. (1994). *Built to last: Successful habits of visionary companies*, New York: HarperCollins Publishers.

Geursen, S. (1994). *Virtuele Tomaten en Conceptuele Pindakaas: Hoe interactiviteit, zelforganisatie en bewustzijnsverruiming de marketing op z'n kop zetten*, Deventer: Kluwer Bedrijfswetenschappen.

Hammill, A., and Besancon, C. (2007). Measuring peace park performance: Definitions and experiences. In: Ali, S.H., Hammill, A., Besançon, C., Lejano, R., Duffy, R., et al. (eds.) *Peace parks: Conservation and conflict resolution*. Cambridge, MA: MIT Press, pp. 23–39.

Nielsen, D., and Thurber, S. (2016). *The secret of the highly creative thinker*, Amsterdam: BIS.

Nijs, D. (2014). *Imagineering – the butterfly effect*, Den Haag: Eleven International Publishing.

Nike. (2018). About Nike. At: https://about.nike.com/ (accessed July 22, 2018).

Oregon Live. (2017, January 29). Nike CEO condemns Trump refugee ban as threat to values. At: https://www.oregonlive.com/business/index.ssf/2017/01/nike_condemns_trump_ban_on_ref.html (accessed March 31, 2017).

Roberts, K. (2006). *Lovemarks: The future beyond brands*, New York: Powerhouse Books.

Senge, P. M. (1990). *The fifth discipline: The art and science of the learning organization*, New York: Currency Doubleday.

Senge, P. M. (2014). *The fifth discipline fieldbook: Strategies and tools for building a learning organization*, London: Crown Business.

Senge, P. M., Hamilton, H., and Kania, J. (2015). The dawn of system leadership. *Stanford Social Innovation Review, 13*(1), 27–33.

Sinek, S. (2009). *Start with why: How great leaders inspire everyone to take action*, London: Portfolio Penguin.

Starbucks. (2018). Our mission. At: https://www.starbucks.com/about-us/company-information/mission-statement (accessed July 22, 2018).

Van der Loo, H., Geelhoed, J., and Samhoud, S. (2007). *Kus de Visie Wakker: organisaties energiek en effectief maken*, Den Haag: Sdu Uitgevers bv.

Virgin. (2018). Our brand. At: https://www.virgin.com/virgingroup/content/our-brand-0 (accessed July 22, 2018).

Volvo. (2018a). About Volvo cars. At: https://group.volvocars.com/company (accessed July 22, 2018).

Volvo. (2018b). Aiming for zero. At: https://group.volvocars.com/company/vision (accessed July 22, 2018).

Wikipedia. (n.d.). Burning Man. At: https://en.wikipedia.org/wiki/Burning_Man (accessed July 22, 2018).

Wyatt, J. (1994). *High Concept: Movies and marketing in Hollywood*, Austin, TX: University of Texas Press.

8

D-eveloping: how to deal with the challenge of making it real and involving others

Geoff Marée

8.1   Balancing the development act

You will have seen from the previous chapters that Imagineering is all about stimulating emergent change to make things better. The word *emergent* here is key. The Imagineering development process evolves as it proceeds and thus it demands flexibility and adaptability from you as an Imagineer. It helps if you see yourself as a facilitator of innovation engaged in a complex challenge, rather than as a problem solver or troubleshooter. The change is realized in Imagineering by engaging the people involved and inspiring them to act. Thus, every step in the Imagineering process must be made real for them. As an Imagineer, you will need to be able to shape ideas and concepts into real, meaningful experiences. But there is more. The emergent nature of Imagineering means that everyone involved should feel inspired to act and be able to build on the ideas and concepts as they develop. The Imagineer facilitates the emergence through a continuous development process of iteration, repetition and refining. This chapter focuses on the creative skills you will need to manage the development process towards real and meaningful experiences.

8.2   The creative process

Creativity is the ability to come up with something new and valuable and it is a key skill for Imagineering. Let us explore how creativity works.

Here is a little experiment for you to try when you are next with a group of people: ask who among them would consider themselves to be a creative person. Most of the time you will find that only about 20 percent of the group will raise their hand. Yet we use creativity every day. It takes creativity to do grocery shopping on a tight budget, for instance. And we surely use creativity to organize a birthday party for a friend or family member. It is a common misunderstanding that creativity can be found only in works of art and that you have to be a very talented person to be creative. This led Mihály Csíkszentmihályi (1996) to introduce "Creativity with a capital C" to describe creation of exceptional quality, leaving space for all the other types of creativity for the rest of us. Some experts even say that creativity is an essential aspect of what makes us human. If this is the case why do so many of us feel that we lack the magical skill of creativity?

Ken Robinson, known for his famous TED talk in 2006, "Do schools kill creativity?", answers his rhetorical question with a sad "yes". He maintains that the main aims of education today are to reproduce knowledge and develop rational reasoning (Robinson and Aronica, 2015). Tom and David Kelley, the cofounders of design company IDEO, note in their book *Creative Confidence* (2013) that most of us lose our childlike perspective as we grow up. They go on to argue that in many cases we need that childlike combination of spontaneity and naivety to be able to combine apparently unrelated ideas into new creative solutions. We referred to this phenomenon as "bisociation" in Chapter 7. Our attempts to find new solutions often lead to a dead-end; creativity is a risky road. As a critical, rational, grown-up we tend to want to avoid repeating fruitless experiences. A child, on the other hand, does not see the outcome as the most important part; instead they enjoy the journey towards the outcome, playing with all the possibilities that turn up along the way. They do not feel the same disappointment or embarrassment at an unsuccessful outcome. It is this playful, carefree approach that we tend to lose as we grow up. The lesson that the child teaches is that to be creative we should focus on the *process* of trying out new ideas, instead of focusing on the *outcome*.

There is more to creativity, however. Tina Seelig, a Professor at Stanford University, introduced the "Innovation Engine" in her book *InGenius* (2012). This model describes three inner qualities (Attitude, Imagination and Knowledge) and three contextual requirements (Culture, Habitat and Resources) that are needed for the creative process (Figure 8.1).

The qualities and requirements are intra- and inter-connected and together they weave through the entire creative process. A creative culture can stimulate the right attitude towards creativity for example. The habitat (environment) that we find ourselves in can stimulate our imagination (or not!). And the right resources can help us gain the knowledge we need to drive a creative process.

So how do you build your creative qualities? It all starts with awareness. The moment you make creativity a significant part of your work or your life, you will

Source: Seelig (2012).
Reproduced with permission.

Figure 8.1 The Innovation Engine

BOX 8.1

IMAGINEERING SNAPSHOT: EL BULLI

Restaurant El Bulli in Rosas in Spain was voted the number one restaurant in the world five times in the period 2002 to 2009. Head chef, Ferran Adrià, was creator of the famous dishes and more than anyone else he championed "molecular cuisine" in the world. He changed the way Spanish cooking was perceived. He knew that if they were to create a new type of restaurant he had to inspire his team to think beyond the traditional way of doing things and to become a creative team. He wanted his kitchen staff to think about creativity rather than be focused only on serving meals. In 1994 he renamed his team "the Development Squad" (El Bulli, 2011). He made it possible for his staff to consider the creative process as their main responsibility. He facilitated the circumstances for them to come up with pioneering new concepts and techniques. They would not have engaged so successfully without the conscious reframing of their role.

---

begin to perceive the whole thing differently. And often you can achieve this with a simple change of words (Box 8.1).

Awareness also supports the right attitude. You need to be curious and persistent if you want to come up with something new. You need curiosity to help you continually focus on what else is possible, to open yourself up to new information. Curiosity not only helps you prepare for ideation but also supports you throughout the innovation process. You need persistence to make ideas happen. The creative process will often be frustrating and persistence helps you to make it through to the end. Innovation requires a certain dogged determination not to give up despite frequent setbacks. Persistence also helps you to overcome critical attitudes towards new ideas (and that goes for both your own critical view as the one of others). Alf Rehn (2011) notes that too many books on creativity forget to mention that introducing new ideas or new ways of doing things can be experienced as dangerous or threatening by others. Innovation demands that people adapt to something new and that can make them feel insecure. Persistence will give you the energy to overcome their fears.

Imagination and knowledge are the drivers of the generative process towards alternative solutions. Your power of imagination to envision possibilities is based on your deep understanding and knowledge of the challenges that you face. Inspiration for new ideas can come from similar situations in related habitats (environments) that you can copy. You can also dig deep into your memories to look for possible solutions. As you read this you are probably thinking: "Copy? Should I not be original to be creative?" The answer is yes and no! It depends. It is impossible not to take the past with you. All your creative ideas will be based in some way on your previous experiences. You will be familiar with the well-known quote often attributed to Isaac Newton: "if I have seen further than others, it is by standing upon the shoulders of giants". You can only do what you do thanks to the work that has been done before you; you create by building on previous creations. Austin Kleon became well known with his book *Steal like an Artist* (2015) that builds on this concept. He maintains that you should copy but only when you observe the following rules: (1) honor the original work, don't degrade it; (2) study it carefully, don't just skim through it; (3) "steal" from many sources, not just one; (4) give your sources credit, don't plagiarize; (5) transform, don't imitate; and finally (6) remix, don't rip off. In the context of Imagineering you can read "remix" as "bisociate".

A final important insight about the creative process is that you should start with a thorough understanding of the problem or challenge, but that the phase of creating ideas should not focus on the problem. Ideation is a playful process of creating solutions and it should be protected from ending too quickly. You will find that an inviting trigger question will ensure that the process is playful. The trigger question should relate to the problem or challenge, but should be open-ended. It should not be closed or restrictive suggesting just one "answer". It should leave room for many different solutions to emerge. It should also be fun and interesting to work on so that you do not get bored and give up quickly. You will find that most of the time, a question that starts with "How . . ." is the most effective. A "how" question invites you to generate a large number of possible solutions, it invites *divergence*. Later on in the process when you want to move towards the optimal solution, you will *converge* your thinking. The CEO of IDEO Tim Brown (2009) puts it this way: first you want to create choice, so that later on you have a choice.

You need to understand what you are aiming for before you can choose the best option. In the context of Imagineering the aim is meaningful experiences.

8.3 The meaningful experience

Joseph Pine II and James Gilmore (1999) discovered that it was helpful to distinguish between various types of experiences. They asked themselves what dimensions can be observed in the experiences. They found that one dimension was the degree to which the experiencer participates actively in the experience. Some experiences, like playing in a football game, require intense participation. Other experiences, like watching TV, can be done in a much more passive way. You can all imagine that this makes a difference to the experience. Another dimension they defined was based on how immersive the experience is. Watching an elephant in the jungle is a different experience from reading a book that describes the behavior of elephants. When you read about the elephant, you tend to absorb the information. When you enter the elephant's habitat, you feel immersed in the experience.

They combined these two dimensions in order to characterize four types of experiences, or as they call them: "realms of experience". Each realm represents a recognizable feeling everyone can relate to: Entertaining, Educational, Esthetic and Escapist. Passive participation while absorbing information is Entertainment. If the activity level is increased, the experience becomes more Educational. A passive yet immersive experience is Esthetic. Combining immersion with active participation results in an Escapist experience. Pine and Gilmore suggest that a fulfilling concept is one that has a balanced combination of all four realms: the experience "sweet spot" (Figure 8.2).

Source: Based on the model in
Pine and Gilmore (1999).

Figure 8.2 Four
realms of experience

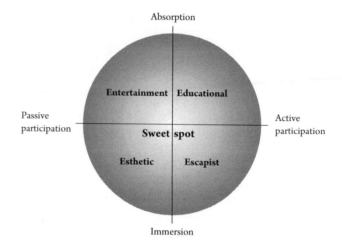

This model can help you think about the experience type (or types) that would be most helpful in your analysis. For instance, you can use the model to help you design a creative session; one in which the participants move between different realms of experience in order to keep them engaged.

Indeed, the Escapist realm can be compared to the state of Flow as described by Csíkszentmihályi (1990, 2003). Flow is when you are challenged to a degree that matches your level of skill. If your challenge is greater than your skill, you will likely become frustrated. If your skill is greater than the challenge, you will probably become bored. Flow is the optimal experience between frustration and boredom. You lose sense of time (and sometimes also place), you are focused and in control, and you are able to develop your skills. This is very similar to the description of the Escapist realm by Pine and Gilmore. Csíkszentmihályi also argues that the enjoyment of an experience depends on increasing complexity. Thus, Flow can be seen as an important indicator for meaningful experiences.

Pine and Gilmore consider experience as something that happens within yourself. However, they also highlight how a focus on experience can help organizations and even society to become more effective and meaningful. John Falk and Lynn Dierking are two more authors who have spent a long time trying to understand, evaluate and influence interactive experiences.

8.4   Influencing the interactive experience

In their book *The Museum Experience Revisited* Falk and Dierking (2012) look back at their groundbreaking book *The Museum Experience*, which was published two decades earlier in 1992. One of the features of the earlier book was the "Interactive Experience Model", which illustrates the three key contexts that influence an interactive experience (Figure 8.3).

This model leads to the three questions you should always ask when trying to analyze or create a specific experience:

Source: Based on the model in
Falk and Dierking (1992).

Figure 8.3 The
Interactive Experience
Model

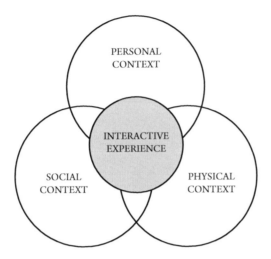

1. Who is involved in the experience?
2. In what type of environment does the experience take place?
3. Who are the others who participate in the experience in some way?

If you can answer these three questions, you will have a good picture of the impact of the experience in question.

The first question explores the influence of personal characteristics on the experience. You need to understand the background, motivation, interests, needs, intentions and previous experiences of the person involved. The more you know about them, the better you can predict how they will respond to the experience and the better able you are to tailor the experience to them. This is what the Personal Context is all about.

However, you also need to know how the physical aspects of the environment influence the experience. All sorts of physical features are relevant here. Just think of the smell of freshly baked bread at a bakery. Or how a perfect view of the stage in a concert creates a VIP-feeling. Or consider that a restaurant can influence the time a guest wants to spend there, just by choosing more or less comfortable chairs. Another interesting example is the architecture of the new wing of the Jewish Museum in Berlin, designed by Daniel Libeskind. It is intended to make the visitor feel uneasy and disoriented in order to illustrate Jewish history. There is, of course, a famous example from literature too: Marcel Proust writes in À la recherche du temps perdu of the smell of a madeleine cake that brought back strong childhood memories. Sensory elements, such as visual cues or sounds, can have a very strong effect on your experience. This is the Physical Context.

Finally, it is clear that other people influence your experience as well. Are you alone or in a crowd, with friends or a loved one? All of these situations influence your experience. You are probably happy to go to a theme park with your friends or family, but being in a large crowd could negatively affect your experience: think of those long queues, the noise, feeling a bit panicky. Or imagine a romantic dinner for two in a restaurant where the table next to yours has a group of overly enthusiastic students celebrating their diplomas with loud singing. On the other hand, you might feel very strange if you and your two friends are the only guests at a dance event. All these are examples of the Social Context.

This model is an excellent tool for you to analyze an experience that has already taken place. It is perhaps even more useful as a tool for you to design new experiences.

Falk and Dierking believe that this model is still valid more than 20 years since they first proposed it. The only adjustment they suggest is to rename the Social Context as the Sociocultural Context. They note in their follow-up book that since their first book the literature on how to understand experiences has grown greatly. Although they developed their theory based on the experiences of visitors to a museum, subsequent work has shown that their approach is applicable to other environments such as theme parks, shopping malls, special events, and so on. Nevertheless, the model does have one shortcoming in that it describes only a snapshot view of an experience. Falk and Dierking acknowledge that experiences take place over time and that it is important to look into the situation *before* and *after* an experience. The *before* and *after* also influence the effect of an experience itself and the memories that stay with you afterwards.

Adding the dimension of time to the Interactive Experience Model turns it into the "Contextual Model of Learning" (Falk and Dierking, 2000). The process of learning from each experience helps you develop a personal understanding of the world. Moreover, each experience gives you added meaning time and time again. Understanding this process in terms of the three contexts can help you become a more effective designer of meaningful interactive experiences.

Finally, there is one more aspect of interactive experiences that can help you as an Imagineer and that is *participation*. Susanne Piët (2006) argues that there is a causal relationship between participation and how meaningful you think an experience is. She uses a counter-example to illustrate this. She observes that consumers who try to find fulfillment by zapping through entertainment will often be disappointed by the experience. This should not be surprising to you. Remember the Escapist realm that combines immersion with active participation and how it is related to Flow. If you can stimulate people to become part of a process to improve their current situation, it is much more likely that it will be meaningful to them. It is part of your role as an Imagineer to help the participants work together to co-create meaningful experiences (Box 8.2). The next chapter will go into this in more detail.

8.5   The customer journey

It is often something intangible like a service that leads to a great experience, but how can you describe a service in the real world?

Let us start with the time-aspect that Falk and Dierking introduced into their experience model. You can then begin to think of a service process as a series of short experiences. Some of these experiences involve an interaction between the user or customer (or experiencer) and the service. These are commonly known

---

BOX 8.2

IMAGINEERING SNAPSHOT: THE CONSTELLATION

The Constellation was the name given in 2004 to a spin-off organization from the United Nations AIDS reduction program (UNAIDS). One of the experts involved in UNAIDS, Jean Louis Lamboray, recounts (2016) how the Constellation came about. He discovered that facilitating local communities to solve the AIDS problem using their strengths worked much better than copy/pasting the standard UN methodology of an injection of cash. The Constellation team does not arrive with money. It comes with an appreciative method of tapping into the community to help them discover how to work things out. In this way, they have been successful in many regions and the number of participants in the worldwide Constellation community is growing daily. An example of this type of approach is the switch by a notorious drugs-criminal in Papua New Guinea into a distributer of medicine using his skills in a positive manner and restoring his respect in the local community. The philosophy of this approach is to act only as catalysts for the process and to leave as much as possible of the solution to the participating stakeholders.

---

as "touchpoints". An example of a touchpoint would be the waiting time at a hospital, or a picture of your rollercoaster ride, or the moment you show your ticket at the entrance gate of an event and so on.

The overall experience is then a series of sequential steps with some touchpoints along the way. This process is commonly referred to as a Customer Journey or sometimes a Guest Journey. Take, for instance, a visit to a museum. Your Journey will likely start with planning your visit, followed by actually travelling to the museum, entering, then perhaps taking part in some exhibition-related activities, then maybe having lunch or taking a break for coffee. Finally, you depart and return home. You could map this Journey on a timeline and it becomes a sort of visualization of the storyline of your visit to the museum. Cutting the whole experience into smaller parts allows you to look more closely into each individual activity and how they make the user or customer feel. For each step and for each touchpoint, we can check what we know about the three contexts of Falk and Dierking and how they influence the user/customer.

Marc Stickdorn and Jacob Schneider describe a set of tools for service design in their book *This is Service Design Thinking*. One of the most important of these is the Customer Journey Canvas (Stickdorn and Schneider, 2010). The Canvas allows you to sketch the *before*, the *during* and the *after* experience of a service encounter and to note how the touchpoints have worked out. Having analyzed the experience in this way, you can develop a timeline that relates the touchpoints to the organization using a Service Blueprint. The Blueprint identifies the User Interaction (what the user sees, hears, smells, feels, does), the Frontstage (the visible part of the service organization) and the Backstage (the part that is invisible to the user). In this way the journey can be related to the *how* and the *what* you need to get right in order to deliver a superior customer experience.

8.6   Scenarios

The Customer Journey Canvas helps you imagine the ways you can create a meaningful experience for the customers or users. Scenarios are an excellent way for you to dig deeper and to gain an insight into the variety of experiences that could occur. Scenarios are detailed descriptions of possible interaction processes. Some scenarios describe desirable situations and some describe those that should be avoided. For example, a pair of scissors should be sharp enough to cut paper easily, but not too sharp so that it would injure the user. Scenarios help you generate a check-list of demands you need to live up to as you develop the experience further (Box 8.3).

One of the pitfalls in writing scenarios is that you write them from your own perspective describing your own needs, values and expectations. This pitfall was recognized in the early days of software development. Software developers had such a deep knowledge of the use of digital hardware that they found it hard to imagine how the average non-technical user might behave when faced with the new products. The result was that the user experience (or "UX" as it is referred to by developers) they created did not fit the perspective of the average user. Alan Cooper described a solution to this problem in his 1999 book *The Inmates are Running the Asylum*. He had the developers create imaginary descriptions of people who would need to be able to use their software. He called these descriptions "Personas". Having created the Personas, the developers would then build software to match their needs, expectations and technical abilities. Since then the concept of Personas has also been integrated into service design. You can create Personas from research that empathizes with the user. You should always write your scenarios with the relevant Personas in mind.

BOX 8.3

IMAGINEERING SNAPSHOT: RITZ-CARLTON

Ritz-Carlton is a hotel chain that puts a great deal of effort into delivering high-quality service. Their motto is "Ladies and Gentlemen serving Ladies and Gentlemen". They use a design concept they called "Scenography" in order to raise their service to the level that they aim for. Michelli (2008) describes the Gold Standard of Ritz-Carlton and explains how scenarios of the intended experiences lead the way when they develop their hotels. Ritz-Carlton asked the design company IDEO to facilitate "an experience culture to scale across all of the fifty luxury hotels in the Ritz portfolio" (Brown, 2009:122). Brown, the CEO and president of IDEO, describes this Scenography-method that they introduced as two phases. In the first phase general managers of the hotels were asked to create inspirational examples of their view on great experience culture. They used visual language like scenes, props and photography. The second phase offered them the option to pick from the imagined scenarios and create scenes that related to their own locations. In this way they told "a story through an experience" (Brown, 2009:123). IDEO learned from this scenography process that it is important to facilitate the transformation of the culture of an organization and that empowering employees to seize opportunities is essential in the process.

Creating multiple scenarios is easier said than done. If you have a rich imagination, you might come up with too many different stories. How do you know when enough is enough? Fortunately, you will find after a while that even though the scenarios are different, the effect they have on the list of demands diminishes. In other words, they become variations on a theme rather than entirely new themes. At the point you reach saturation of demands you can safely say that you have done enough. It is time then to start connecting the dots and describe the experience in a more detailed manner by determining the building blocks. Can you ever be certain you have captured all the scenarios and demands? Unfortunately not; there may always be effects that you overlook and have not predicted. This is one reason why it is recommended that the development process is iterative. When you retake steps several times over, you will find that your insight deepens and progresses; the chance that you miss something important decreases too. It is also advisable to create a way to test situations in order to compare theory with practice. This is where prototyping can help.

8.7 Prototyping and iteration

Most managerial books describe successful strategies and they often make for interesting reading. However, for each success story there are many more untold stories about failures. A book on failures would probably be an even better read and you would likely learn more. Indeed an oft-repeated mantra in the hotbed of innovation that is Silicon Valley is "fail fast, learn faster". It is, of course, less attractive to fail when a new product has been launched on the market and a large investment already made. Thus, it makes sense to create test situations before product launch. This is prototyping. Prototypes can also be used early on in the creative process to create deeper insights into possible solutions. In fact, you will find that prototypes are a crucial element throughout the development phase.

Prototypes allow you to fail safely and to learn from it. A prototype is usually some form of tangible representation of the new situation or experience that you want. You test the prototype to see if it has the effect you were aiming for. Your observations of how the testing goes reveal information that can help you improve your design or your plan. It is likely that you will need more than one prototype and more than one test to get the desired results. Indeed, you will find that iteration is especially important for prototyping. One helpful side effect of prototyping is that it can further unlock your creativity. New ideas that would otherwise not have occurred to you pop into your head when you are confronted with tangible results of your imagination. It follows that prototypes can be used as a part of both a divergent process and a convergent process. In other words, prototypes can help you come up with even more ideas, but they can also help you select or combine ideas (Box 8.4).

Prototypes not only give you feedback on how useful something is, they can also prepare users and customers for future development. Think about the concept cars that you see at the large automotive fairs. The big brands offer the

---

BOX 8.4

IMAGINEERING SNAPSHOT: ALESSI

Alessi is a third-generation family-owned company in Italy that produces kitchen and house-hold equipment with an ambitious level of design. The company has a very interesting philosophy on failure. They aim for design that is "on the edge". Their products stand out as examples of how world-renowned designers experiment with the constraints of func-tion and meaning. In order to stay on the edge, CEO Alberto Alessi formulated a strategic driver to aim for "one, possibly two, fiascoes per year" (Wylie, 2001). They gain on several levels from this. To start with, they argue that how else would they know if they are indeed operating on the edge, if they did not cross that line every now and then? This is how they measure their ambition in design. In addition, this driver offers a safe environment for their designers to experiment in. The designer does not lose face when the product does not work out because it simply confirms that Alessi is still on the edge. The famous French designer Philippe Starck delivered a big hit for them with his iconic citrus juicer but before this he had designed a thermos can that had production problems. If Alessi had responded negatively to the thermos can design, they might have missed out on what has become one of their most famous products.

---

audience a sneak preview of features that are still years away from production. They are looking not only for feedback on these features but also to prepare future customers for what is to come and to set expectations. This is especially interesting for the Imagineering process, where we aim to inspire emerging improvements. Prototypes can ignite stakeholders in the same way as a narrative or a generative image does.

3D printing has revolutionized the prototyping of physical products: manu-facturers can now produce single versions of an industrial product cheaply and easily. Creating a prototype for an experience or a service, however, requires some extra creativity. The key is to ask yourself what questions you need to have answered in order to make the improvements you want. You then create prototypes to help you answer these questions. As a result, your prototype might sometimes be very different from the final concept you have in mind, since it is created to answer one question along the way.

Prototypes can often be quite rough and ready. Cardboard cutouts or just some tables and chairs in a certain position can be enough to do the trick. Fortunately, most people are gifted with enough imagination to interpret simu-lated situations as real enough. All you have to do is support them through the process. Remember, too, that prototypes may well stimulate people to come up with suggestions you would have never thought of yourself. This is something that is very important for the Imagineering process.

On the other hand prototypes can also be very close to the real thing. If you are close to your final concept, you might want to create a prototype that simu-lates the desired experience as if everything is already up and running. It could pilot your plans before the real launch.

8.8   Get others involved

The moment you decide that you have created something that is ready for others to hopefully experience as meaningful you must move to the next step in the process. You must surrender your control of the experience design and leave it to others to actually make it meaningful. This does not mean that your work is over nor that the interesting part is finished – quite the reverse is true.

It is inspiring, for example, to see how "Meatless Monday" in the United States (which was launched in 2003) and "Meat Free Monday" (initiated by Paul McCartney in the UK in 2009) have led to numerous creative initiatives by many other individuals and organizations. The goal is co-creative participation in the evolution towards improvement and innovation. As an Imagineer, you are back in facilitation mode, acting as a catalyst in the process to enable those involved to interact and inspire. More about this in the next chapter.

References

Brown, T. (2009). *Change by design: How design thinking transforms organizations and inspires innovation.* New York: Harper Collins Publishers.

Cooper, A. (1999). *The inmates are running the asylum: Why high tech products drive us crazy and how to restore the sanity.* Indiana: Sams Publishing.

Csíkszentmihályi, M. (1990). *Flow: The psychology of optimal experience.* New York: HarperCollins Publishers.

Csíkszentmihályi, M. (1996). *Creativity: The psychology of discovery and invention.* New York: HarperCollins Publishers.

Csíkszentmihályi, M. (2003). *Good business: Leadership, flow, and the making of meaning.* New York: Viking.

El Bulli. (2011). *1994. The birth of the concept of the creative team.* Retrieved from http://www.elbulli.com/historia/index.php?lang=en&seccion=4 (accessed October 7, 2018).

Falk, J. H., and Dierking, L. D. (1992). *The museum experience.* Washington, DC: Whalesback Books.

Falk, J. H., and Dierking, L. D. (2000). *Learning from museums: Visitor experiences and the making of meaning.* Plymouth: Altamira Press.

Falk J. H., and Dierking, L. D. (2012). *The museum experience revisited.* New York: Routledge.

Kelley, T., and Kelley, D. (2013). *Creative confidence: Unleashing the creative potential within us all.* New York: Crown Business.

Kleon, A. (2015). *Steal like an artist: A notebook for creative kleptomaniacs.* New York: Workman Publishing.

Lamboray, J. (2016). *What makes us human? The story of a shared dream.* Bloomington: Balboa Press.

Michelli, J. (2008). *The new Gold Standard: 5 leadership principles for creating a legendary customer experience courtesy of The Ritz-Carlton Hotel Company.* New York, Chicago, San Francisco: McGraw-Hill Professional Publishing.

Piët, S. (2006). *The Emocode: Designing branded personalities and bringing them to life.* Amsterdam: Pearson Education Benelux.

Pine, B., II, and Gilmore, J. (1999). *The experience economy: Work is theater & every business is a stage.* Boston, MA: Harvard Business Press.

Rehn, A. (2011). *Dangerous ideas: When provocative thinking becomes your most valuable asset.* Singapore: Marshall Cavendish Business.

Robinson, K., and Aronica, L. (2015). *Creative schools: The grassroots revolution that's transforming education.* New York: Viking Penguin.

Seelig, T. (2012). *InGenius: A crash course in creativity.* New York: HarperCollins.

Stickdorn, M., and Schneider, J. (2010). *This is service design thinking.* Amsterdam: BIS Publishers.

Wylie, I. (2001). Failure is glorious. *Fast Company Daily Newsletter.* Retrieved from http://www.fastcompany.com/43877/failure-glorious (accessed October 7, 2018).

9

E-nabling: how to enable co-creation

Angelica van Dam

9.1   Introduction

In the E-nabling step it is time for you as an Imagineer to arrange for the stakeholders to interact with one another and to co-create. It is more than simply interacting, however. You need to establish a creation space that allows the emergence of new combinations and new interactions, just as Nike Plus did (Box 9.1). This creation space is also called 'a platform'. It is important nowadays to think in terms of platforms rather than products. Platforms enable communities to engage and unite around a High Concept or a Creative Tension Engine. In this way, you can tap into the imagination of everyone allowing new opportunities to arise.

Platforms like Nike Plus are conquering the world. You probably know more of them than you think. Twitter, Facebook, YouTube, Instagram, and WhatsApp are all platforms. So are places where the sharing economy has influence, for example app stores, Airbnb and Uber. These platforms enable people to share valuable services and experiences ranging from a taxi or renting a room in someone's home to posting a selfie during your holiday. The common factor is that sharing is at the heart of all of them.

Interactions between consumers and/or between consumers and producers are essential for all platforms. It is noteworthy that the boundaries between consumer and producer are blurring; we are more often either adopting both roles or effortlessly switching between them.

The E-nabling step in the Imagineering process is all about co-creation and involvement using a platform. The platform sets the stage, both digitally and physically, for the generation of a new reality through inspiring interactions. This leads to collective creativity from which new actions can emerge. You will have realized by now that the boundaries between the Imagineering A–B–C–D–E–F steps are not always clear. Moreover, facilitating interactions and co-creation is key for every step. You should not be surprised if you have already come up with ideas and a design for your platform in the preceding D-eveloping step. In that case, the E-nabling step serves the purpose of refining your designs and plans.

Platforms are revolutionary because they are associated with new markets

---

BOX 9.1

IMAGINEERING SNAPSHOT: NIKE PLUS

In 2006 Nike introduced the Nike Plus platform based on the High Concept of 'Get connected to your running experiences'. It consisted of a sensor that fitted in a running shoe and an iPod carried by the runner. The system collected and stored data such as the elapsed time of the run, the distance traveled, the pace and the calories burned by the individual. After every run you could upload your own running experience to the website and share it with a wider community of runners. You could monitor your own progress and share it with friends. You could also contact other runners to find people to run with or to discover when running events were being organized. The smart shoe sensor was an indispensable part of the platform. It connected the offline and online interactions, and enabled connections between individuals and between individuals and the community. Through the platform Nike was able to multiply the ways in which individuals could influence their running experience. It also inspired the development of new domains and products, for instance the Nike Run Reporter platform, the wear testing platform (for testing out new shoes) and the voiceover of Olympic athletes on your iPod who monitored your progress. This made it possible to tap new sources of potential users for co-creation inside the greater ecosystem.

In short, Nike Plus became a platform that facilitated the creation of value for all the stakeholders. It integrated itself into the daily lives of individuals and groups. Close relationships were established and trust between people was built. In addition, Nike gained a profound understanding of their users' values and needs. This allowed Nike to generate new ideas more rapidly and to repeatedly refresh the co-creative opportunities. Nike no longer sees itself as a seller of products but as a driver of social change where sport acts as a means to an end rather than an end in itself.

---

and new rules; consequently, they change the current way of working and thinking. We touched upon this in the first part of this book and it is high time that we explore this phenomenon in more detail.

9.2   Platformization

9.2.1   Definitions

There are a lot of definitions of platforms but central to all of them is the notion of an interactive environment for interlinked stakeholders where co-creation is enabled and value creation is the objective.

Platforms are not islands; they are part of an ecosystem of interconnected platforms. This kind of ecosystem is having more and more influence on the way that social and economic interactions are organized in society. Van Dijck et al. (2016) refer to this trend as platformization. The dynamic of the platform can be a guiding force in society and have a significant influence on public values.

Platforms are penetrating our society at a breathtaking rate today and changing our traditional ways of thinking. Moreover, knowledge and skills can be mobilized very quickly with the result that new players can cleverly position themselves in the market in a short space of time. The upshot is that the number of players in a market is growing exponentially and that the emphasis is on social interactions rather than more traditional differentiators such as price. In addition, platforms enable every individual to organize and profile themselves in new ways without needing interventions from private or public bodies. If you want to be able to stay afloat in this uninterrupted stream of changes, you need bravery and creativity, you need to embrace continuous learning and be ready to experiment freely.

9.2.2 Different types of platform

A distinction can be made between different types of online platform (Van Dijck et al., 2016), which largely holds true for offline platforms as well:

- **Platforms with a profit motive** such as Facebook, Google and Amazon. They form a complex ecosystem in which all kinds of commercial parties are involved. As regards offline you can think of the Build-A-Bear Workshop, for example, where you can create your own personalized soft toy.
- **Neighbourhood platforms**, for example Nextdoor, which is operated by a cooperative of members of the public and users.
- **Crowdfunding platforms** are platforms whose development has been funded by external parties and in some cases through government grants. These are primarily online.
- **Platforms developed by government agencies**. SynAthina, winner of the Eurocities Award, encourages residents to improve their quality of life and to extend the democratic process. Members of the public and groups of initiative takers can post activities and ideas on the platform via a website such as Twitter, Facebook or Pinterest.

9.3 Online or offline

Although the exponential growth in platforms has largely occurred online, it is perfectly possible to create an offline platform. Indeed offline platforms can intensify the sharing experience. We are familiar with offline platforms because people have been trading goods and services for centuries. Charity shops and car boot sales are still very popular despite the rise of online platforms. However, the reach of the internet is so much greater that in many cases online platforms have become more interesting than offline ones. Cross channelling, in which several interrelated channels are used, is becoming increasingly important. You can think of focus groups, meeting places and live events that have online components added to them. An offline platform can sometimes be more inclusive than an online one. More and more cities and local authorities are becoming convinced that a bottom-up process, in which local participation and cooperation are enabled, is an effective way to make and implement policy. The key feature of all platforms, whether online or offline, is the interaction between all the stakeholders that engenders a rich experience which creates value.

You will need to choose between online, offline or a combination of the two (see Box 9.2) for your platform. You will need to choose what fits best with the target group, desired direction, vision, and the Creative Tension Engine or High Concept chosen.

The case in Box 9.2 clearly shows the emergent, joined-up process that the generative image of SEATS2MEET (S2M) has set in motion. It inspired the collective creativity of the participants, which led to a creation space in which many actors in the system were enabled to orchestrate a new reality. Using poetic language changed mindsets and behaviour and new initiatives could emerge. This expanded the capacity of the whole system.

You might want to reflect on the differences in approach between Nike Plus and S2M. Nike are and remain the main orchestrators of their process. In contrast, S2M offers more space for self-organizing activities; they let the system take over by making use of the creative human interactions.

9.4 Platforms versus engagement platforms

We have included a number of examples of platforms in this chapter so that you can have a better understanding of them. You might be asking yourself whether all platforms are automatically Imagineering environments. The answer to this question is a resounding no! We want to do more with Imagineering than simply bringing supply and demand together. We want to add value and bring about change by inspiring people to embark on collective creativity. You have seen from the first part of this book that it is essential to design for emergence in times of complexity. Engagement is crucial to achieving this.

Vargo and Lusch introduced the term service dominant (SD) logic into the marketing literature in 2004. They offered a new perspective on relationships and interactions between organizations and their customers. It is clear from their articles on the topic that engagement is not the same as participation or involvement. People who are engaged are in a special psychological condition that is created by interactive, relational and co-creative experiences in networks. Engagement leads in turn to loyalty, long-term relationships and value creation. Engagement creates the ideal breeding ground for ambassadors as you saw in the S2M case. Accordingly, we call the outcome of the E-nabling step in the Imagineering process an 'engagement platform'.

9.4.1 ACTIVE: criteria for engagement platforms

The ACTIVE model (van Dam and Ouwens, 2015) can be used as a starting point for constructing and evaluating a platform. The letters ACTIVE stand for the following criteria: Appreciative, Co-creative, Transformative, Imaginative, Values-based and Experience-focused.

This model is designed to provide insight into the platform and allow you to fine-tune it. It also initiates a dialogue about the direction in which the platform should go. Table 9.1 illustrates some of the questions that you may well find helpful for this model.

BOX 9.2

IMAGINEERING SNAPSHOT: SEATS2MEET

SEATS2MEET (S2M) provides a combination of an online and an offline platform. It started in 2007 with just one table in Utrecht that provided up to 20 people with free workspace and lunch. The table was at Meeting Masters, where hundreds of professionals met each other on a daily basis. The philosophy behind the free workspace and lunch was that the table was free anyway and lunch for 20 extra people was barely noticeable compared with hundreds served each day. It was a success.

However, the founders, Mariëlle Sijgers and Ronald van den Hoff, resisted the temptation to convert the experiment into a linear business strategy. Instead, they welcomed newcomers with open arms and enjoyed the lively working atmosphere that was created and the subsequent social media buzz that emerged from it. They believed that access to networks and social capital was more important than possession and ownership.

The participants experienced the free lunch and workspace as a gift and as a result an immediate strong social bond was created. The only request for something in return was a contribution to the 'social capital'; the 'when' and 'how' was left entirely up to the participants. S2M describe this as asynchronous reciprocity. The upshot was that people stopped thinking about equivalent sorts of repayment and set about surprising one another with special actions in return.

Social capital was used as the currency because S2M believed that knowledge and creativity are created through the right connections and the right social network.

S2M asks for an open attitude in return for a free lunch so that knowledge will be shared within the social networks. This attitude extended to S2M itself. The viral marketing created by the texts, emails and posts about S2M proved to be enough on its own to ensure its survival. In this way, S2M was able to create a social capital business model based on the power of digital technology and social media.

Expansion of the platform

S2M has extended the platform with much new functionalities since 2012. They are using a Strategic Generative Image (SGI) and use inspiring words and images such as Seats4locals and Seats4silence:

- An online booking system lets you see which people with which knowledge are working at the same location at a particular moment. S2M links like-minded people to each other using The Serendipity Machine. In this context S2M takes serendipity to mean unexpected and surprising encounters that add value.
- S2M went international in 2013. In 2017 there were over 2,500 workspaces in nearly 400 meeting spaces worldwide.

➡

- In 2015 it also became possible for the first time for private individuals to offer workspaces via Seats4locals.
- Seats4silence offers workspaces surrounded by nature.
- Ambassadors and hosts regularly have discussions through their S2M global meetup about topics such as World 3.0 and The Serendipity Machine.
- All the various initiatives are supported through event calendars, social media, blogs etc. There are plenty of opportunities to share photographs, experiences and adventures. There is also a magazine and an app.

Table 9.1 The ACTIVE model

Question: Does or did the platform . . .	
Appreciative	– use positive language and images?
	– build upon the strengths, energy and potential instead of the problems and impossibilities?
	– create new inspiring perspectives for the future?
Co-creative	– build upon the power of the stakeholders?
	– keep the dialogue open and alive and catalyse interactions?
	– let the involved stakeholders create/design themselves or does it invite them to create themselves?
Transformative	– focus on some kind of desired change?
	– inspire people to think or act differently?
	– lead to a sustainable, desired and valuable change or future?
Imaginative	– appeal to the imagination of stakeholders?
	– consciously use creativity or invite stakeholders to use creativity?
	– create or trigger new ideas or combinations that don't exist yet?
Values-based	– work from (shared) values?
	– reflect or make visible which (shared) values are used?
	– add meaning for stakeholders?
Experience-focused	– inspire participation?
	– evoke positive emotions? (for example by the design of the platform: look and feel, colours, the way they trigger the senses, storyline etc.)
	– create a long lasting impression and resonate with stakeholders?

You will by now have realized that value is always created jointly. In the next section we will look in greater detail at co-creation.

9.5   Co-creation

Co-creation has become the way for companies to differentiate themselves from their competition. The word is used all the time in marketing campaigns and on websites. It can refer to basic user customization, for instance by allowing customers to select a favourite colour or design. But nowadays users want much more than this. They want to be involved in the production process itself.

Source: Prahalad and
Ramaswamy (2004);
Ramaswamy and Ozcan (2014).

Figure 9.1 The DART
model

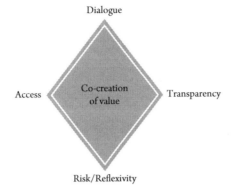

Organizations see co-creation as a way to build trust with their users by allowing them to provide input into their operations.

The way in which people think about co-creation has evolved over time. The focus ten years ago was on the cooperation between users and organizations to deliver personalized experiences, whereas now the emphasis is on platforms of engagement. These platforms seem to spring almost spontaneously from ecosystems but it is, of course, not as simple as that. Co-creation is not a targeted strategy with clear rules; it requires constant adapting to changing circumstances. As an Imagineer you will have to navigate through a fog of opportunities, changing course as you build new connections and create new engagements.

Prahalad and Ramaswamy are usually given the credit for bringing co-creation to the business community in 2000. In 2004, they introduced the DART model (Figure 9.1). They described how Dialogue, Access, Risk assessment (in 2014 this was changed to 'Reflexivity' by Ramaswamy and Ozcan) and Transparency are the building blocks for the interaction between company and consumer.

Dialogue is more than simply listening to consumers. Dialogue implies learning, interaction, engagement and communication between two equal partners. Dialogue creates and maintains a loyal social community.

Access begins with information and tools. Businesses are becoming increasingly data aware and learning how to share their data with customers. As a result, everyone can be given access to a huge amount of knowledge for things like quality procedures, prices, design and manufacturing processes. It also works the other way around. Consumers can choose to close the channels through which companies can approach them; they can opt out. So organizations need a different attitude towards their customers if they want to have access to them.

Risk assessment or **R**eflexivity. In the original DART model, the R represented 'Risk assessment', but Ramaswamy replaced it with 'Reflexivity' in 2014. Risk referred to the possible damage to the consumer. If co-creators are also responsible for risks, companies must correctly inform them of those risks. Consumers will have to learn that co-creation is a two-way process and that they have responsibilities too. Reflexivity puts more focus on thinking about the outcomes of the process. It is about using the continuous flow of feedback from all stakeholders to make the platform better. This involves tools, information, insights, recommendations, meanings, lived experiences and the valuable creations of others.

Transparency – we saw in the early chapters of this book how coping with hyperconnectivity comes down to transparency and openness. There should be visibility in the flow of information and openness that builds trust. Interactions must be transparent in order to better access information and knowledge.

9.5.1 Forms of co-creation

Two parties come together on a platform: the stakeholders and the organizations or companies to which they are connected. Stakeholders can be customers, employees, suppliers, partners, financiers, residents or any other interested party. Stakeholders have access to their own resources, those of their network, and public and social resources too. You can think, for example, of personnel, buildings, technology, equipment, hardware, knowledge and contacts.

The type of co-creation is determined by the degree to which one or other of the two parties is in the driving seat. Crowdsourcing, collaboration and open innovation are types of co-creation where the values and objectives of the organization are more dominant than the stakeholder values. The main objective here is to sell or market a product. The organization embraces the stakeholders and to some extent they become almost part of the organization; some refer to this as 'bringing the outside in' (Ramaswamy and Ozcan, 2014).

If, however, the stakeholder values are given priority over the organization values, the inside is brought out. Resources that belong to the organization are made available to stakeholders. The role of the stakeholders is more dominant and consequently more determining for the process and the result of the co-creation. It is usually necessary for the stakeholders involved in this type of co-creation to have a substantial degree of ownership to guarantee sufficient engagement.

The moment in the overall process when co-creation takes place is also an important factor in distinguishing different types of co-creation.

The SnappCar platform brings car owners and those who need transport together. SnappCar has no cars of its own. Their vision is for the world to make better use of the cars we already have. After all, the average car is parked unused for most of the day. The role of the stakeholders in this process is very dominant. The reviews of the cars, their owners, and the renters play a significant role in ensuring the continuing quality of the experience. High ratings create trust, and trust creates engagement. SnappCar is all about co-creation from the very beginning of your experience with them.

9.6 Building the platform

Now that you know more about co-creation and the forms that it can take, your next challenge is to create environments and platforms that enable co-creation. You need to design something that invites participation, that inspires interaction and creates value for everyone involved. Comprehensive guidelines are useless because platforms are complex systems with shared values and convictions at their core. Designing a platform is a continuous process of discovery and experimentation. The generative image, High Concept or Creative Tension Engine engenders inspiration that brings the platform to life and helps to maintain it so that co-ownership is created among the stakeholders.

The plug-and-play character of a platform is essential (Choudary, 2015). The platform should be designed as an open system so that external producers and consumers can easily plug into it. The platform must be relevant with a guaranteed level of quality. Furthermore, the design must not fall back to more conventional forms of design where the user is at the centre. Altogether it is not a simple challenge to create a platform that involves complex systems with different users who have widely different roles, relationships and forms of interaction. In fact, knowing how to start can be the most difficult challenge. Imitating other successful platforms is a pitfall best avoided; your situation will always be different from any other in some fundamental ways even if the differences are not obvious to you. As an Imagineer, you need to draw inspiration from everything that you see around you. You should associate and combine, but never imitate. Remember that every context is different and you will need to adapt your approach every time.

9.6.1 The building blocks of a platform

Interactions should be at the heart of a platform based around three simple ingredients: the what, the why and the how; these are also known as the building blocks (Choudary, 2015). See also Figure 9.2.

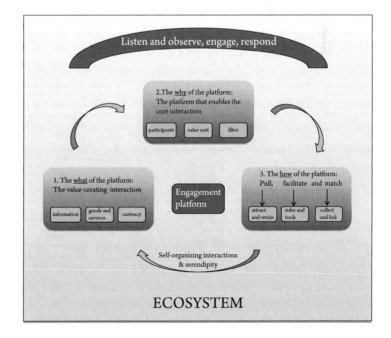

Figure 9.2 The ecosystem of the engagement platform

The what of the platform

There is usually sharing in three dimensions:

1. **Information**: the sharing of information is often at the core of a platform. The platform must be designed so that it can facilitate easy sharing of information.
2. **Goods and/or services**: these usually follow as a result of the information sharing. Note that it is not a requirement of a platform that goods or services be exchanged. You may indeed choose to limit your platform to just the sharing of information and experiences with no role for goods and/or services.
3. **Currency**: traditionally we use money to pay for things. However, payments on platforms often use other 'currencies' such as attention or influence. Think for example about liking YouTube videos or retweeting messages, or submitting ratings and reviews. Services or knowledge can be exchanged on offline platforms. It is also possible for users to agree with one another on their preferred currency. In the case of S2M the currency is 'social capital'.

The why of the platform

It is important to identify the core interaction on the platform; something of value that attracts users to join in. The core interaction of LinkedIn, for instance, is networking by professionals. It immediately tells you all you need to know. If you can, try to come up with a theme that is relevant for people and that appeals to their pride. Alternatively, make sure that it provides some social value like improving the user's network, identity and reputation.

There are three elements you should consider after you have established the core interaction:

1. **The participants**: generally speaking there are two types of participants – producers who create value and stakeholders who consume value. However, it is very important to note that the same person can take on the role of a producer or a stakeholder depending on the context and the interaction. On Nike Plus you can be a runner in one situation and a coach in a different one. On Facebook you post photographs of yourself and like the photographs of others. Obviously it is important that there are enough users on your platform (critical mass), but above all else it is key that the platform attracts the *right* people (Evans and Schmalensee, 2016). Indeed, you may choose to use a screening tool for your platform to make sure that the users are the ones you are aiming at. You should try to attract users who are intrinsically motivated. Extrinsic benefits, such as a prize that can be won, can provide an additional stimulus but should never be the main reason for participation for a user.
2. **The value unit**: every interaction begins with the sharing of information that has value for the users. So you need to find the unit of information that will be created on the platform that is of value for the users. This can be a

generative image or a High Concept/Creative Tension Engine. For Uber it is the taxis available to you to hire, for YouTube it is the videos, and so forth. Users will decide to participate in a platform on the basis of the value unit. Ask yourself what your users value?

3. **The filter**: the filter is there to make sure that users are only provided with the information that they need or are looking for. On Facebook, for instance, as you type a name it preferentially looks first in your list of friends. On Booking.com you get relevant hits by entering a city, country or a specific hotel name.

The how of platform design

1. **Pull**: pull is the continuous inspiration to participate. Attracting users to platforms differs from conventional forms of marketing. There are two main challenges:

    i.   There is a chicken and egg situation with regard to platforms. Users do not come to a platform unless it has value and yet a platform has no value without users. Failing to figure out a way to cope with this situation is a major reason for platform failure.

    ii. As soon as there are users on your platform you have to keep their attention. Giving feedback to users and inspiring them to take action can play a significant role here. You can think of offering value units, or interventions and triggers that generate a form of response. These reactions can, in turn, give rise to new interactions, with the result that the platform remains dynamic.

2. **Facilitate**: unlike conventional enterprises, platforms have no direct control over the process of creating value. Instead, platforms provide a place where value can be created and exchanged. Platforms facilitate the process of value creation and value consumption, but the usage of the platform is impossible to predict. There will be occasions in the lifetime of your platform when you will add new interactions to extend the platform in some way. Some of these interactions will take hold and some will come to nothing, but it is impossible to predict this ahead of time. You will find that it is a good idea to sow several interaction seeds and to carefully watch what happens. You should look for those interventions that generate energy and have a multiplying effect on other interactions. You will need to be flexible and adaptive and have an open attitude to serendipity. Look especially for pleasant surprises and discoveries unearthed by users that could lead to new interaction possibilities. It follows that you should make the process of sharing and exchange on your platform as simple and transparent as possible for all users and limit any barriers to a minimum.

    It is important to note that, although you have little or no control over the interactions that take place on the platform, you must nevertheless keep the platform alive and functioning effectively. You will need to maintain tools and enforce rules. Tools can include the technological infrastructure or the design of an offline platform. The rules ensure that there is some structure to user behaviour. A good example is Twitter. The initial rule was that a tweet has a maximum of 140 characters. At the same time Twitter was open to self-organizing actions such as the hashtag, which was introduced by a user. After a while hashtags were incorporated in the Twitter rules.

3. **Match**: you must find a way to link the right users to one another. To do this you need to collect relevant data about your users. There are a number of ways you can do this: by offering rewards, or asking questions, or adding game elements, or introducing apps, and so on. A search button can be a simple and highly effective way to collect data and is often used on platforms. You can gain a profound understanding of your users' needs and values through collecting data. You will find that new ideas can emerge more rapidly as a result.

Let's have a look at a closed platform for employees (Box 9.3).

A number of additional skills are important during the process of building a platform. Bhalla (2011) considers engaging, listening and responding as important. As an Imagineer you will need to engage with users and listen carefully to their reactions and feedback. You will also need to respond with immediate action both internally and externally. Internal action might include making sure everyone at the organizational level is pulling in the same direction. An external action might be to modify the design of your platform or to make new interventions. We would add the skill of observing to Bhalla's list. It is essential for you to observe where energy and emergence are created and where initiatives fade away. So, in summary, you need to:

1. Listen and observe to what happens.
2. Engage in the energy.
3. Respond for emergence.

The platform must provide incentives, such as S2M's free lunch, and it must encourage behaviour that ensures stakeholders continue to interact for an extended period. You will find that it is essential for you to acquire a thorough understanding of the ecosystem in which operations take place. Systems thinking plays a significant role here because it involves reviewing the entire system and its relationships instead of looking only at isolated interactions or problems. Processes of emergence are not created spontaneously in complex contexts. You will find that sometimes trigger actions are needed to inspire users to behave in ways that benefit the platform and the ecosystem as a whole.

Makers rules

Finally, we have some additional tips for you. These are collected into three rules that we think you will find are most important during the building of your platform:

BOX 9.3

IMAGINEERING SNAPSHOT: CENTER PARCS

Center Parcs is a European network of holiday villages with more than 8,500 employees who are mostly active on the ground in the villages. One of their core values is: 'Create happiness and live the expectations of our guests'. This value is articulated in the High Concept 'Happy' and can be found in every step the organization takes. The Happy programme aims to make the employees happy and, according to the employee satisfaction survey, the programme has been successful – except for one aspect: communication always scored low. The employees had no company computer and no work email address. This is hardly surprising since almost all of them are in front-line positions interacting directly with guests. However, this did make it difficult for them to stay connected with their organization. To address this Center Parcs introduced App@work in 2015 as part of a hAPPy programme and all employees received a tablet. The programme was extended in 2017 to provide smartphones for Housekeeping, Technical Services and Guest Service. Center Parcs strongly believes that in order to make a platform come to life, employees should be intrinsically motivated and engaged to participate. Let's take a closer look at the what, why and how of the App@work platform.

- **The what of the platform**: there is sharing in all three domains (information, goods/ services and currency). Some information is uploaded, such as work schedules, birthdays, calendar events, brief video clips with instructions on housekeeping and safety, and so on. However, employees are also able to upload information themselves. They make their own brief video clips, they give each other tips and they upload pictures of defects in the cottages so that the technical departments can see them and respond quickly. They can nominate fellow employees for the award of 'employee of the year'. The department with the most valuable feedback can win the award of 'department of the year'. The platform is integrated into the new employee onboarding process. Newcomers are given an assignment to use the tablet to get to know the Parc on their first day. There is a even a small marketplace where you can buy goods such as old furniture or stuff from the lost and found department. You can conclude that the currency on this platform is a combination of money, attention and influence.
- **The why of the platform**: the platform appeals to the pride of all the employees of Center Parcs. There are many diverse interactions on the platform, but the core interaction is the sharing of information that is work related with the goal of improving the wellbeing of employees. The High Concept of 'Happy' plays a decisive role, since it inspires everyone to move into that direction. The platform filter makes sure you only receive the information that is important.
- **The how of the platform**: the key factor in building the platform was that it had to be accessible for every employee. The language, the layout, the look and feel must be as appealing for management as it is for housekeeping. The content feels valuable to everyone and is not 'forced' on the employees even though some of the information is uploaded top-down. However, most of the content comes from the employees themselves i.e. bottom-up. The idea of uploading pictures of defects in cottages was an initiative from the employees themselves.

➡

The ecosystem of Center Parcs has become more effective and efficient as a result of this platform. Moreover, new ideas are updated and generated rapidly. The platform allows the emergence of new combinations and interactions by tapping into the collective imagination of all employees and thereby opens up a new reality. The tablet ensures that the offline and online activities are more connected. A good example is the online award nominations that feed the offline gala award event that in turn inspires employees to upload movies and pictures of the gala. There are more than 30,000 actions per month and the employee satisfaction around communication has increased greatly. In addition, they feel more connected not only with each other, but also with the organization as a whole. They are 'hAPPy'.

Source: Dezeure (2018).

1. **Small and simple**
   - Act small: be flexible and adaptable in trying out minor interventions in and around the platform. Do not be discouraged when some of them fade away but continue to try new ones out and observe where energy is created. For example S2M deliberately put a coffee machine on the other side of the space so that people would be forced to walk to it; they saw more spontaneous encounters happen as a result.
   - Keep it simple: the interaction process should be much more direct and transparent since the users themselves are in control. It follows that it is important to keep your platform simple and clear so that it is completely obvious how it works and what users can expect.
   - Use existing platforms: look at existing networks and platforms and see what you can learn from them. Many existing organizations have significant assets that cost money to maintain and that hold them back. Take, for example, a hotel with its building maintenance requirements and compare to Couchsurfing with no physical assets.
   - Ambassadors: when users act as ambassadors and inspire others to participate, the impact is greater than conventional forms of marketing. Try to make the best possible use of social networks and social capital.
2. **Experiment**
   - Make small bets: encourage experimentation as a way of stimulating innovation on your platform. Google, for example, spends a great deal of time and money trying new things out, most of which do not appear to lead anywhere. However, they know that major breakthroughs can only be achieved by starting from small discoveries and inventions.
   - Embrace risk and uncertainty: playing safe has become risky. It is simply not sustainable in a complex world. It is limiting, predictable and too often produces only minor improvements. You should embrace change and not be afraid to take risks.
3. **Know when to act**
   - If something fails, do not spend too much time trying to make it work. Stop it and move on to try something else.
   - Breadth trumps depth: continue to develop yourself and evolve in step

with the changes around you. Google started as a search engine, but in the meantime has broadened its offering to include mail, calendars, docs, chrome, maps, and much more.

- Move quickly and decisively when spotting an opportunity or energy: get into the habit of continuous reflection so that you are agile and efficient in what you do. Build processes that support fast decision making. Try to avoid overly complicated organizations on your platform.
- Temper expectations: the construction of a working platform takes time; patience is the magic word! Remember that building a website is not enough; the platform has value only when meaningful interactions begin to take place.

9.7 Takeaways

You have seen in this chapter that networks of relationships and interactions are all around you. Platforms have become the new way for users to create value together. You have also seen how platforms provide opportunities for emergence because they are continuously in a process of transition. You have learnt that as the facilitator of the processes you make it possible for the users to co-create by triggering their imagination. This cannot be managed or controlled and it often occurs spontaneously and sometimes as a way to repair the system if needed. You have seen how it is possible to inspire people to head in a particular direction by means of a Creative Tension Engine or a High Concept.

Finally, you have seen that it is important to create an environment that can handle change and that can support emergence so that co-evolution can proceed in a sustainable way. In the next chapter we will show how this sustainability can be orchestrated and monitored; how to nurture the system into becoming a learning community.

Bibliography

Benkler, Y. (2006). *The wealth of networks: How social production transforms markets and freedom.* New Haven, CT: Yale University Press.

Bhalla, G. (2011). *Collaboration & Co-creation: New platforms for marketing.* New York: Springer.

Boudreau, K. J., and Hagiu, A. (2008). Platform rules: Multi-sided platforms as regulators (working paper). *Social Science Research Network,* SSRN 1269966.

Choudary, S. P. (2015). *Platform scale: How a new breed of startups is building large empires with minimum investment.* New York: Platform Thinking Labs.

Choudary, S. P., Parker, G. G., and Alstyne, M. W. van. (2015). *Platform revolution: How networked markets are transforming the economy and how to make them work for you.* New York: W.W. Norton & Company.

Dezeure, E. (2018). Interview with Erwin Dezeure, CSR Director Center Parcs Europe at Groupe Pierre & Vacance Center Parcs, 17 February 2018.

Evans, D. S., and Schmalensee, R. (2016). *Matchmakers: The new economics of multisided platforms.* Boston, MA: Harvard Business Review Press.

Glind, P. van de, and Sprang, H. van. (2016). *Share: Kansen en uitdagingen van de deeleconomie.* Amsterdam: Uitgeverij Business Contact.

Kamp, K. op den (2009). *Viable business models for corporate co-creation communities.* Retrieved from http://timreview.ca/article/300 (accessed September 25, 2013).

Kreijveld, M. (2014). *De kracht van platformen: Nieuwe strategieen voor innoveren in een digitaliserende wereld.* Den Haag: Rathenau Instituut.

LSE Enterprise. (2009). *Co-creation: New pathways to value.* Retrieved from http://personal.lse.ac.uk/samsona/CoCreation_Report.pdf (accessed October 1, 2013).

Mitleton-Kelly, E. (1997) Organisations as co-evolving complex adaptive systems. Paper presented to the British Academy of Management Annual Conference.

Olma, S. (2013). *The Serendipity Machine: A Disruptive Business Model for Society 3.0.* Amersfoort, Nederland: Van Lindonk & De Bres.

Prahalad, C. K., and Ramaswamy, V. (2004). Co-creation experiences: The next practice in value creation. *Journal of interactive Marketing, 18*(3), 5–14. Retrieved from http://www.interscience.wiley.com (accessed September 3, 2013).

Ramaswamy, V. (2009). Co-creation of value – towards an expanded paradigm of value creation. *Marketing review St. Gallen, 6,* 11–17.

Ramaswamy, V., and Gouillart, F. (2010, October). Building the co-creative enterprise. *Harvard Business Review, 88*(10), 100–109.

Ramaswamy, V., and Ozcan, K. (2014). *The co-creation paradigm.* Redwood City, CA: Stanford Business Books.

van Dam, A., and Ouwens, F. (2015). *Let's get ACTIVE.* Breda: BUas (internal publication).

Van Dijck, J., Poell, T., and de Waal, M. (2016). *De Platformensamenleving: Strijd om publieke waarden in een online wereld.* Amsterdam: Amsterdam University Press.

Vargo, S. L., and Lusch, R. F. (2004). Evolving to a new dominant logic for marketing. *Journal of Marketing, 68*(1), 1–17.

10

F-lourishing: how to nurture the system into becoming a learning community

Liliya Terzieva

10.1   Introduction

In this book so far you have seen how, with creativity and imagination, you can involve everyone in transforming today to tomorrow through analyzing **A**ppreciatively, blissful **B**reathing, collective **C**reating, dynamic **D**evelopment, and **E**nabling engagement. It is time to dive into the **F**lourishing futures: how to sustain what you have created so that it continues into a limitless future.

You are not designing houses or chairs with Imagineering, but something that is here to stay and that will also develop and evolve over time. You cannot entirely steer the processes you set in motion since you are not controlling them; but you can influence them. You will come to realize that these processes are never-ending. Imagineering, at its heart, is about creating a continuous learning community.

Let us start by taking a look at an intriguing example: the Harry Potter books, a series of seven books that tells the story of "The Boy Who Lived" created by author J. K. Rowling. The books were hip, fashionable and non-traditional; they broke the mold of so-called "traditional children's fiction". They galvanized the movie industry and the imagination of producers and actors alike. They inspired theme parks. They rejuvenated tourism and tourism destinations. Communities sprung up, creating experience platforms. Movements were established. Harry Potter stimulated dialogue on human values, learning and knowledge. However, slowly but surely the power of the brand faded away. The moment all seven books were published, filmed, the theme park open, the communities created, the entire system reached a stable position. Then suddenly J. K. Rowling signed a contract with the Palace Theatre in London, Great Britain to stage a new Harry Potter story. This was to be a transformation from movie to real-life theatre performance, where "all the heroes actually come alive" and there it was again – Harry Potter – breaking news, a best-seller, translations into more than 15 languages, the invitations for the "real-life actors" to perform all over the world, and so on. The magic had been brought to life again.

What happened here? How is this relatively minor intervention by J. K. Rowling able to cause such turbulence? How can doing something new have such an impact compared to improving what is already there? The lesson here is that the "magic" disappears unless it is fed regularly. A system must be "shaken" out of its equilibrium to avoid it becoming stable and static. This is what the Flourishing step in the Imagineering design process is all about: how to design, sustain and facilitate a flourishing future for your platform.

The goal of the Flourishing step is to provide the conditions for a continuous process of Imagineering so that the power of dynamic transformation continues into the future. This chapter starts with the "essence of Flourishing" from the Imagineering perspective. The specific terms are defined and the central theme of "flourishing futures" is explained together with the implications for the management and leadership context. The chapter continues with a specific example of what is happening in the world today. The example shows the value of what the Flourishing futures step can mean when well orchestrated and properly designed. The chapter then focuses on the central theme of how to continuously nurture the transformation and keep it flourishing or, in other words, how to keep the magic going. Some specific tools are presented and explained in detail.

10.2   Essence

You have seen in the previous chapters how extremely dynamic Imagineering is as an approach and as a process. Imagineering as such cannot be translated into a procedure that comes to a final point; it is renewed endlessly as it moves ever onwards. Imagineering is never repeated but it is continuously rethought and further elaborated. Imagineering always looks forward into the future shape of things and uses simple rules to influence the process to move towards a desired direction – a flourishing future.

10.2.1 Which terms do we need to define?

There are several terms that we need to define when we talk about Flourishing that is continuous and unending. The first one is "follow-up". The English *Oxford Living Dictionary* (Oxford Dictionaries, 2016) provides the following definitions:

- "a continuation or repetition of something that has already been started or done"; and
- "a piece of work that builds on or exploits the success of earlier work".

You will realize immediately that follow-up can have a static or a dynamic meaning. In Imagineering we use the dynamic form of follow-up to indicate something that allows further (never-ending) transformation and innovation to happen. Follow-up is key to Flourishing. A great generative image, if badly managed, can fail to inspire, while a mediocre High Concept, if well orchestrated, can turn into a great success.

The second term that needs some explanation is "dynamic sustainability". The simple idea behind this term is that the involvement and engagement of everyone (all the actors) in a process will continuously bring value to them all. The concept of dynamic sustainability requires a shift in your perspective from self-interest and shareholder interest to the interests of our communities, nations, regions and, ultimately, all members of society. This is the stakeholder perspective, which we introduced in Chapter 1, and which drives dynamic sustainability.

While the future may well see a flowering of wondrous sustainable technologies, we will also need to find ways to re-envisage the point and purpose of enterprise and economics. We call this "rejuvenative innovation" (Tantram, 2016), another term that deserves some further explanation. It is questionable that we can solve the problems of tomorrow with the tools of today. Moreover, if we want different outcomes in the future than in the past, we will need to do something different to achieve them.

Most of the rejuvenation happening today is connected in some way to technology. However, in Imagineering we use the term rejuvenation to describe the approach to sustaining and nurturing value. Continuous innovation happens when organizations and companies are enabled to experiment freely through facilitation, rather than when being managed in a closed and controlled environment.

A simple truth in today's world is that organizations can only innovate in co-evolution with their environment. Entire industries, sectors and economies innovate; individual organizations in isolation do not. Innovation today lives in systems that are creative, conscious, committed, networked and hyperconnected. It follows that is the stakeholders who we need to activate and involve (Ditkoff, 2016) and it is the entire living system that has to be out of its "stable comfort zone" (Nijs, 2014) in order for it to stay dynamic. This can only be done when is everyone engaged and ready to learn and experiment. We can only innovate our systems together.

10.2.2 Why "flourishing futures"?

Perhaps as you read the previous chapters and followed along with the Imagineering process, you might have had the feeling that E-nabling was the last step. You will recall that the E-step is all about creating a platform where the stakeholders can interact with one another and co-create. It seems reasonable to imagine that the moment the experience platform has been created, your work as an Imagineer ends and you can leave it to the users to self-organize. However, as we have seen in this chapter already there is no end but even this must be designed for, if it is to be sustainable over time. The F-step allows for the continuous learning, generative processes and dynamic experimentation that keep everything alive. You have to find ways to observe what is happening in the systems now that the engagement platform is working. You need to provide answers to questions such as what type of leadership is necessary to enable the organization or the company to develop further in the desired direction? You need to design a flourishing future.

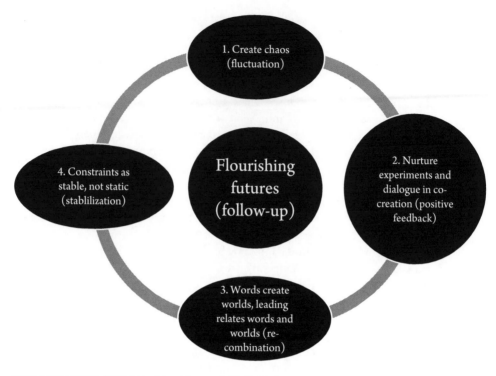

Source: Based on Prigogine (1980); Lichtenstein and Plowman (2009); Nijs (2014).

Figure 10.1 The four conditions of the Imagineering F-lourishing step

We will use the "leadership of emergence" (Lichtenstein and Plowman, 2009) and the four dynamics of Prigogine (Prigogine and Nicolis, 1977) to help explain the Flourishing step. You are living in a time of tremendous change. It is no longer sufficient to rely on planning, organization and control in order to innovate and improve. You need to allow imagination to flourish and this, in turn, means that leadership is also going through a transformation. Nowadays, you are required to collaborate, to be open, to create space for dialogue, to inter-act, to learn and to experiment. These demand specific types of behavior and attitude, especially when it comes to continuous innovation and the free flow of design. Lichtenstein and Plowman (2009) define four main conditions for helping organizations and companies to develop as a community and space for experimentation. The four conditions are shown in Figure 10.1 using the lan-guage of Imagineering.

To help us explain these four conditions we will use the example of Breda University of Applied Sciences (BUas) in The Netherlands, which has "Discover Your World" as its generative image. We will show what it means to use this image as a dynamic driver for innovation that does not come to an end but becomes more sustainable with time.

Innovation in education is complex and requires the active collaboration of each and every stakeholder as well as people that you would not necessarily think of as being especially relevant. BUas took this into account when they chose a generative image that would invite everyone to participate and co-create. It is interesting to mention here that when the university designed "Discover Your World" they did not do so by looking internally for a catchy slogan. On the contrary, they realized that their context was the whole educational system. The scope went far beyond the university. It is about education in general and what it means for the students, the teachers, the staff, the alumni, the partners, the prospect students, the city, the province, and the country. Each of these actors is somehow involved and engaged with the professional process of making learning happen. It is this thinking that led them to "Discover Your World" as a generative image that resonates and inspires both internally and externally.

It is interesting to make a comparison between the multi-layered meaning of "Discover Your World" and the High Concept of the University of Tilburg, namely "Understanding Society".

"Discover Your World" suggests a hands-on approach; it suggests the direct practical and applied competencies that one can master at BUas. "Understanding Society", on the other hand, directly relates to the perspective of a scientist within the system looking outwards to society. Let us now consider the example in terms of the four conditions.

The first condition is "create chaos" or fluctuation (Nijs, 2014), which shakes the organization out of its stable comfort zone. The introduction of "Discover Your World" caused people within the organization to reflect on their experiences and to rethink the way they looked at their own organization. They were pushed to think about the way they were articulating the values and the core principles of BUas. For the external environment, "Discover Your World" meant a complete transformation of what an educative institution can be and can come to mean. The image suggests discovery, opening new worlds, creating expeditions rather than a more traditional linear pathway of educational levels. There was chaos and confusion because of a lack of understandable logic. The image did not fit the comfortable pattern of education that everyone was familiar with. The result was that the organization began to move beyond its usual behavior of teaching in classes using traditional methods and known technologies.

The second condition is "Nurture experiments and dialogue in co-creation" or positive feedback (Nijs, 2014). Here time and space are provided for people to dive into their limitless imaginations. They interact and design new pathways and create new possibilities. Positive feedback reactivates energy in the organization that has been always been there but that has never been allowed to come to the surface. Now this energy can be used to realize the full potential of an organization and even beyond. For BUas this condition was the moment when the actual activation of the system took place. Creative sessions were conducted for all the stakeholders already involved in developing, designing and constructing the educational institution together with experts in areas far from what a university usually offers. This was also the moment when special innovation labs and hubs were created both centrally as well as decentralized at the academy and program level. Together these actions stimulated an unexpectedly open, rejuvenatived and incredibly creative arena that generated potentially valuable ideas. One example of this is the so-called Performatory that emerged as a new educational concept and laboratory resulting in a new way of learning at the university. Performatory is hosted by the Academy for Leisure. Several programs have been developed including a three-year bachelor program in Social Innovation, an Honors program in Imagineering and several design courses. Programs are offered both as 'open sign ups' and 'in company'. The Performatory works on real-world challenges brought in by the participants themselves. Learning is seen as a collaborative hands-on process of giving meaning to theory in practice through co-creation in a lab environment. The Performatory facilitates this process by adding education, working space, experiences, network, knowledge and young entrepreneurial talent.

The third condition is "Words create worlds, leading relates words and worlds" or re-combination (Nijs, 2014). This is the condition of employing language, symbols, stories and High Concepts in order to activate diverse interpretations of the ideas generated as a result of the second condition. In this way innovative ideas move towards reality and implementation. Leaders at all levels in the organization step in and take the generative potential of the idea further by finding High Concepts that invite and activate stakeholders. "Discover Your World" led to the emergence of a number of High Concepts. One of them was "Shaping Society", which was designed by the Academy for Logistics and Built Environment. It brought to life an abundance of initiatives among diverse stakeholders. At the same time it allowed for an expansion of the horizon of what mobility, traffic, the built environment, logistics, and so forth can mean for an individual as well as for the entire society. This High Concept transformed the learning process into real discovery for everyone involved.

The fourth and last condition is "Constraints as stable not static" or stabilization (Nijs, 2014). Here the idea is that once innovation has been recognized and implemented, and everyone has in one way or another claimed ownership of it, it cannot be suffocated or cannibalized by the next big thing. New concepts no longer require a huge effort to make them happen. The values of the organization now support continuous development and evolution. It does take a certain amount of time and space for the first concept to be embedded and fully accepted (stabilized) by the organization. Stabilization can be seen as a guarantee for the dynamic sustainability of the organization. This in turn is an opening for the A-ppreciative analysis step of the Imagineering process to start all over again. The "Discover Your World" generative image has resulted in "discoveries" and "new worlds" becoming logically as well as intuitively perceived as the true nature of BUas. The various departments and stakeholders have then introduced policies and procedures of their own based on the "Discover Your World" principles. If at that very moment a new concept had been introduced, all that has been achieved so far would have collapsed.

The four conditions explained above show that there is a certain rhythm that can be followed when striving for flourishing futures. You can think about the following logic as you apply the four conditions over and over again:

- Creating and facilitating chaos/Breaking open/Shaking/Igniting/ Awakening the potential for new ways of being and doing (CHAOS – fluctuation).
- Nurturing/Feeding/Holding/Facilitating this new way of being and doing (EXPERIMENT – positive feedback).
- Flourishing/Evolving/Implementing/Improvising this new way of being and doing (FEEDBACK – re-combination).
- Stabilizing/Allowing for recognized and perceived rejuvenation and at the same time opening space for new chaos again (STABILIZE – stabilization).

10.2.3 What does this mean for management/leadership?

The new organizations of the future require a completely different management style and attitude (Mitleton-Kelly and Davy, 2013). They need a style of management that creates space and enables the free flow of ideas; a style that encourages experimentation, learning, innovation and unpredictability. They need leadership that uses a shared sense of purpose as a guide, and that understands the open, expansive, creative and energizing nature of involving everyone. It follows that competencies of coaching, facilitating and designing become vital to support self-organization and experimentation. Furthermore, they must allow learning communities to develop and grow. Leaders and managers must become comfortable with chaos. Organizations must become more human places where everyone is valued, empowered and engaged.

It is important to realize that this type of leadership is not about one person, who as some sort of *übermensch* possesses all the features that we are talking about. This is about leadership as a process based on interaction among people within the organization. A process that creates an environment where people are led to learn, encouraged to experiment and stimulated to share. An environment where everyone feels able and is invited to take the lead when needed.

10.3 What is happening today? An example

There is already a lot happening today when it comes to flourishing futures. Although not everyone is consciously using the Imagineering methodology, we can still find instructive examples in many and varied sectors. For this example, let us look at what politics, economy and social work can do when integrated into a powerful generative image, namely Barack Obama's "Feeding the Future" (see Box 10.1). It is interesting to note the continuous re-activation of the generative image in this example as well as "the chaos" that was needed for the system to continue to innovate, experiment and learn. "Feed the Future" shows the process of innovating on a global scale with a strong emphasis on the sustainability of the system to continuously co-generate future innovation and allow for each and every actor to step in, feel invited and contribute.

BOX 10.1

FEED THE FUTURE: BARACK OBAMA'S AGRICULTURAL PROMISE

Feed the Future is the US Government's global hunger and food security initiative launched in 2010. It aims to establish a foundation for lasting progress against global hunger with a focus on smallholder farmers, particularly women. Feed the Future assists millions of vulnerable women, children, and family members to escape hunger and poverty.

The United States Agency for International Development's (USAID's) 2017 Progress Snapshot showed that progress on hunger is possible. By bringing partners together to invest in agriculture and nutrition, they have helped millions of families around the world lift themselves out of hunger and poverty. This means more families are able to feed themselves, and more children are able to reach their full potential. This progress is helping them meet Feed the Future's goal of reducing poverty and stunting by an average of 20 percent in the areas where the initiative is operating.

Through the Feed the Future Innovation Labs, USAID is working with the world's leading universities to scale up proven technologies and activities, expand nutrition interventions and programs, and conduct research to create the next generation of innovations that can change the lives of food producers and their families.

The Peace Corps is one of 11 federal departments and agencies that contributes to Feed the Future, with more than 3,500 Peace Corps volunteers in 55 countries working to bring important food security messaging and practices to their communities.

Recognizing Feed the Future's proven approach in working with partners across a variety of sectors, global leaders affirmed their support of a country-driven model for food security that includes a cross-section of government, NGO, and private sector partners.

Agriculture has been critical to America's growth as a nation, and today, demonstrating the continued commitment to agriculture globally through Feed the Future is one of the most important and successful ways America is leading in the world. As it has been managed to connect more farmers abroad to the global economy, the work brings benefits back to the USA, too, generating knowledge to help America's farmers stay ahead of new pests and diseases, boosting incomes in developing countries and increasing demand for US products, and reducing the risk of instability and turmoil often driven by a lack of access to food.

Today more than ever, through Feed the Future's whole-of-government approach, the USA is one step closer to a world without hunger, creating a dynamic momentum for what it means on an open, global, systemic rather than on a closed, regional level.

10.4   Tools for flourishing futures

10.4.1 The nine leadership behaviors (Lichtenstein and Plowman, 2009)

You will have gathered by now that the Flourishing step requires a new style of leadership, but how do you actually lead in this way? In addition to the "leadership of emergence" that we described above, Lichtenstein and Plowman (2009) have also developed nine very practical leadership behaviors. These relate directly to the four general conditions from the theory of Prigogine (1980).

In order to help us translate these nine behaviors into the Imagineering context we will use an interesting example of a generative image that was designed to reframe the role of the library in modern society. The world of libraries is very different today. Not only has user behavior changed but also the needs of users. Information still plays an important role and it is still considered as a crucial condition to civilize and elevate society. However, it is no longer taken for granted that people gather information through books, newspapers and magazines. Nowadays there are many more ways to provide information. New technologies have made it easy to share information, create knowledge and increase the speed of interaction. It is clear that the relevance of libraries is no longer just in lending books. The needs, expectations and requirements of society have changed. If the library wants to play a role in future, then it has to face up to the changes that are needed and live up to our modern expectations of an information provider.

The Master in Imagineering academy experts and students joined with seven libraries from the North Brabant region of the Netherlands in a research expedition to investigate the changing role of libraries. The goal was to identify the core of what a library can mean in today's world. They looked especially at those people who never usually go to a library and yet do not want to see it closing down, and how they could identify with a library in future.

The outcome of the research expedition was the design of a powerful generative image, namely "From collection to connection". The value of this image was immediately recognized and it has been taken up on a national and international level as a transformational tool for the future role of libraries. Libraries may look to you like something old-fashioned, a place not open for experimentation and creativity, and possibly a symbol of the past. However, we are now beginning to see a transformation of what a library can mean and we can only be proud of what the Imagineering methodology has contributed to that transformation. It should be clear too that libraries can only change and transform in a systems way, when the entire environment is co-evolving.

Let us now follow the nine steps, map them into the context of Imagineering and apply them to the library example (Table 10.1).

Now that you have seen the example of using the nine leadership behaviors as a tool, you can apply them to any generative image that you have designed. You will find that these behaviors will stimulate people to experiment further, to learn and to contribute to the innovation. Do not forget that Imagineering does not end

Table 10.1 The nine leadership behaviors in an Imagineering translation

General condition	Behavior	F-step translation	Example – the role of libraries today
1. (Fluctuation)	1. Embrace uncertainty	Step out of the comfort zone; enter into the unknown.	Having introduced "From collection to connection" the library is no longer only a distributor of diverse collections of books and a provider of sophisticated knowledge. How to move further? How to relate to the new roles, which are emerging out of the generative image?
	2. Bring conflict to the surface and create controversy	Facilitate free and constructive dialogue and enable people to come to findings that are illogical, unreal, even strange and impossible.	Allow for, and further enable, such questions to find meaning and interpretation among all players within and outside the library: Why not become a social place of interaction? Why not open a café/restaurant? Why not offer training programs? Why not cater for talents to be developed? And yet still be a library.
2. Nurture experiments and dialogue in co-creation – cater for completely new ideas to be shared (positive feedback)	3. Allow experiments and fluctuations	Enable and facilitate people to test, taste and apply something that has never happened before without setting the scene or introducing limits and requirements.	Activate creativity in action for example: Let us design the first workshop on 3D-printing. Let us team-up with secondary schools where students and teachers can use the library for space of experiments.
	4. Encourage rich interactions in a "relational space"	Provide time and space for people to discuss, to question, to socially communicate, to exchange ideas, and to interact. Provide totally different, unknown, and interesting environments as well as the known ones.	Sustain dialogue and interaction in reality by, for example: opening the library for everyone, making its services transparent and its nature – one of cherishing ideas and imagination.
	5. Support collective action(s)	Create possibilities where tasks are executed collectively and not on an individual basis; where people can consult each other, rely upon each other, talk and listen to each other while doing their job or coming up with ideas and novelties.	What could be possible collective actions in relation to the generative image and its translation to the libraries' core principles: three new partnerships generated by every employee, groups of employees who never worked before together, now finding common ground on new ideas and translating them into reality.

3. Words create worlds, leading relates words and worlds – here is the moment to start giving names and explanation to what has been generated as ideas, new behaviors, new types of action (re-combination)	6. Create correlation through language and symbols	Open the space for interpretation; what do the new ideas mean in the language of the organization; what kind of symbols can be derived and associated with what has been achieved so far.	Creating a vision and allowing for dynamic narrating of the generative image itself, bringing it to understanding to each and everyone involved (all actors).
	7. Re-combine resources	Enable diverse combinations of people, information, finance, technology, etc. – one that has not been seen or introduced before and cater for it.	Catering for the new ideas to grow further, not setting limits; freeing resources.
	8. Leaders accept "tags"	Facilitate "flat" organizations with almost no hierarchy where everyone in a specific context can take the "hat" of being the leader/initiator/facilitator and drive the process of innovation further.	The chair of the leader being open for everyone to step in – relational leadership models catered for.
4. Constraints as stable not static (stabilization)	9. Integrate local constraints	Here is the moment to "hold the magic", simply meaning that every innovation, in order for it to remain viable and practical, needs a certain amount of time and space to be bedded down into the organization and a new one to further grow alongside it.	Being able to clearly and shortly state what the new role of the library has become as a result of the designed generative image (Adaptive or Creative Tension Engine) and its perceived interpretations; how further; why not this or that; opening for further meanings to be generated.

Source: Based on Lichtenstein and Plowman (2009).

with the completed concept or with the designed platform. Imagineering must continue to thrive in your system and the process repeated over and over again.

10.4.2 The learning launch

The next tool is one that you can use immediately to keep your society, your organization, or your business active. It is called the learning launch. It is a tool that you can use when you want to test the potential of a particular generative image. You can use it to encourage open learning where every possible actor is invited and can participate. The learning launch is a quick way to engage potential customers, start-ups, organizations, and diverse stakeholders in the creation, design and testing of new ideas. It also stimulates learning and innovation as you go.

When used in the Flourishing step, this tool helps to create a free and open space for innovation and experimentation. It helps to create an environment where ideas can be tested without judgment in different situations and contexts. This tool allows everyone to learn.

Learning is a core value in organizations today where being dynamic is crucial for survival. The learning launch is a hypothesis-driven approach based on the idea of learning rather than knowing. As a result, it is particularly useful under conditions of uncertainty when we do not know as much as we would like to.

You will undoubtedly recognize the link with the new style of leadership whereby experimentation is a day-to-day process. A new business idea is nothing more than a hypothesis waiting to be tested.

We will explore the five stages of a learning launch using a generative image that was created by an alumna of the Master in Imagineering program at BUas. The project looked at whether an Imagineering approach could help to transform the way people think about death (Duarte Barata Feio, 2014). The assignment was to create opportunities for new business models for a funeral agency business in Portugal. The alumna's research showed that in many cultures talking about death before it happens is seen at the very least to be a touchy subject; some cultures even consider it as a taboo topic. The result is often that these discussions happen at the very worst time, namely when a loved one has just passed away and funeral arrangements must be made. How can people be stimulated to talk about death before it actually happens?

The generative image that the alumna created to address this question was "Make a wish". It enabled the funeral agency business to become an actor in life instead of death. It allowed people to be co-creators of the services that funeral agencies provide to their closest family and relatives. Suddenly, they have an active role in anticipating and designing their own pathway to the unknown.

Learning launch stage 1: immerse yourself in the existing data, looking for patterns and possibilities

Begin by taking a strategic look at what you already know. What do you think will likely be important to the new way of acting, processing and serving that you have in mind. Take a close look at the essence of what the organization or business stands for using the lens of the generative image. To use the example, articulate what it actually means for the people in the funeral agency to be able to make wishes come true. How can they transform the saddest experience of one's life into a form of celebration of human existence?

Learning launch stage 2: generate a new business idea

Take an educated guess about an opportunity you see. Open your mind to the new world of possibilities that the generative image brings in. Translate the opportunity into tangible actions; how will you actually do this? In other words, restate the hypothesis in the form of a new business idea and make it real by specifying the value proposition for a particular customer, the execution strategy, and the likely competitor reaction. Taking the example of "Make a wish", what are new things that the business can do? What kind of behavior is then required? What kind of key messages does the business send out? Who are the potential stakeholders and actors to be involved and why? Some of the ideas that "Make a wish" inspired were: approach elderly people in nursing homes to talk about their funeral plans; encourage people to live a full and healthy life; reframe the experience from dark and serious to light and celebratory, and more.

Learning launch stage 3: articulate the assumptions on which the success of the new business idea is based

It is essential in this stage to separate out the unknowns that matter from the ones that do not. In other words, what are the critical assumptions upon which the new business relies? You should go further and consider the future steps you have laid out to realize the new business: what will be the critical points along the way? What could be the short-term victories for the business and what are the long-term goals? Try to be as realistic as possible in your modeling. For instance, the idea of engaging the elderly makes the assumption that despite the taboo they will be invited in to do this.

Learning launch stage 4: design and conduct a learning launch to test assumptions

Now design a hypothesis-testing experiment. This is a series of small actions that will allow you to gather data to test your assumptions as you launch the idea. You will need some form of prototype in order to do this; something that will engage the stakeholders. It must feel like a real launch to the stakeholders and key actors who have been invited to the learning launch. Everyone should be welcome to test, explore and elaborate on the prototype, be it a new business model, a new service, a new behavioral model, or whatever. For "Make a wish", the alumna created a booklet with stimulating questions and a checklist of ideas for funeral arrangements. She took this to nursing homes and used it to engage the residents. It went so well she was invited back thus validating one of her assumptions.

Learning launch stage 5: kill or sustain (scale) the idea

Once you have completed enough research through the learning launch to convince yourself that the new idea is sound, you will start to roll the idea out. You will need to change your focus from learning to growing. Think about how to scale it so that more and more people become involved. This is also the moment when you might decide based on your findings that the idea has little or no merit and it is better to kill it. In our "Make a wish" example, the funeral agency chose not to continue to engage the elderly since it proved too difficult to scale, but they did change their image into something much more modern and light. This had a big impact not only on how they were perceived but also on their own working environment. However, the biggest change was that the funeral agents saw how many external people were interested in their work and they heard all their innovative ideas for improvements. They felt valued and inspired and motivated to change.

10.4.3 Human Resource Management cycles within an organization

Dealing with organizations is to deal primarily with people; people who need to be encouraged, stimulated and enabled to grow. What kinds of instruments are there to help you do this? The Human Resource Management (HRM) cycle has the objective to guarantee and sustain the performance quality of the employees. At the same time it should provide clarity and room for improvements and further development. HRM cycles traditionally use key performance indicators to measure how well planned targets and objectives have been met. There are usually annual or biannual reviews to track and assess progress. Contrast this with an Imagineering approach, which would focus on the process and the dynamic nature of employee performance and create opportunities to experiment and learn. So how can the HRM cycle be transformed so that it inspires collective creativity? To answer that question, let us take another look at "Discover Your World", the generative image of BUas, and discover what this can mean for the HRM cycle. "Discover Your World" is a multi-layered High Concept, i.e. it can have many different meanings and interpretations from the point of view of an employee such as:

- How is BUas as an employer enabling employees to discover their world?
- How can employees of BUas expand their horizons through discovering their world? How can they obtain more international experience, more multicultural awareness, and teach in diverse international environments?
- How do employees of BUas enable the students to discover their world?
- In what way is discovery more oriented towards the inner nature of the employee, the students, the staff and the stakeholders; and in what way more oriented towards the "the world out-there"?
- Does discovering your world allow for talent development and, if so, how?

Returning to the HRM cycle, the generative image can be used as the guiding principle for:

- Setting dynamic targets at the planning stage around what "Discover Your World" means for the employee in relation to his or her own tasks/roles during the planning period.
- Using the performance review to analyze, reflect on and receive feedback on how the plans are being implemented.
- Extending the assessment to include not only the measurement of outcomes but also a personal development plan. The development plan should at the very least stimulate a new interpretation of what the generative image should achieve and preferably it should describe a complete re-design/ transformation of their role.

10.5 Conclusion

Congratulations! You have come to the end of the Imagineering design process or rather, as you now know, you have come to a new beginning. In this chapter you have learnt how to experiment and you have seen how to open up spaces for learning communities to grow and evolve. All being well this is enough to sustain innovation. However, should you find that you or your organization comes to a standstill then you know what to do. Find a way to bring the system slightly out of equilibrium, slightly out of its "comfort zone". Create some chaos so that the system can start again to imagine a better future. This is how you design for continuous sustainable and meaningful innovation.

Bibliography

Antal, A. B., and Strauß, A. (2014). Not only art's task – Narrating bridges between unusual experiences with art and organizational identity. *Scandinavian Journal of Management*, 30(1), 114–123.

Ditkoff, M. (2016). *The heart of innovation*. Free Press.

Duarte Barata Feio, J. (2014). *The role of funeral planning in improving one's attitude towards death/dying*. Imagineering Academy, The Netherlands.

Gergen, K., and Gergen, M. (2004). *Social construction: Entering the dialogue*. Taos Institute.

Hess, E. D., and Liedtka, J. M. (2016). *The Learning Launch: How to grow your business with the scientific method. Design thinking, entrepreneurship, innovation and growth*. University of Virginia, Darden School of Business.

Lichtenstein, B. B., and Plowman, D. (2009). The leadership of emergence: A complex systems leadership theory of emergence at successive organizational levels. *Leadership Quarterly*, 20(4), 617–630.

Mitleton-Kelly, E., and Davy, L. K. (2013). The concept of 'co-evolution' and its application in the social sciences: A review of the literature. In: Mitleton-Kelly, E. (ed.) *Co-evolution of intelligent socio-technical systems: Modelling and applications in large scale emergency and transport domains. Understanding complex systems*. Springer Berlin, pp. 43–57.

Nijs, D. (2014). *Imagineering the butterfly effect*. Den Haag: Eleven International Publishing.

Oxford Dictionaries (2016). Follow-up. *English Oxford Living Dictionaries*. At: https://en.oxforddictionaries.com/definition/follow-up (accessed 20 May 2016).

Prigogine, I. (1980). *From Being To Becoming*. New York: Freeman.

Prigogine, I., and Nicolis, G. (1977). *Self-organization in non-equilibrium systems*. Wiley.

Scharmer, C. O. (2010). Seven acupuncture points for shifting capitalism to create a regenerative ecosystem economy. *Oxford Leadership Journal*, 1(3). At: http://www.ottoscharmer.com/sites/default/files/2010_Oxford_SevenAcupuncturePoints.pdf (accessed May 20, 2016).

Tantram, J. (2016). *Sustainable change: Natural philosophy in the 21st century*. Terrafiniti LLP.

Afterword

Diane Nijs, Breda University of Applied Sciences,
the Netherlands

Besides ranking highly on the Global Innovation Index (number 3 in 2017), the Netherlands also tops other indexes such as the European Innovation Scoreboard, has innovation hubs across the country and focuses firmly on innovation in education. Innovation is an important engine for the wellbeing of a country. Now, more than ever, focusing on innovation in all its diversity in education is a critical task, as innovation is required in many of our systems and institutions. The more (young) people understand that we now live in a world that is complex and turbulent, the more they can accept and engage in the collaborative experiments that are needed to flourish in this world. The broader and deeper the view (young) people have of innovation in all its diversity, the more constructively they can act upon it.

This book intends to make a very specific contribution to the field of innovation by embracing complexity science to further our design thinking in order to cope with socially complex innovation issues. Growing complexity comes with its challenges and with its opportunities and those who can see both are in a position to make the best of this structural shift in society. The transition from the industrial era with its mechanical and material focus on expert innovation to the networked era with its ecological focus means innovation and design thinking are increasingly important for social science and management schools. By complementing conventional 'expert innovation' as we know it from the technical universities with 'experience innovation' as whole system innovation, this book invites management and business schools to explore their own route and to discover their own design thinking and implementation to effectuate good business as business for good.

As your colleagues, we hope that this book will be a great source of inspiration for you and we hope you will join the movement of Imagineering. As creativity not only engages people but also increases their wellbeing, let us use this opportunity to set the stage for collective creativity to make the world a better place. Let's unleash and harness innovation as collective creation!

Index

1G innovation model 4–6, 10, 13–14, 16, 72
3D printing 148
5G innovation model 4–7, 10, 13–14, 16, 41–3, 72

A-B-C-D-E-F model 17, 74–7, 86, 89, 117, 151, 167
   A-phase 74–5, 90–103, 107, 167, 172
   B-phase 74–5, 103, 105–17, 167
   C-phase 74–5, 117, 119–36, 167
   D-phase 74–5, 138–49, 151, 167
   E-phase 74–6, 151–65, 167, 169
   F-phase 74–6, 167–81
active breathing 107–12, 117
ACTIVE model 154–6
actor mapping 86, 105, 111–17
adaptive creativity 53
Adrià, F. 140
Age of Design 38, 60–61, 77–80
Age of Science 60, 77
Airbnb 2, 10, 30, 151
ALCOA 67–8
Alessi, A. 148
Amazon 153
A-phase 74–5, 90–103, 107, 167, 172
Apple 67
appreciative analysis 74–5, 90–93, 105, 107, 124 see also
   A-phase
   resources for exploration 96–102
   trends 96
Appreciative Inquiry Summit 14
appreciative interviews 97–101
aspiration 8–11, 13–15, 47, 50, 60, 71–2, 119–22,
   124–32
Atlee, T. 14, 68
atoms 134–6

Bank of North Dakota 33
Bechky, B. A. 64–5
Beltagui, A. 1
Ben & Jerry's 1
Bernhard, Prince of the Netherlands 132
Bettis, R. A. 29
Bhalla, G. 162
Bieber, J. 36–7
big data 25

bisociation 134, 139, 141
BlackRock 32
Booking.com 160
boomerang effect 111
boredom 107, 141–2
Boulton, J. G. 51
B-phase 74–5, 103, 105–17, 167
Braun, S. 36–7
breathing 74–5, 105, 117 see also B-phase
   active 107–12, 117
   passive 106–7, 111–12, 117
   as trigger to insights 111–12
Breda University of Applied Sciences 170–72, 178, 180
Brown, J. 17
Brown, T. 72–4, 141, 146
Bruner, J. 61
Build-A-Bear Workshop 153
Burning Man Festival 127–8
business model 2, 11, 26, 34, 74, 86–8, 155, 178–9
butterfly effects 47
Buurtzorg. NL 54, 56, 76

Candi, M. 1
Capra, F. 43–4
Center Parcs 163–4
century of complexity 25–9
CEOs 32–3, 55–6, 60, 72, 122, 141, 146, 148 see also
   leadership
chaos 7, 36, 47, 78, 170–71, 173, 181
cities 3–4, 28–9, 78, 153
Clarke, T. 113
co-creation 151, 156–8
Co-Intelligence Institute 68
Colander, D. 7, 79
collective
   action 15, 50, 69, 176
   creation 2, 5, 6, 9, 10, 14, 16, 30, 41, 47, 53, 57, 68,
      71, 77, 85–8
   creativity 29, 31–2, 34, 53, 60–64, 69, 70–73, 77,
      85–6, 88, 183
   focus 4, 8, 9, 10, 14, 69, 70
   intelligence 29, 31–2, 44, 68
Collins, J. 123–4, 126
community of creation 2

complex adaptive systems 7, 43, 45, 69, 75
complexity 5–10, 15–17, 22–5, 27, 29, 37–8, 44–5, 48, 50–53, 56–7, 61–2, 66–78, 105, 111, 183
   culture of 25–9
   and design thinking 66
   process of 61
   and systems thinking 61, 66
   systems thinking *see* systems thinking
complexity science 41, 57, 88
   complex systems lens 44–9
   management and leadership 49–52
   and whole system innovation 52–7
   worldviews and their evolution 42–4
concept 126–36 *see also* C-phase; High Concepts
Concept Continuum 127, 129–31
Conklin, J. 35–6, 60, 77, 79
Constellation 145
Cooper, A. 146
Cooperrider, D. 14, 90, 92
corporate innovation 23
Corporate Social Responsibility 122
Couchsurfing 164
C-phase 74–5, 117, 119–36, 167
creative
   industries 15–16, 61–5, 67–9, 86
   process 138–41
   tension 10, 13, 71, 119–20, 128
Creative Tension Engine 10, 13, 15, 47, 53–4, 65, 68–72, 74–7, 79, 85–6, 88, 129–36, 151, 154, 159, 161, 165
   characteristics of 132–4
   creative industries as 15
   the Molecule Principle 134–6
   and whole system innovation 13–15
Csíkszentmihályi, M. 139, 142
cultural innovation *see* whole system innovation
cultural probes 99–101
customer experience design 60
customer journey 144–5 *see also* journey mapping
Customer Journey Canvas 145–6
customer journey mapping 74, 86

DART model 157–8
Dawkins, R. 45
de Block, J. 54
Declaration of Corporate Values 74
design 66, 69, 75–6, 85
   Age of 60–61, 77–9
   Systemic Design Approach of Imagineering *see* Imagineering
   two modes of 62–5

design thinking 60–62, 65–7, 72–4, 80, 85
desk research 97, 99
development 138–49
Dierking, L. 142–5
Disney Company 63, 68, 123
Dollar Shave Club 2
Double Tree Hilton 129
Dougherty, D. 52
D-phase 74–5, 138–49, 151, 167
dream scenarios 120 *see also* 'I have a dream' speech
dynamic sustainability 169

ecological worldview 43–4, 57
education 2, 22, 54, 85, 91, 108–10, 115, 132, 139, 141–2, 170–72, 183
Einstein, A. 41
El Bulli 140
emergence 7, 46–7, 52–4, 60–67, 69, 87–8, 111, 125, 170 *see also* generative emergence
emergent innovation *see* whole system innovation
emotions 63–4, 99, 101, 107, 120, 134, 156
empathy maps 93–4
employee experience 60
enabling 74, 151–65 *see also* E-phase
engagement platforms 154–6
entrepreneurial innovation 4, 7, 8, 67, 85
E-phase 74–6, 151–65, 167, 169
European Innovation Scoreboard 183
Experience Dominant Logic 6, 32, 70
Experience economy 2, 60
experience innovation 1–10, 13–14, 119, 129, 183
experience vision 60
expert innovation 2–6, 10, 13, 71, 183

Facebook 74, 151, 153, 160
Falk, J. 142–5
Family by Family 78, 131
Farmer, D. 71
Fashion District Arnhem 3–4, 7–10, 15, 71
Feed the Future 174
financial crisis 22, 33, 51
Fink, L. 32
Florida, R. 29
flourishing futures 76, 167–73 *see also* F-phase
   tools for 175–81
fluctuation dynamics 48
follow-up 168
food management 91–2
forecasting 27, 47, 50
F-phase 74–6, 167–81
Fredette, J. 25
FSG 113–14

Gandhi, M. 120
Garud, R. 10, 53, 62, 79
Gaver, W. 100
generative
    conversation 14, 70
    creativity 53
    emergence 1, 4, 6–10, 16–17, 52, 57, 60–62, 66–70,
        90–91, 98–9, 113, 133
    innovation practices 5
Gergen, K. 90
Gergen, M. 90
Geursen, S. 121
Gillette 2
Gilmore, J. H. 2, 35, 60, 141–2
Global Innovation Index 183
golden nuggets 102–3
Goldstein, J. 6
Goods Dominant Logic 6, 32, 70
Google 153, 164–5
Gopal, S. 113
Gouillart, F. 36
Grameen Bank 33

Hagel III, J. 22, 29
Hamel, G. 54–6
Hargadon, A. B. 64–5
Harley-Davidson 1, 130
Harmeling, S. 41
Harry Potter books/movies 167–8
Harvey, L. 128
Hatch, M. J. 62, 66
Hawken, P. 85
Hawking, S. 25
Hazy, J. K. 66
healthcare 12, 22, 42, 52, 54–6, 76, 85
Hietanen, J. 33
High Concept thinking 61–3, 69, 85
High Concepts 63, 69, 85–6, 93, 129–35, 151–2, 154,
    159, 161, 163, 165, 168, 171–2, 180
    characteristics of 132–4
    the Molecule Principle 134–6
Holmes, O. W. 10
human resource management 71, 88, 126
Human Resource Management 180–81
Hutter, M. 15
hyperconnectivity 22, 25–7, 33–4
    challenges and potential of 27–9
    implications of 29–37

'I have a dream' speech 13–14, 120, 126
Ideation phase 74, 86–8, 105, 141
IDEO 139, 141, 146

imagination 7, 10, 62–4, 87, 103, 133, 139, 147
Imagineering 4, 6–7, 9–17, 22–3, 45, 47, 51, 53,
    56–7, 61–3, 65–9, 78, 80, 85–6, 138, 141, 175–6,
    180–81
    definition of 69–70
    design approach to 66–76 *see also* Creative Tension
        Engine
    illustration of 75–8
    Imagineering Design Approach 86–8, 94, 96, 102–3
    Imagineering design room/corner 88
    Imagineering design team 87–8
    snapshots 3, 11–12, 78, 128, 132, 140, 145–6, 148,
        152, 155–6, 163–4
Implementation phase 73, 86–7
Industrial design 60
Information and Communications Technology 25
innovation
    1G model 4–6, 10, 13–14, 16, 72
    5G model 4–7, 10, 13–14, 16, 41–3, 72
    A-B-C-D-E-F model *see* A-B-C-D-E-F model
    as collective creation *see* collective creativity
    corporate 23
    entrepreneurial 4, 7, 8, 67, 85
    evolution of 4–6
    experience 1–10, 13–14, 119, 129, 183
    expert 1–3, 10, 13, 183
    narratives 14, 61–3, 80
    paradox of 53
    policy 5–7, 11, 46, 51, 57, 66, 85, 126, 153
    process of 86–7 *see also* Ideation phase;
        Implementation phase; Inspiration phase
    public 3, 4, 6, 23, 26, 41, 67, 79, 85
    social 4, 23, 67, 85
    system 1, 23, 36
    user-driven 31
    whole system 4–6, 13–17, 27–8, 35–6, 38, 41, 52–7,
        65–7, 183
Innovation Engine 139
Inspiration phase 73, 86–7
Instagram 151
interactive experience 142–4
Isaacs, D. 17
iteration 147–8
iTunes 2

Jernsand, E.M. 1
journey mapping 86, 88, 101, 144–5

Kelly, D. 139
Kelly, T. 139
Kennedy, J. F. 124–5
King, M. L. 13–14, 120, 126

Kleon, A. 140–41
Kodak 121
Koestler, A. 134
Kraff, H. 1
Kreitzer, M. J. 54
Kupers, R. 7, 79
Küpers, W. 33

Laissez-faire activism 79
Lakeland Health 54–6, 76
Lamboray, J. L. 145
Landry, C. 38
Lane, D. 52
language 90–91, 95, 126, 134–6
    daily 87
    plain 126
    poetic 76–9, 80, 87, 126, 154
leadership 49–52, 79, 170, 173
    CEOs 32–3, 55–6, 60, 72, 122, 141, 146, 148
    nine leadership behaviors 175–8
learning launch 178–80
Libeskind, D. 143
Lichtenstein, B. B. 4, 6–9, 16, 47, 49, 52–3, 56, 170, 175
Liljedahl, P. 63–4
linear thinking 105–6, 113, 116
LinkedIn 28, 160
Linux 78
living systems 6–7, 16–17, 41, 43–8, 50, 52, 56, 66, 69, 73, 77–9, 87–8, 169 *see also* systems thinking
    science of *see* complexity science
Lockwood, T. 65
Luisi, P. L. 43–4
Lusch, R. F. 32–3

MacLean, D. 62, 66
managerial logic 34–7
Mandel, M. 28–9
Mandela, N. 132
mapping
    actor 86, 105, 111–17
    journey 86, 88, 101
    systems 50–51
marketing 11, 32–5, 63, 101, 124, 126, 130, 135, 154–6, 160
Martin, R. 72–3
McCartney, P. 149
McKenzie, F. 46
meaningful experiences 141–2
Meatless/Meat Free Monday 149
mechanistic lens 51–3, 57, 88
mental models 46, 50, 67, 68–71,
metaphors 42, 43, 45–7, 72

Metcalfe's Law 28
Michelli, J. 146
microfinance 33
Mindfulness 133–4
Mintzberg, H. 52
modeling 56 *see also* business model
Molecule Principle 134–6
mood boards 126
Morin, E. 42
Mossberg, L. 1

NASA 125
national park 10–12, 13–15, 71, 120, 131
Netflix 2
networks 28–9, 31, 33, 37, 43, 112, 164
Newton, I. 6, 42–4, 57, 140
Newtonian worldview 6, 42–4, 57, 65, 85
Nextdoor 153
Nijs, D. E. L. W. 1, 4, 6, 10, 16, 53, 61, 64, 66, 71, 76
Nike 122, 124, 131, 135
    Nike Plus 151–2, 154, 160
non-linearity 49

Obama, B. 174
Obolensky, N. 44
Oliver, J. 120
One Laptop per Child initiative 105–6
one-liners 134–6
open systems 47–8
operating logic 29–37
order through fluctuation 48–9
organization analysis 93–4
Osterwalder, A. 88
Ouwens, F. 102

p^3 model 122–5
Parker, M. 122
participant observation 99
passive breathing 106–7, 111–12, 117
Peace Parks 132
peer production 31
Peñaloza, L. 33
Performatory 172
Peters, F. 1
Piët, S. 144
Pine, B. J. 35
Pine II, J. 2, 35, 141–2
Pinterest 153
platforms 151–2, 165 *see also* E-phase
    building 158–65
    co-creation 151, 156–8
    definition of 152–3

versus engagement platforms 154–6
online or offline 153–4
types of 153
Plowman, D. 49, 170, 175
poetic language 76–8, 87, 126, 154
policy 6–7, 11, 46, 51, 57, 66, 85, 122, 126, 153
Porras, J. 123–4, 126
positive feedback dynamics 48
Potts, J. 7, 15–16, 53, 57, 69
Prahalad, C. K. 2, 29, 34, 157
Prandelli, E. 2
Prigogine, I. 43, 48, 170, 175
principles 123–4, 126 *see also* values
proactive creativity 8, 47
promises 124–5
prototyping 147–8
Proust, M. 143
public innovation 2, 23, 41, 67, 85
Puchert, W. 60
purpose formulations 122–3

Quinn, R. E. 79

Ramaswamy, V. 2, 36, 157
Ramirez, R. 23–4, 30, 34
Random Corporate Serial Killer scenario 123
Ratcliffe, J. 68
realms of experience 141–2
recombination dynamics 48–9
Red Bull 131, 135–6
Rehn, A. 140
rejuvenative innovation 169
research and development 1
retentive creativity 53
Riedel, J. C. K. H. 1
Rittel, H. W. 23
Ritz-Carlton 146
Robinson, K. 139
Rothwell, R. 4–6
Rowling, J. K. 167–8
Rupert, A. 132

Sanders, E. B. 61, 73
Sawhney, M. 2
Schembri, S. 33
Schneider, J. 145
Schops, I. 11–12, 14, 120
Schumpeter, J. 5
science of the living systems *see* complexity science
Seelig, T. 139
SEATS2MEET 154–5
Senge, P. 13–14, 16, 50, 70–71, 85, 87

Service design 60
Service Dominant Logic 32–4, 70–71, 154
Sijgers, M. 155
Simon, H. A. 8, 10
simulating 56
slow-food movement 1, 10, 92
smart governance 26
Snapchat 2
SnappCar 158
social
capital 155, 160, 164
entrepreneurship 31
innovation 4, 7, 78, 85, 172
media 26, 35, 126
SocietyOne 2
Sontag, A. 60
Spotify 2
stabilization 49, 74–6, 172–3, 177
Stacey, R. 53
Starbucks 1, 123
Starck, P. 148
startups 2, 26, 42
Stevenson, H. 41
Stickdorn, M. 145
storytelling 98–9, 102, 130, 146
strategic generative images *see* Creative Tension Engine
Suitner, J. 68
Surplus 76, 85
SynAthina 153
system innovation 4, 6, 13, 23, 36
Systemic Design Approach of Imagineering *see*
Imagineering
systems
mapping 50–51
systems
thinking 28, 44–52, 61, 65–6, 105, 109–10, 116–17,
164 *see also* living systems
Szostek, A. 60

TACSI 78
tame problems 23
thinking
design 35, 60–62, 65–7, 72–4, 80, 85
High Concept 61–2, 69, 85
linear 105–6, 113, 116
systems 28, 44–52, 61, 65–6, 105, 109–10, 116–17,
164
twice 106–9
two modes of 61–2
Total Quality Management 46
touchpoint 74, 101, 145
tourism 167

transparency 26–7, 33, 37, 88, 122, 164 *see also* DART
        model
trigger questions 141
Triodos 33
Trosten-Bloom, A. 90
Trump, D. 122
Tsoukas, H. 43, 51, 62, 66
Twitter 26, 151, 153, 162

Uber 2, 30, 151, 161
UNAIDS 145
uncertainty 23, 27, 29, 46, 99, 164–5, 176, 178
user-driven innovation 31
user experience design (UX) 60

value
    chain 30
    creation 2, 5–6, 11, 17, 22, 26–37, 41, 60, 88, 96, 133,
        135, 152–4, 161
value-driven innovation *see* experience innovation
values 94–7, 119, 124, 127–8, 167, 169 *see also*
        ACTIVE model
van den Hoff, R. 155
Van Dijck, J. 152
Vargo, S. L. 32–3
Vasconcelos, F. C. 23–4
Venkatesh, A. 33
Veritas 71

Virgin 124
vision 74–5, 119–26 *see also* C-phase
        and concept 126–7
Volvo 124
VUCA 27–8 *see also* complexity

Webber, M. M. 23
Weick, K. E. 64, 79
Wentzel, A. 68
WhatsApp 151
Whitney, D. 14, 90, 92
whole system innovation 4, 6, 13–17, 27–8, 35–6, 38,
        41, 52–7, 76, 183
wicked problems 23
WikiLeaks 26
Wikipedia 28, 70, 79
Wilden, R. 33
Wilson, I. 32
World Cafés 79
World Economic Forum 54
worldviews 42–4
    ecological 43–4
    Newtonian 6, 42–4, 65, 85
Wyatt, J. 130

YouTube 44, 151, 161

Zuckerberg, M. 74